Howard Stern

A *to* **Z**

Howard Stern

A to Z

The Stern Fanatic's Guide to the King of All Media

Luigi Lucaire

St. Martin's Press ☞ New York

Design by Bonni Leon

This book and its contents have not been authorized or endorsed in any way by Howard Stern.

Library of Congress Cataloging-in-Publication Data
Lucaire, Luigi.
  Howard Stern, A to Z : the Stern fanatic's guide to the king of all media / by Luigi Lucaire.
    p. cm.
  "A Thomas Dunne book."
  ISBN 0-312-15144-6
  1. Stern, Howard, 1954- —Dictionaries. I. Title.
  PN1991.4.S82L83 1997
  791.44'028'092—dc20   96-44781
                        CIP

First St. Martin's Griffin Edition: February 1997

10 9 8 7 6 5 4 3 2 1

Acknowledgments

Paul Colford's seminal biography of Howard Stern, *Howard Stern: King of All Media,* was an indispensable source for this book. His superb reporting provides the public with everything they might want to know about Stern's life to date. Thanks also to Thomas Dunne, Neil Faber, Neil Farber, Gary Gold, Sandra Gonzalez, Adam Hanft, Alex Hoyt, Murray Hysen, Melissa Jacobs, Jeremy Katz, Bonni Leon, Steve Levitt of Marketing Evaluations, Seth Poppel, Jason Rekulak, Jesse Sanchez, Allan Tepper, Lisa Vecchione, Bruce Wolff, and especially Luis E. Villegas. Of course, I alone am responsible for any errors which may have crept into this book.

My mother thinks that I'm playacting. Which I'm not. I mean, everything I say is true.

—*Howard Stern in a* New York *magazine (11-20-95) interview with Maer Roshan*

I'm locked in my own world. I spend all my time in my basement. I rarely come out of there except for meals.

—*Howard Stern*

Abortion   Howard Stern is beyond pro-choice—he is pro-abortion and will not support any political candidate who is against abortion. On air he has said, "We have got to execute the people who are against abortion." He rephrased the statement seconds later, "There should a a law passed—anyone against abortion should be executed." About the fetus, Stern told his audience, "It's soulless . . . That's an insect that needs vacuuming out . . . It's mucus . . . It's a phlegm ball." **See Tiny Tim.**

Abraham, F. Murray   The Oscar-winning actor *(Amadeus),* who handled Stuttering John's oddball questions quite well, picked his well-endowed Syrian-American nose on cue and placed the "booger" on John's shoulder. He had the presence and acting ability to kiss John on the cheek.

Adams, Cindy   The New York–based gossip columnist who Stern said was among "the lowest of life-forms." Adams sports an affected accent that sounds like a highly polished combination of less affluent sections of Brooklyn and Philadelphia, but she means no harm and is making a decent living (on Fifth Avenue). Born Cindy Heller, she was Miss Bagel of Brooklyn and Miss Bazooka Bubble Gum in her early days. **See Adams, Joey.**

Adams, Joey   The Brooklyn-born husband of columnist Cindy Adams and a fixture on the New York comedy scene. Stern likes to kid about Joey, an octagenarian borscht belt comedian, who, according to Stern, "falls asleep in his soup" at the Friars Club during lunches. When Stuttering John asked him, "How many times have you seen Halley's Comet?" Adams (né Abramowitz) unintentionally uttered one of his best lines ever. "What?" he asked, "What? . . . Danny Thomas?" as wife Cindy quickly whisked him away.

Adlman, Jane   Stern's Rockville Centre South Side Senior High School classmate who married classmate Mark Young. Howard and Alison ran into Mark at a Transcendental Meditation (TM) class in Virginia in 1981. (Young was a TM instructor at the time.)

Adelphi University   The alma mater of Stern producer Gary Dell'Abate and Mike Gange. Located in Garden City, Long Island, Adelphi's major claim to fame is that its president, Peter Diamandopoulos, is one of the highest-paid ($524,000) university presidents in the world, second only to the president of Howard's alma mater (See Silber, John). From 1991 to 1995, Diamandopoulos also ran up expenses of

$625,289.52, including trips to Greece and tips to employees at the $1.15 million condominium on East Seventy-second Street in New York City, which Adelphi maintains for him. As of April 1996, the New York State Attorney General was looking into whether the Adelphi board had financed "extraordinary personal spending" by President Diamandopoulos in violation of state law. University officials defended their actions, claiming the charges were inaccurate. **See Boston University, Dell'Abate, Gary, and Gange, Mike.**

Adler, Jack   A Stern relative who painted the covers of Superman comic books. Adler's grandson sold all of the covers for $15,000 when, according to Howard, they were "worth three or four hundred thousand dollars."

The Adventures of Fartman   The Stern movie that was supposed to be produced by New Line Cinema and written by Jonathan Lawton *(Pretty Woman, Under Siege)*, but the deal soured because the studio wanted a PG-13 rating and merchandising rights, and Stern wanted the flexibility of an R rating, and he wanted to retain the merchandising rights.

Advertising   The field that Howard entered before broadcasting. He worked for an ad agency (Benton & Bowles), and then for a bartering service in Queens, which he has described as shady, before he got a broadcasting job in Westchester County (NY), at the encouragement of his wife and mother.

AIDS   The dreaded disease about which Stern announced one morning that people having it should be made to have tattoos on their genitals.

Air Florida   After an Air Florida flight plunged into the Potomac River in January 1982, near Fourteenth Street in Washington, DC, Stern tactlessly pretended on-air to call the airlines to find out the cost of a one-way ticket to the Fourteenth Street Bridge.

Alan   The name of a childhood friend in Roosevelt, Long Island, a black boy who was beaten up by other blacks for hanging around with Howard, a "honkie." Also Howard's middle name, but spelled with two Ls.

Alex   No, not Johnny Carson's wife but a five-foot-ten-inch stripper and guest of the Stern show. From Pottsville, Pennsylvania, Alex lost her virginity at age fourteen and is "very horny" but has sex only two to four times a week. Her boyfriend fixes automobile transmissions for a living.

Alexander, Jason   Born Jay Greenspan, the *Seinfeld* star told Howard at his forty-second birthday party at the Plaza Hotel that he received $1 million for his next movie.

Alexander, Michael   The general manager of WWOR-TV who was responsible for discontinuing Stern's second attempt to conquer television. Alexander maintained that although the Stern show sometimes beat *Saturday Night Live* in New York ratings, stations in other parts of the country were dropping the show because of the vulgarity factor. He also explained to the press that the program was seen in 56 percent of the United States, and advertisers generally seek an 80 percent level of penetration. Stern hoped that he and another executive would get stranded at sea and be "forced to drink their own urine."

Alford, Bill   The engineer at WMMS radio in Cleveland who cut the cable to Stern's broadcast celebrating his early-drive-time victory in the ratings. Alford was sentenced to ten days in jail and a fine.

Alison   A nice Jewish girl (née Berns) from Newton Centre, Massachusetts, who found the "mother lode" when she decided to go to college at nearby Boston University, where she met Howie. Alison is Stern's attractive but occasionally kvetchy five-foot-six-inch wife since 1978, and the mother of their three daughters. She is a graduate of Boston University and has a masters in social work (M.S.W.) from Columbia University. Alison has such a great life! She doesn't do any housework—a housekeeper does it. She does not shop for groceries—she or the housekeeper orders by phone. She rarely cooks—they have meals delivered to their house. (They eat a lot of Chinese food—especially popular fare for Jewish-Americans and other New Yorkers!) She has a personal trainer and also plays a lot of tennis. Howard complained one morning that "I have to pay twenty-seven people to keep my wife off my ass." As Howard's income has increased, Alison's hair has gotten blonder— soon she will have platinum blond or gilded hair! Howard has kidded that for this great life all she has to do is have sex with him once a week! According to Howard, she likes being stimulated by a vibrator of unknown size or dimensions. Stern tells his audience daily that Alison is the only woman he has had sex with since they got married—a rare accomplishment for a red-blooded celebrity millionaire, who gets hit on by women on a daily basis. In his book *Private Parts*, Howard thanks her for letting him "finger her on the first date." Stern has commented, "She doesn't do anything wild" but did mention that he got her to suck one of his toes in January of 1993. Regarding her bra size, Howard said she was a "large A or small B." On his April 27, 1990, radio broadcast, Stern explained some of the details of his sex life with his wife. He likes her in a pink T-shirt and Calvin Klein briefs. She urinates before and after sex "to avoid urinary infections." Until late October 1996 Alison did not know the joys (the oys?) of third-input sex, and she has only swallowed once or twice. The vibrator is always nearby. Howard likes Alison's pubic area to be well trimmed. Alison is extremely tolerant of Stern's on-air shenanigans, but she hit the roof when she had a miscarriage and Howard did an on-air bit on it. (He joked that he took pictures of the aftermath from the toilet seat so he could give them to her parents, who always ask for photos of the grandchildren.) Alison goes to a few psychics, prompting Howard to complain, "I spent two thousand dollars on tea leaves last year." About Howard she once said, "He doesn't need to be the life of the party, but he needs to be famous. When he's not performing, he's rarely on—he's a real stick-in-the-mud." Alison, by the way, snores but doesn't think she snores. All told, she is the Princess of Old Westbury, Long Island.

All Folked Up   Jackie Martling's band, the name of which was changed to Big Orange Marble (the sun) in mid-1996, according to a flyer that Stern received in the mail.

Allen, Marcus   The pro football player, friend of O. J. Simpson, and former date of Nicole Brown Simpson. When Robin and Liza, coauthors of *You'll Never Make Love in This Town Again,* appeared on the Stern show, they said that Allen had "the biggest private parts you've ever seen on a man." One of them said, "I screamed when I saw it!"

Allen, Sandy   The World's Tallest Woman and Stern guest. She is 7 feet 7 1/4 inches tall and weighs about 320 pounds. She was 6 feet 3 inches tall when she was only ten years old and wears size twenty-two shoes. She is forty years old and still a virgin.

Allen, Steve   The television pioneer who is a favorite senior-citizen target of Stern's wrath. According to Stern, Allen has the "world's worst toupee . . . It looks like a knit cap," and "claims to have written three hundred thousand songs," although the *TV Guide* theme song is the only one Stern knows about. (He also wrote "This Could Be the Start of Something Big" and at least one other decent song.)

Allen, Woody   The film director-writer for whom Stern has low regard, especially since he began an affair with Soon Yi, his stepdaughter. Stern has called him a "vile *meeskite*" (Yiddish for "ugly person or thing") and "ugly, miserable, sad, pathetic." He also said, "Any girl who'd give herself to Woody Allen is sick."

AllOverTan   One of Howard's cyber chicks, a "D cupper," who turned out to be a guy, turning off the King of All Media from computer sex for a while.

Alt, Carol   The fashion model whose "supermodel" status was debated during several shows. Stern producer/writer Fred Norris did not think she merited the epithet, which, he contends, has been overused. Alt, by the way, is married to former hockey pro Ron Greschner. Hoping to ingratiate himself sexually in the AIDS era, Stern told her, "I am the cleanest guy in America." In his second book, Stern named her as his number one sex fantasy because she's "real tall" and "a real Goody Two-shoes." Alt once dated realtor Donald Trump.

Altered States   One of Stern's favorite movies, directed by Ken Russell, about which he said, "That was the coolest movie . . . That thing rocks! William Hurt's the best!"

American Flatulators   A novelty comedy video and Stern sponsor. It features such characters as "Gaseous Clay" and "The Ripper." In their "Wind-a-bago" they tour America's "Fartland." Their phone number is 1-888-PASS-GAS.

Amos, John   The black actor who, according to ex–K-Rock intern Sandy, was verbally abusive when he showed up for a WNBC-TV interview.

Amsterdam, Morey   One of the early television comedians, Morey had a great run on *The Dick Van Dyke Show* as Maurice "Buddy" Sorrell. Morey told Howard, "I wrote for Will Rogers . . . for five presidents."

Amy   The six-foot-one-inch-tall, attractive young model from Washington, DC, who licked honey off Stern's thighs one October morning. The next morning Howard revealed that he masturbated twice, with Amy's ministrations in mind. Amy later returned in conjunction with a visit to try out for a part in Howard's movie *Private Parts.* He asked her if she wanted "to eat chocolate pudding off my butt cheeks," which she declined, offering instead, "I could lick whip cream off your nipples." They "compromised" and she suggestively ate a banana from between his thighs. Amy stopped by the studio two days later and not only "gave good banana" but also licked peanut butter off his thighs and ate two Raisinettes out of his navel.

Amy Lynn   *See Baxter, Amy Lynn.*

Anal fissures   An ailment suffered by Stern but cured, according to him, by altering his diet. Howard also loves to give advice on proper use of toilet paper ("no more than three wipes," etc.).

Anal sex   A form of sex that Stern likes to ask his female guests about (e.g., "Are you a three-input woman?"). When a caller asked him (8-5-96) if he ever had anal sex with his wife, Stern commented, "I've never had the privilege—I'm not even sure I have the desire with her." He added, "I know with some of the young girls that I meet I would like to do that to them . . . but I've never been one of those guys who's into the buttocks." However, on November 28, 1996, Howard announced to his crew and audience that he invaded Alison's third input that weekend.

"Anus"   One of Stern's nicknames for deejay Don Imus.

Andersen, Kurt   The magazine editor who wrote a major *Time* magazine article entitled "Big Mouths" (11-1-93) about Rush Limbaugh and Howard Stern, comparing and contrasting them. He described Limbaugh as "a fat, baldish, old-fashioned middle American guy . . . a conservative idealogue who has never owned a pair of jeans, gorges on $250 meals of caviar and steak, revels in drinking 'adult beverages,' and gets embarrassed when a friend makes a bawdy crack about a female reporter interviewing him." He described Stern as "a skinny, 6-ft. 5-in. longhair who wears jeans, dark glasses and five earrings, a teetotaler who eats no red meat and whose radio shows and book inevitably include stretches of Butt-head uncensored sex raps." *See Limbaugh.*

Anderson, Pamela   The sexy, saline *Baywatch* actress who admitted that she is usually completely shaven (you know where), that she lost her virginity at age sixteen, had her first orgasm around the age of seventeen, and she took a photo of a boyfriend's penis and kept it. She dated actor Scott Baio for over a year. When she gave birth to a child in mid-1996, Stern remarked that the baby looked like the late Doug Bady, not a flattering comment. *See Bady, Doug.*

Andrea   Howard's college classmate who owned a "Naked Passion" bus. She had a "big can" and was "tall and thin." She invited Howard to a party, but he was afraid to attend because it was the week after he met Alison. Andrea thought that Howard in his college days was "nice, sweet, friendly, intelligent . . . not a geek, not a dork . . . a real nice guy." She now works for a movie production company and has written screenplays, one of which is a "Chinese romantic comedy."

Andy the Intern   The intern who bought baked potatoes for Howard at a Roy Rogers restaurant. At last look, he was attending the Western New England School of Law in Springfield, Massachusetts, and intends to be an entertainment lawyer. Stern called him the station yenta.

Ankle bracelets   One of Stern's turn-ons (". . . makes me nuts . . . sexiest thing in the world").

Anti-Defamation League of B'nai B'rith   The Jewish organization that received a surprisingly high number of complaints about Stern during his days at WNBC radio.

Anti-Semitic   A word meaning "anti-Jewish," Stern mispronounces it as if it were written anti-Semetic ("suh-mettick" vs. the correct "suh-mittick").

Antonelli, Pam   The Weslaco, Texas, librarian who got into "hot water" for ordering a copy of Stern's first book, *Private Parts*, for the local library. The city's commissioners voted to remove the book from the shelves.

April 24, 1987   The day of Stern's protest rally against the FCC outside the United Nations building.

Aqualung   A fixture on the New York rock scene, who Stern says "looks like the cover of the Jethro Tull album." Aqualung hobnobs with rock stars and usually hits them up for freebies to concerts (e.g., the "Rain Forest Concert"). He can be seen hanging around in front of the K-Rock studios, the Four Seasons Hotel, and other celebrity-driven locations.

Armenian girl   The "Armenian chick" with whom Stern admitted he had sex—she made "funny noises" during sex and had a "bad case of 'bubbles' [acne] on her back," which is why she did not like her blouse removed.

Arnaz, Desi   The Cuban band leader and costar and producer of the classic *I Love Lucy* television shows. Desi is one of Stern's best imitations, so he likes to do spoofs based on the *I Love Lucy* characters.

Arnold, Tom   The ex-husband of comedy star Roseanne Barr Pentland Arnold, he was badmouthed for years by Stern. Stern ridiculed the couple on his television show when he played a slovenly Tom Arnold to Judy Tenuta's Roseanne. After Arnold appeared in the Schwarzenegger hit movie *True Lies,* Stern admitted that his performance was commendable, and soon thereafter Tom was a "mystery guest" and the two enemies made peace. They both were surprisingly gracious to each other.

Aron, Ylyse   A Long Island friend of Alison Stern, she appeared on the show and looks like a cherubic younger sister of Edward Koch, former New York mayor, wearing a woman's wig. Her husband is "in computers."

Artie   The rehab counselor who helped Ken, the Albany Stern show producer, get cleaned up. Artie "pleaded the Fifth" when Howard asked him if he ever had sex with any female patient.

Ashley   The youngest of Stern's three daughters—a name suggested by fitness guru Richard Simmons, who, by the way, owns a dalmatian dog named Ashley. Her full name is Ashley Jade Stern. When Nancy Sirianni and Jackie Martling gave her a blue baby outfit and a nightlight as a present, Howard found thirty minutes of comedy material, a public exhibit of bad manners. He complained that the outfit was blue (blue is for boys, pink is for girls) and that it was made of polyester, as if polyester were a form of asbestos. About polyester, he said, "It's a fire hazard!" Howard wants cotton for his future princess! (At six months of age, she uttered "dah dah," and Howard declared that "she has my intelligence," adding, "My kids seem very bright . . . My father made feel like a moron, and I turned out all right." Howard pointed out that Ashley was still not "potty-trained" at just under three years old, but she called Howard one April morning off-the-air and told him, "I go poopie . . ." Howard was *kvelling,* promised her piano lessons, and then realized that he was the victim of a "phony phone call." The perpetrator appeared in the studio the next day at Howard's invitation to replay the audiotape for the listening audience's enjoyment. A few weeks later, Howard declared that she did a "poopie" in preschool in mid-April 1996. (Hey, she's going to get the piano lessons anyway!)

Athena   The Scores nude dancer who looks like Pamela Anderson. Her real first name is Lonnie, but Scores's manager, Lonnie Hanover, didn't want her to use the name. She has also used the names Nico and Pamela. **See Scores.**

Attila the Thumb   What Howard called himself after a Saturday night sex session with his wife, Alison. He proudly commented about a weekend's dalliance, "I had two busy thumbs!"

August 8, 1952   Robin Quivers's birthday—she is a Leo.

August, Miles   The pseudonym Howard used on the Boston University radio station for a brief time. (It was the name of a classmate's brother.)

Aunt Jemima   A brand of pancake mix and syrup, named after a black woman. Stern told television personality Geraldo Rivera on the air, "The closest I came to making love to a black woman was when I masturbated to a picture of Aunt Jemima on a pancake box . . . I did it right on her kerchief."

Aura Recordings, Inc.   The name of a recording studio that Howard's father, Ben, co-owned.

Austin   The Texas capital where Stern's major competitors are Dudley, Bob, and Deborah on KLBJ-FM, John Boy and Billy Big on Z-102, and Allen and Karen on KHFI. Stern entered the market in early April 1996 on station KUTZ-FM (98.9).

Autographs   Stern does not like to sign autographs, although he signed thousands of copies of his books to promote them.

Avildsen, John G.   The movie director *(Rocky)* who was announced by Rysher Entertainment as the director of *Private Parts*. Because of script differences, Avildsen bowed out of the deal, and so did Rysher.

Aykroyd, Dan   Stern likes the comedic actor but calls him "a dick" because "he hasn't treated me with any respect" and basically ignores Stern's existence. Comedic actress Fran Drescher, a good friend of Aykroyd and his wife, Donna Dixon, once undressed with the married couple ("I went first . . .") at a Martha's Vineyard beach. Drescher said of Aykroyd, "He's got a huge joie de vivre," which sounded very much like a double-entendre reference to his zest for life *and* his organ size!

Baba Booey   The nickname of Stern's radio producer, Gary Dell'
Abate. Gary mentioned that he collected cartoon cell art (frame-by-
frame drawings used in cartoon movies) and wanted a "Baba Booey."
(Baba *Loo*ey was Quick Draw McGraw's little burro sidekick in the car-
toons.) Stern was fascinated by Gary's collecting these cells and kept
playing with the name and knew he had a great nickname for his producer. Gary introduced a line of Baba Booey T-shirts and caught grief
because the teeth, lip, and mustache graphic was not as effective as it
could have been. **See Dell'Abate, Gary.**

Babylon 5   One of Stern's favorite television shows, a science fiction
drama set in the year A.D. 2258. The series stars Bruce Boxleitner and
Claudia Christian.

Bacon, Kevin   The film actor *(Animal House, A Few Good Men)* who
is separated by no more than six degrees from all other movie actors!
See "Six Degrees of Kevin Bacon."

Bady, Doug   The good-natured eighty-pound, three-foot-tall small
person and occasional Stern guest who had muscular dystrophy. Bady
related the not-very-pleasant story about almost losing his rectum ("I
grabbed a handful of flesh, lots of blood . . .") while defecating, not exactly breakfast conversation. He also participated in a bit in which he
was put in a steamer trunk on Madison Avenue and asked passersby
to let him out. He died in August 1996.

Baer, Max, Jr.   The second-generation actor who played Jethro Bo-
dine on television's *The Beverly Hillbillies* (1962–71), one of Howard's
favorite shows in his youth. He told Stern that he was paid $500 per
episode the first year and $600 the second year. Baer wrote and pro-
duced the movie *Macon County Line,* and made a few bucks on other
low-budget movies. Max dated actress Sharon Tate, but, unlike Roman
Polanski, never scored with her. He also let Stern's not-so-secret fantasy love Amy Lynn Baxter live at his house when she was only seventeen years old. Baer said he never touched her and later fixed her
up with actor James Woods, a golfing partner, whom she dated for
several months. Baer was famous for throwing big parties at his two-
and-a-half-acre Beverly Hills home, complete with real palpitating
magazine centerfold women, hot tubs filled with champagne, etc.

Bagel   One of Howard's favorite comestibles, which he sometimes
eats with tuna fish or smoked salmon. (At the 9:00 A.M. or 10:00 A.M.

break, you can usually hear Howard smacking his lips while trying to read a commercial.) When he periodically mentions his boring daily diet (e.g., shredded wheat, rice cakes, steamed chicken, hot water, etc.), he rarely mentions his beloved bagels, although he said that he ate twelve bagels on June 4, 1996!

Bailey, F. Lee   When the famous lawyer was jailed in early 1996, Stern began calling him F. Lee *Jailey* and said that O. J. Simpson was now giving Bailey legal advice. When Bailey was arrested for drunken driving long before the Simpson trial, Robert Shapiro was his lawyer, and Bailey was acquitted.

Baio, Scott   The former child actor *(Happy Days* and *Joanie Loves Chachi)* who told Stern that he had sex with some of the actresses on television's *Baywatch*, including Pamela Anderson whom he dated off and on for four years. He also had a fling with actress Erin Moran, who Gary Dell'Abate said had told them that Scott was "Quick Draw Mc-Graw." When Howard later probed Anderson on this matter of sexual quickness, Pamela hesitated, and Howard declared, "That's a yes!" Baio also dated Heather Locklear.

Baked potatoes   Stern often eats four baked potatoes a day.

Baker, Dr. Daniel   The plastic surgeon who performed Robin Quiver's breast reduction.

The Baldwins   The fabulous Baldwin brothers (Alec, Billy, Daniel, and Stephen) from Massapequa, Long Island, about whom Howard said during an interview with Chynna Phillips, wife of brother Billy, "My goal is to 'deep-hump' every Baldwin wife!"

Baldwin, Alec   The movie actor and husband of sexy blonde Kim Basinger. Howard is dying to smell Alec's fingers after a hanky-panky session with sultry Kim. He also likes Alec's liberal Long Island political stance, although they probably have not voted for the same people lately, except for Bill Clinton in 1992. His full name is Alexander Rae Baldwin III.

Baldwin, Billy   One of the Baldwin boys—an actor and husband of singer Chynna Phillips, who told Stern that Billy had a big shoe size (she said size fifteen, he claims fourteen), prompting Howard to ask if he had a large love organ. She said nothing but smiled. Jackie Martling quickly chimed in, "That's a yes!"

Baldwin, Stephen   The Baldwin who plugs his Pool-Aid AIDS benefit on the Stern show every year. Contributors pay $250 and get to play with some actors and actresses of marginal marquee value. When Stern asked Stephen about actor William Shatner, with whom he acted, Baldwin said, "He's a prick."

"Baldy, Baldy"   The Stern song parody about Philadelphia deejay John De Bella, sung to the tune of "Louie, Louie," the rock classic.

Ball, Lucille   The comedic movie and television actress (*I Love Lucy* and others) whom Howard liked to spoof. Since her death, Stern has "visited" her in heaven. The imitation (voice by Billy West or Robin Quivers?) sounded more like Leona Helmsley than Lucy.

Balon, Rob   The author of the Austin *American-Statesman* article (4-4-96) about the Stern show introduction in the Austin, Texas, market. Balon wrote, "Stern never sets himself above his target audience. His ongoing laments about his deficient genitalia and his poor love life serve to create a conduit between those in the audience who have their own problems and see Stern as a regular guy. He is also wickedly funny."

Barbara, Dominic   The heavyset Long Island lawyer who came to Jessica Hahn's defense after hearing Stern's on-air ramblings on behalf of Hahn. In the process, Stern befriended Barbara (and Hahn) and now plays cards with him, and other guys, on occasional Friday nights. Dominic said that Stern "complained for an hour when he lost a nine-dollar pot." He also unsuccessfully defended Joey Buttafuoco in his statutory rape case—Joey spent some time behind bars. Stern complains that Dominic clings to him too much at certain events ("bachelor" parties at Scores and book-signing events) and he calls him "The World's Fattest Lawyer."

Barbara the Comedy Doctor   The woman who is trying to help Stern intern "Smelly James" develop a comedy act, a near impossible task. She formerly was with the "First Amendment" improvisation group, to which Bruce Willis once belonged. For stand-up advice, her number at Comedy Elite Talent Booking is (212) 864-6620.

Barbarella   The 1965 Jane Fonda movie that Howard's father took him to when his mother was away visiting relatives in Florida. The movie was considered racy at the time, but Jane's Vassar-educated breasts were more perception than reality. Her opening striptease is the highlight of the movie.

Barnett, Donald Jay   Stern's general manager and program director at WRNW-FM, his first paying radio job in Briarcliff Manor, New York. Barnett also deejayed at WKTU-FM in New York City, which was later renamed WXRK, Stern's current flagship station since 1985. Barnett almost fired Stern his first day on the job when "the board jammed," according to Howard. About Stern, Barnett said, "He followed instructions very very well."

Barrows, Sidney Biddle   The "Mayflower Madam" who had 180 prostitutes work for her (on whose services she received a 40 percent commission) before she was busted in the late 1980s. Unlike Heidi Fleiss, who was convicted for federal tax evasion, Barrows filed taxes and received no prison sentence. She developed the SAT (no, not the college entrance test!)—the Swallowing Avoidance Technique for prostitutes who didn't want to ingest the sperm of their "johns." Barrows is now married to a lawyer and told Stern that she gives her husband sex "whenever he wants it." Barrows called Stern "low-rent," according to one listener who had attended her book-signing.

Barry, Marion   The off-and-on mayor of Washington, DC, and frequent target of Stern's humor, especially when Stern broadcasted from DC and after Barry was arrested for possession of crack cocaine. On-air Stern asked one of Barry's aides why he was named Marion, noting, "That's a girl's name."

Barrymore, Jaid   Actress Drew Barrymore's mother, who posed for *Playboy* at age forty-eight and has been an occasional Stern guest. She is playful, flaky, and in good physical shape for her age—Howard seems to find her very attractive. She wrote him a "gushy" letter after her first appearance in which she called him "completely brilliant, sexy, handsome, talented, and sassy." He told her that he would like to make love to her, promising, "I'd be so busy with you for an hour that you wouldn't even see my face." When she uncrossed her legs, Stern kidded, "I just saw where Drew came from!" Jaid, by the way, is her maiden name. Is it a coincidence that Ashley Stern's middle name is Jade?

Basch, Richard   A lawyer-agent who does work for Stern at Don Buchwald's talent agency. *See Buchwald, Don.*

Basement   Not many multimillionaires spend much time in their basements, but Howard does. It is his office and his refuge. Wife Alison uttered one of her best on-air lines when she (on the December 13,

1995, broadcast) asked Howard, "When are you going to get out of the basement?"

Basile, Jonathan Stern's personal fitness trainer. He has also credited Steve Basile as the man who taught him aerobics and the importance of nutrition.

Bassett, Angela When Robin Quivers was asked during the York, Pennsylvania, press conference who she would like to play her in Stern's movie (if she didn't get to play herself), she said Angela Bassett, the Yale-educated actress *(Malcolm X)*.

Bat Mitzvah A Jewish religious ceremony for girls on their thirteenth birthday. It is sometimes called a Bas Mitzvah. It culminates in a social event that often costs more than an average wedding. About a year before the event, Howard said on-air that the Bat Mitzvah for his oldest daughter, Emily, would cost $50,000. He discussed who would be invited (Robin Quivers, Jackie Martling, Gary Dell'Abate, Ralph Cirella, Don Buchwald, and Neil Drake) and who would not (Donald Trump, Joan Rivers, Wayne Siegel, Dominic Barbara, Tom Chiusano, Dan Klores, and Infinity Broadcasting chief executive officer Mel Karmazin). In the same monologue Stern complained that he didn't like Bar and Bat Mitzvahs or wearing yarmulkes (Jewish skullcaps), and kidded that the theme of his daughter's Bat Mitzvah should be "I Hate Jews." (No mention of Emily's *Bat Mitzvah* was ever made after that broadcast, suggesting that wife Alison was disturbed by Howard's talking about the topic.) After Emily's *Bat Mitzvah* in May 1996, there was no mention of it by Stern or crew, although they made vague references to a "party" that they had been to the previous weekend. For some reason, Stern, who holds few topics sacred (e.g., his own income), did not want to announce this significant family event to his audience.

Bates, Janet See "Janet from Another Planet."

Baxter, Amy Lynn Known as Amy Lynn, she is a very attractive blond topless dancer, a *Penthouse* Pet, a regular guest on Stern's show, and one of Stern's favorite women. With Tempest, she posed topless with an almost naked Howard for the cover of his book *Private Parts* but the photo was left on the "cutting room floor." Amy's mother helped sell photos of Amy nude standing next to patrons at her various dancing engagements. When Howard found out that Amy Lynn smokes, he said, "Behind those beautiful breasts are black lungs." If Stern's wife, Alison, died tomorrow, Amy Lynn would be at Howard's lapside and poolside in about a week, give or take a minute.

Baywatch   One of Stern's favorite television shows, which starred David Hasselhoff and included a bevy of beauties such as Pamela Anderson, Yasmine Bleeth, Nicole Eggert, and Susan Anton. *Baywatch* was first seen as a made-for-TV movie on April 23, 1989. The network show lasted only one season (1989–90) on NBC but has been in syndication since September 1991 and is the most popular television show on the planet. The show has also been called *Babe-watch* and *Baio-watch*. **See Baio, Scott.**

Beanstalk Restaurant   A former sponsor of the Stern show and the location of the Imus funeral that four thousand people attended in New York.

Beastie, Elaina   The woman who went out with Mike as a "prize" after he ate the marshmallow from Jackie Martling's buttocks crack. In a discussion about lovemaking ("My wife hardly moves . . . even with the vibrator!"), she told Howard, "I could give you a heart attack . . . I'm famous for scratching people and scarring."

Beatty, Warren   The legendary lover, movie actor, and director whom Stuttering John asked, "What's bigger, the Oscar or your penis?" Always confident, Warren answered, "That's a very, very good question." Beatty has a reputation for having long lovemaking sessions, although the authors of *You'll Never Make Love in This Town Again*, Stern guests, impugned his sexual talents.

Becker, Gretchen   The woman who accompanied actor Martin Landau to the 1995 Academy Awards ceremony when he won an Oscar. She beat Howard in a one-on-one basketball game (21 to 17) after spotting him fifteen points! Howard finds her very attractive.

Becker, Sandy   A kiddie television host omnipresent in the 1950s and 1960s, whom Stern liked. "Sandy Becker was a cool man . . . really bizarre and good." Stern enjoyed his characters Hambone, Norton Nork, Dr. Gesundheit, and Big Professor. Becker was a radio announcer in the 1940s, who later appeared in 1955 as host of the extremely popular television kiddie show *Wonderama*, later replaced by Sonny Fox.

Belushi, Jim   The comedic actor and occasional Stern guest. Belushi admitted that his ideal woman would have "seven vaginas" and that his late brother John Belushi "didn't get along" with Chevy Chase. When Belushi punched some guy out for spitting on him, his lawyer was Robert Shapiro, O. J. Simpson's defense attorney. Belushi admitted to having sex with two girls at a time "many times" and told Howard that during a nude scene with actress Tuesday Weld, he got an erection—he apologized, and she said, "I'm flattered."

Belzer, Richard   The cynical, pockmarked comedian, actor, and a Stern regular. He wears his liberal politics on both his "sleeves" and his "cuffs." As Stern is quick to point out, Belzer has only one testicle (he lost one in a cancer operation), prompting one Stern fan to call him the "Uniballer." His wife, Harlee McBride, starred in what were considered to be "pornographic" movies (*Young Lady Chatterley* and its sequel) in their time. Belzer doesn't vote and admitted that he had one homosexual experience ("we didn't consummate") in the late 1960s when he was drunk. Belzer's father committed suicide in 1968 when Belzer was nineteen—he found him slumped in the family garage, dead of asphyxiation and carbon monoxide poisoning. Belzer was kicked out of Hebrew school as a kid.

Ben's Deli   The delicatessen next to the Barnes & Noble bookstore in Coral Park, Long Island, which handed out free hot dogs to Stern fans on line to buy their copies of *Miss America*.

Bennett, Alex   An irreverent, candid liberal radio commentator by whom Stern was influenced in the early 1970s. Bennett, for example, did a dial-a-date routine and accepted rapid-fire phone-ins, long before Stern did. Stern later complained that Bennett "ripped me off."

Bennett, Tony   Italian-American singer, born Antonio Benedetto, and a guest on Stern's October 5, 1991, television show. Bennett's "people" stipulated: no singing, no spokesmodel on set, don't mention Pat Cooper, no skits or parodies, and don't bring up anything embarrassing.

Benrubi, Asher   *See Smasher, Adam.*

Benton & Bowles   An advertising agency that Stern worked at for a brief period before he launched his career in radio.

Benza, A.J. The *New York Daily News* "Downtown" reporter who is a Stern booster and frequent phone-in guest. **See West, Billy.**

Ben Wah See *Ryder P.I.* and Wah, Ben.

Berger, Larry The program director at WPLJ-FM, a New York radio station, who tried to recruit Stern for a nighttime slot when he was about to leave Washington, DC.

Berglass, Marc A writer on the Stern WWOR-TV show, about whom Howard kidded, "He's the only writer who never contributes anything to the show."

Berkowitz, Susan Stern's "Shadow Traffic" reporter in his early days at WXRK. He called her "Susan Berserkowitz" for a while. She adopted the name Susan Berkely and left her job in 1987 to start a broadcasting school.

Berle, Milton The octogenarian comedian whom Stern likes to kid about the legendary size of his penis ("He can't fall . . . his wiener is like a kickstand!" "He has the penis of a black man!"). During one broadcast, a prompted caller asked "Uncle Miltie" if it was true that his organ was so large that it has a "fiveskin." It was a good comedic line, but Berle, being Jewish, doesn't even have a "threeskin." Berle responded, "It's not the size of your penis, it's what you do with it." When Stern introduced Berle as a comic, Berle quickly corrected him, "I'm not a comic, I'm a comedian," an old Friars Club cliché, clarifying, "A comic says things funny, a comedian says funny things." Berle, who turned eighty-eight on July 12, 1996, exchanges cigars with Bill Cosby, who was also born on July 12 (1937). Stern sometimes refers to him as "Uncle Wiltie." Berle claims to have been the model for the Buster Brown logo. He appeared as a young child in the Mack Sennett 1914 classic silent comedy *Tillie's Punctured Romance,* starring Charlie Chaplin, Marie Dressler, Mabel Normand, and Chester Conklin, so Miltie has been in show business for a few years. Berle is also one of the early entertainers to get a nose job!

Bernhard, Sandra A mousy-looking comedic actress and former manicurist/pedicurist. Stern finds her "sexy" for reasons unknown even though he likes to remind his listeners that she prefers the company of women. When Bernhard began appearing on the Roseanne show, she was officially banned from the Stern shows. In a spoof of the

Hollywood Squares, one question was, "What out-of-the-closet actress is now on Roseanne's show?" Bernhard was a phone-in guest in November 1995, after a long hiatus, to plug her latest media appearances. She told Stern, "I'd have sex with you if you weren't married." Stern, a bit cynical, replied, "If a guy had a vagina, she'd do him!" Regarding his question about her proclivities, she said proudly, "Honey, I swing, I go, I have a blast!" After her appearance on a music award show in early 1996, Stern remarked that she looked better than any other woman there, prompting one listener to call in and complain, "Now I know why people hate New York Jews!" A few months later, Stern's daughters Emily and Debra showed up at the studio for "Take Our Daughters to Work Day" when Bernhard was a guest. The girls said that Bernhard was "mean," "ugly," and had "big lips" and an "annoying nose." Emily and Debra rested their cases, but Howard still says, "I love Sandra, I really do."

Berns, Bob   Stern's father-in-law. **See Bob and Norma.**

Berns, Bruce   Howard's brother-in-law who lives in Georgia and owns Leisure Club International, a travel agency. A woman listener called in and claimed that Bruce had a dinner party and asked people to bring their own food and wine. Stern agreed that his brother-in-law is "a cheapskate's cheapskate" and "never picks up a tab." He is "the prince of Georgia . . . a real sport." The agency's phone number is (800) 723-1717.

Bernsen, Corbin   The *L.A. Law* television actor who told Howard that he had sex with Heather Thomas when he was a student at UCLA. They were on a double date, but when she threw up, her date left, and Bernsen nursed her back. They began a relationship, about which he said, "She was good the first couple of years . . . then she became a TV person." He also picked up Vanna White at a New Year's Eve party and went home with her. Occasionally a gentleman, he admitted that "we took a shower together" but he "didn't baste the turkey . . . We took a couple of days." He also admitted that he had "amazing sex" with "this wolf girl" who covered up her low Hispanic-forehead hairline with a bandana. On his honeymoon with his first wife, he had sex with another woman. He believes that "sex will drive a cold off" and "jerking off doesn't do it." He espouses the "Sperm Deposit Theory," which says that man has to place his seed in many places.

Bernstein, Richard   The *New York Times* reviewer (12-4-95) of Stern's book *Miss America*, who wrote, "If you can take what the movie ratings people call coarse language, you will laugh out loud at Mr. Stern's antic audacity, though the laughter may be guilty because the humor is cruel." He conjectured that "Stern must have been a quick mean kid, the kind who sniggered a lot at the discomfort of others." He further noted that "Mr. Stern has achieved his [godlike status] because he raucously legitimizes the dark side, the anarchic impulse, the savage beast in all of us."

Berry, Chuck   When Howard showed boxer Joe Frazier (11-21-89) a nude photo of the rock 'n' roll singer, who is well-endowed, he asked the boxer if he thought Berry had a large organ. Joe said, "He can stand on his own!" Howard added, "If Chuck Berry lost one leg, it wouldn't make a difference." Berry's boner has gotten him into trouble. He has spent time in a federal penitentiary for transporting a fourteen-year-old girl across state lines for immoral purposes.

"Bestiality Dial-a-Date"   A controversial routine that Stern performed on WNBC-AM radio, which he thinks triggered his being fired in 1985. **See Bradshaw, Thornton, and Tinker, Grant.**

Beth   Stern's first sexual "score" at Boston University. The relationship lasted a little over a week. She thought that Howard was "sweet, shy, sensitive, one of the nicest guys I've known."

Bey, Richard   A New York talk-show host who called Stern on air when Joan Rivers was a guest to say that Rivers's ratings weren't as high as she said. Howard called him a "creep" and said that Bey steals ideas from him, and hung up the phone. Bey has adopted the format of Stern's old WWOR-TV show, but with more "riffraff" types.

Bianculli, David   The *New York Daily News* critic who was favorably impressed by *The Howard Stern Interview* show on the E! cable channel, noting that "Stern has learned how to handle himself better in a visual medium . . . Stern has matured as a TV personality . . . I never expected to write a sentence containing both the words 'Stern' and 'mature.' "

Big and Tall   The men's specialty clothing chain for extra large and tall men. Stern bought clothing at their Hempstead, Long Island, store.

Big Mouth Award   An award that the National Association of Radio Talk Show Hosts wanted to give Stern, but he turned it down, saying that it was an insult.

Big Orange Marble   Jackie and Nancy Sirianni Martling's band, formerly known as "All Folked Up."

Biggers and Summers   A talk show on the Lifetime channel, cohosted by Sissy Biggers and Mark Summers. When NBC's Katie Couric appeared on the show on November 1, 1995, Stern called in and asked Katie why she was afraid to interview him about his book *Miss America*. She replied that she wasn't afraid to interview him but did, in fact, have a scheduling problem. She said she would talk to him and that her people would call his people.

Biopic   The *Variety* trade magazine word that Stern understandably mispronounced when he was reading their blurb about his upcoming movie. The word looks like it should rhyme with *myopic*, but it stands for "biography picture" and therefore should be printed as bio-pic, as this author recommends.

Bishop, Kelly   The actress who plays Howard's mother, Ray, in the movie *Private Parts*. Her stage credits include *A Chorus Line* and *Six Degrees of Separation*.

Black Like Me   One of few books that Howard has admitted reading. Written by John Howard Griffin, it is about a white man who dyes his skin dark to see what living like a black in the South is like on a day-to-day basis. Veteran actor James Whitmore starred in the 1964 film version of the book.

"Black Jeopardy"   One of Stern's regular routines, which features black contestants and themes. For this bit, Howard sports an Afro and dresses in a dashiki. Typical categories include "Black Bastards" (e.g., Jesse Jackson), "Interracial Couples" (e.g., Quincy Jones), "Black History," and "Stiff, Black, and Dead." Sample prizes have been a "colorized Amos and Andy kinescope," a copy of "The History of Blacks on the *Mayflower*," a scholarship to "The George Washington Carver School of Three-Card Monte," and a double-Dutch jump rope. Among the contestants have been "Louis Farrakoop" (as in Farrakhan), "Bill Avoider" (as in deadbeat), "Will Fare," "Six-Pack Shakoora," "Jesse Jackoff," "Rob Whitey," and "Malcolm X-Ray." "King of the Blacks," a contestant, is a sanitation worker from New Jersey. "Big Blacky," an occasional guest, was seen drinking malt liquor. The background sound track usually consists of "natives" chanting "ungawa, ungawa." The segment has sometimes closed with everyone singing "Swing Low,

Sweet Chariot." One first prize was announced as a ski package (lift tickets, ski rental, and one lesson) but was downgraded to third prize when it was pointed out that "blacks don't ski."

Blacks   Shortly after the O. J. Simpson case verdict and "Million Man March" in Washington, DC, Stern told punk-rocker guest Billy Idol that "our blacks are out of control."

Blackwell, Mr.   The clothing designer who put Stern on the top of his Worst Dressed Women List of 1996, the first male ever to make the dubious distinction. (Milton Berle and Flip Wilson made previous lists, but not the top!) Blackwell said on the CBS *Day and Date* talk show, "Let's face it, Howard. Your Miss America looks like Godzilla impersonating Gypsy Rose Lee." As a Stern guest (and occasional target—"Mr. Blackswell" is one of Stern's impressions), Blackwell openly admitted that he is a homosexual and his first sexual experience was when he was forced to perform an act on a boy at camp. He admitted becoming a prostitute after the camp experience to earn quarters for "food money." His big announcement was that he claimed he had sex with actors Cary Grant and Tyrone Power—and with women. Born in Brooklyn, New York, as Richard Sylvan Selzer, he used the stage name Dick Ellis at one time.

Blair, Linda   The former child star of the 1973 movie *The Exorcist* and one of Stern's former lust objects.

Blaze   The name of the horse that Robin Quivers bought in the summer of 1996 for a rumored $7,000.

Blum, Len   The screenplay writer of the 1997 movie *Private Parts*.

Bleeker, Lt.   The New York policeman who called Stern after he talked down the man who threatened to jump off the George Washington Bridge.

Bleeth, Yasmine   *Baywatch* babe "Yaz-MEEN" is a favorite Stern love object. The foxy five-foot-five-inch-tall actress once lived with actor Luke Perry in their soap opera days, and also dated Grant Show of *Melrose Place*. Yasmine admitted having sex on a beach on the island of Saint Barthélemy, almost did it on a plane, and said that she would kiss another woman on camera.

Blind people   Stern said that he hated "blind people who don't wear sunglasses." He asked, "Don't sighted people have rights?"

23

"Blueberry"   Howard's nickname for one of the teachers at his Rockville Centre, Long Island, high school, so named because of a skin discoloration on his face. **See *Cirella, Ralph.***

Bloom, Andy   As program director of Infinity Broadcasting's Philadelphia station WYSP-FM, he suggested that Stern's New York show be simulcast in the "City of Brotherly Love." He was the program director at the time the funeral for "zookeeper" De Bella of WMMR-FM was held in Rittenhouse Square. He later became program director in Los Angeles.

Bloomfield, Connecticut   The town in which Howard and Alison lived when Howard deejayed in Hartford.

Bob and Norma   Stern's well-intentioned but slightly annoying in-laws, Bob and Norma Berns, from Newton Centre, Massachusetts. Howard always says that he loves them, perhaps because they give him hours of comedic material when they visit Howard at his house on Long Island. Bob, the retired owner of the Pullman Vacuum Cleaner Company, speaks in a monotone and constantly asks Howard kvetchy questions like "How much is a person like Kitty Carlisle Hart or Arlene Francis or Dr. Ruth paid when they come on your show?" and "When did Kitty Carlisle change her name to Kitty Carlisle Hart?" Bob likes to put his feet up on the furniture, puts newspapers on the couch, and lets Stern's declawed cat out of the house. Norma calls Howard "darlinguh" and likes to pat Howard on the head, much to his irritation, as if he were a six-foot-five-inch-tall cocker spaniel.

Bobbitt, John Wayne   The poor young man whose penis was severed by his South American wife, Lorena. To Stern's and Bobbitt's dismay, Bobbitt's ex-wife was exonerated by a jury. His organ was reattached by surgeons, and he later starred in a pornographic movie which he publicized on the Stern show. Bobbitt also appeared on the show with Dr. Melvin Rosenstein, who performed additional surgery to add a couple of inches to the now famous organ.

"Bobbing for Tampons"   A Stern WWOR-TV show game, not quite his finest moment in the annals of comedy. **See *"Man-pons."***

Boggs, Bill   The easygoing, lantern-jawed New York television host whom Stern likes but always ribs for not quite having a stellar career on TV. **See *Comedy Tonight.***

Bogosian, Eric   The actor/playwright who wrote and acted in *Talk Radio*, a play and 1988 movie about an iconoclastic radio personality—sound familiar? (Stern buddy Alec Baldwin, by the way, appeared in the movie.) Bogosian couldn't handle Stuttering John's questions and pushed him up against the wall during a book-signing event. Bogosian told Stuttering John several years later that he liked Stern.

Bon Jovi   The rock group that Stern supported early in their career but who turned against him when other rock stations threatened to boycott their records if they appeared on the Stern show. Jon Bon Jovi became "Jon Bon Phony" in Howard's mind and words. Band member Richie Sambora became the butt of many Stern jokes, especially when he began dating singer-actress Cher. Comedian Sam Kinison promised to reunite Bon Jovi with Stern one morning and didn't deliver, which riled the shock jock. However, Jon and Richie eventually made peace with Howard on his E! channel interview show. They wished him "Happy Birthday" on Howard's forty-first-birthday broadcast! When Stern's daughter Ashley was born, Jon sent flowers, which Howard described as "the worst flowers I ever got." Jon was expelled from a Roman Catholic elementary school for slapping a girl and once worked in a junkyard. He has a tattoo of a Superman logo. His mother is a former *Playboy* bunny.

Bonaduce, Danny   Former television child star *(The Partridge Family)* and former drug user, Bonaduce has been a periodic Stern show guest. He was host of his own talk show, "Danny!" after two years of being a disc jockey (and using Stern-type material) in Chicago. Stern does not fully trust Danny. "There is something about the guy . . . I can't put my finger on it," he says.

"Bone smuggler"   Howard's curious slang term for a homosexual.

Bonet, Lisa   *The Cosby Show* actress who told Howard that she used to go to temple (attend a synagogue) because her mother is Jewish. **See Kravitz, Lenny.**

Bongarten, Randy   One of few NBC executives for whom Stern had any respect ("one of the greatest people who ever lived"). Randall D. Bongarten became the general manager of WNBC in the summer of 1983 and later president of NBC's radio division. He doubled Stern's salary, adding bonus incentives, but, in the end, fired Stern.

Bonilla, Emilio   The nineteen-year old man who was about to jump off the George Washington Bridge in December 1994 when a witness gave him a cellular phone in order to call the Stern show. Thinking the phone call was a hoax, Stern asked his listeners traveling on the G. W. Bridge to beep their horns. When he heard the horns, Stern realized he had a "live wire." He talked Bonilla out of jumping, but sarcastically said later, "The guy was so annoying, at one point I was going to tell him to jump."

Bonnitt, Ted   The weatherman at WRNW radio in Briarcliff Manor, New York, when Howard worked there. (He had been known as "Phil Rodent" in some bits.)

Bo the Lesbian   The blond stripper whom Stern let substitute for Robin Quivers one morning when she was out sick. Robin was livid the next day!

Books   Howard sells a lot of them but claims to read very few, which is especially unusual for a magna cum laude graduate of a major university. He has admitted to reading *Black Like Me*, by John Howard Griffin (about a white man disguised as a black man to see what life was like), "a Carlos Castaneda book in college," *Manchild in the Promised Land*, by Claude Brown (about a black growing up on Harlem streets), "a book by Kurt Vonnegut," "maybe a Kissinger book," a small part of *The Celestine Prophecy*, and the first chapter of attorney Christopher Darden's *In Contempt* (about a black assistant district attorney trying to prosecute a prominent black sports hero).

Boomer, Paul   A name that Stern uses when he's on Prodigy. It comes from a character on an old Canadian comedy record album that he listened to as a child. On the album, Paul Boomer has a farting match with Lord Windesmere and becomes the Farting Champion of the World.

"Boopsy"   One of Ray Stern's nicknames for Howard.

Boosler, Elaine   A Brooklyn-born comedienne and former singing waitress on Howard's hate list—he says she's not funny and is "lame." At the 1989 Grammy awards, after Stern hectored Boosler about why she won't come on his show, Boosler's boyfriend pushed Stern's megaphone into his nose, and hit Gary Dell'Abate in the mouth.

Borriello, Bobby   The young actor who plays Howard Stern at age seven in the movie *Private Parts.*

Boston   The Stern show finally debuted in Boston (home of his in-laws and where he and Alison went to college) in early April 1996. He opened the press conference by proclaiming, "Boston: home of baked beans, home of the Red Sox, home of the Boston Strangler, home of the drunk driver Teddy Kennedy . . ." When asked if he would visit Boston soon, Howard compained, "Boston was a town of rejection for me. Women rejected me. Radio stations rejected me. What am I going to do? Walk around and bum out?" He particularly enjoyed kidding Dixie Whatley, former cohost of *Entertainment Tonight,* about being in a market like Boston for nine years.

Boston University   The university that Stern attended after high school. He graduated magna cum laude with a 3.8 average in 1976 from their school of communications. The school was founded in 1839 as a Methodist seminary. Two-thirds of freshmen applicants are accepted, and the average combined SAT score is 1,158. (Stern says he scored about 1,200.) After getting his SAT scores back, Stern said, "I was lucky to get in Boston University . . . I had to take Basic Studies." (Basic Studies was considered a level or two below the School of Public Communications from which Stern eventually graduated magna cum laude.) He often criticizes John Silber, the president of the school, who is missing one hand and tends to be a tyrant and right-winger politically. He is also the highest-paid university president. As long as Silber is president of the school, Stern refuses to give them money. **See Silber, John.**

Boy George   A Stern guest who proclaimed that "everyone's bisexual." George admitted that he never went all the way with a woman but did say that he liked the "top half" of women in a sexual way. His first homosexual experience was at age sixteen. His first full experience was the same year with a forty-five-year old married Italian man ("I was a messenger boy . . . He undressed me . . .").

Boy Lee   One of Boy Gary's predecessors at WNBC radio, who was made to buy such things as gay magazines, hemorrhoid remedies, suppositories, Kotex, and other embarrassing products for Howard to talk about on the air. Lee is now the general manager of a radio station and makes at least $150,000 a year.

Bozo   The clown who accompanied Stuttering John at the Harley-Davidson Cafe. Bozo is a trademarked clown created by Larry Harmon and franchised on a market-by-market basis.

Bradshaw, Thornton   The chairman of the board of RCA, the parent company of NBC when Stern worked for WNBC radio. Howard con-

27

jectured that Bradshaw was traveling in his limousine and heard his "Bestiality Dial-a-Date" routine and became upset enough to get him fired in September 1985. (Note: Grant Tinker later took credit for the firing. **See Tinker, Grant.**)

Brandmeier, Jonathon The Chicago morning deejay ("Johnny B") on Evergreen Media's WLUP-AM and FM stations when Howard entered the market. He decided to work the afternoon shift.

"Breasts Feed the World" The Stern crew's song parody of "We Are the World."

Brennan, Joe The Libertarian party politician who encouraged Stern to run for governor of New York in 1994.

Brenner, David The nasal-voiced comedian and frequent guest. His legal spats with the mother of his first son have been the subject of several shows. He is owner of Amsterdam Billiards, a pool hall on the Upper West Side of New York at 344 Amsterdam Avenue at Seventy-sixth Street; telephone: (212) 496-8180. Brenner has a good sense of humor and a penchant for attractive blondes. Brenner's current girlfriend (and mother of his latest child), Elizabeth, admitted having a nose job but insisted that she was "blond all over." Elizabeth worked in an art gallery when they met and has never been an oceanographer, as Brenner once said in an interview to change the topic. Brenner was an early defender of Stern's brand of humor. At one time, Brenner made David Wallechinsky's *Book of Lists* for appearing on more talk shows than any other performer. Brenner's press releases indicate that he was born in 1945, but Howard suspects that he is about ten years older.

Breslin, Jimmy The liberal Irish-American New York–based reporter and author who was suspended without pay from *New York Newsday* after appearing on Howard's radio show (5-8-90) via telephone. Breslin had berated a Korean-born reporter, Ji-Yeon Yuh, as a "yellow cur" and a "cunt" the previous week. Editor Don Forst said, "His radio conversation with Howard Stern indicates a lack of sensitivity." Breslin pointed out that his nephew, Donald Noonan, was going to marry a Korean. He asked, "Now, does this mean I can't go to the wedding?"

Brewster, Punky The Stern guest with whom Steve Grillo went rollerskating, much to the consternation of Stern, who disapproves of his people getting too cozy with guests. (Incidently, she wanted to use Grillo's credit card to rent the skates.)

Brisebois, Danielle   One of Howard's love fantasies, Brisebois (her name is misspelled in *Miss America*) appeared as Stephanie Mills on *Archie Bunker's Place* and as Mary-Frances Sumner in *Knott's Landing*. She has a tattoo of what looks like an Aztec sundial on the nape of her neck.

Brokaw, Tom   The NBC newscaster whom Stern considers "despicable" for having revealed the name of the then alleged William Kennedy Smith rape victim on national television. (Smith was acquitted of the rape charges.) Stern railed against Brokaw the next morning, and Brokaw retaliated a week or two later.

"Bronskied," To get   In SternLanguage, the joy of a man having his face pleasantly ensconced between the breasts of a well-endowed woman. **See Colt 45, Gina, and Vogel, Ludwig.**

Brother Electronics   A regular sponsor, especially for their P-Touch labeling machine, fax machine, or laser printer. During one birthday bash, Stern received a pair of Harley-Davidson motorcycle boots from Brother Electronics, and he complained to the executive that they were "only worth a hundred bucks."

Brothers, Dr. Joyce   The noted psychologist and occasional guest, who called in to congratulate Stern on the birth of Ashley. In the same interview, he asked her if she masturbated, and she replied, "Everyone does!" She appeared on *Hollywood Squares* during the week that Stern appeared.

Brown, Divine   The Hollywood hooker who was caught by police while performing oral sex on British actor Hugh Grant, and subsequently a guest on the Stern show. (Robin called it "the lick that would be heard around the world.") Being tactful, Howard opened with, "After a night's work, would your jaw ever get sore?" She replied, "I never worked myself that hard." To show her professionalism, Howard got her to put a condom on a banana—mission accomplished in only three seconds! She plugged her movie *Sunset and Divine: The British Experience,* in which she re-creates the Hugh Grant incident. When Howard asked if she would perform sex on Fred Norris or Jackie Martling, she winced and said that Jackie "looked like a cop" and Fred looked "capable of murder."

Brown, "Downtown" Julie The E! channel *Gossip Show* host and former MTV video jock with an annoying British accent, and occasional Stern guest. She is the daughter of a Jamaican black man in the Royal Air Force and a white mother. Stern said, "She's one of the most attractive black women I know." When Stern asked if she favored dating one race versus another, she said that she goes out with "both species." She complained that Howard's studio is full of photos of himself. She wears a B-cup brassiere.

Brown, James The rock-and-roll singer whom Stuttering John asked, "When you do that famous James Brown split, do you ever bang your testicles against the floor?" Brown has been arrested eight times, resulting in only three convictions and five years in jail. Hey, not everyone is perfect.

Brown, Mark An obsessive-compulsive listener from New Jersey, and Stern guest on the WWOR-TV show. The numbers three, six, and thirteen particularly upset him. As with most guests, Stern ridiculed him on-air, but was very sympathetic toward him off-the-air. **See Obsessive-Compulsive Disorder.**

Bruce The man who recommended Dr. Sarno to Stern to help him with his back problem.

Boobe-myseh A Yiddish phrase that "half-Italian" Stern started using on air in 1996. It means "nonsense" or "something silly or untrue."

Buchanan, Pat About the journalist and occasional presidential candidate, Stern said that he is "a loudmouth like me . . . He's wacky." He has also called him "a piece of filthy garbage." (Stern said that comedian Flip Wilson's drag Geraldine character is more feminine than Buchanan's sister Bay, who was once treasurer of the United States; her name and signature once appeared on all U.S. currency.)

Buchwald, Don Stern's agent since 1984 and the man who has helped steer Stern to multimillion-dollar deals. Buchwald also represents cohost Robin Quivers and other deejays such as Jay Brown (now a comedic actor), Ted Brown, and Dan Ingram. His office is at 10 East Forty-fourth Street in New York City.

Buckley, Kathy The six-foot-tall deaf comedienne and Stern show guest. She admitted to Stern that she was molested at age eleven.

Buckman, Adam   The *New York Post* TV editor who called *The Miss Howard Stern New Year's Eve Pageant* 1993 pay-per-view special "the most disgusting two hours in the history of television."

Buffalo   The market (WWKB) that canceled the Stern show on January 8, 1996, and replaced it with a country music program. **See Detroit.**

Bullock, Jm (no i) J.   **See Hollywood Squares.**

Bush   A guest band in early 1996, they sang their hit song "Glycerine," a song that Stern likes.

Bush, George   Stern voted for George H. W. Bush in the 1988 U.S. presidential election, but not in 1992. He complained that Bush spent too much time at Camp David. (Hey, Howard spent too much time at Camp Wel-Met!) Howard, as listeners know well, has a prejudice against people born to money (especially the Kennedys), and Bush is certainly one of them.

Bush, Howard   After getting a "phony phone call" plugging Howard Stern from the "King of All VCRs," a flustered Larry King asked his Republican spokesperson guest, "Why should we vote for *Howard Bush?*"

Busta Rhymes   A rap singer who mentions Stern in one of his songs (". . . that nigga Howard Stern").

"Busty Dusty"   A woman with *massive* breasts, who has appeared on several Stern shows. Her breasts are so large that model/actress Carol Alt was flabbergasted and said, "I'm in shock!"

Butt Bongo Fiesta   The title of one of Stern's infamous videotapes. It was released in 1992 and features lots of derrieres of women who are invariably not as attractive as Howard describes them on his radio shows! About 260,000 fans plunked down $34.95, so the endeavor grossed (so to speak) $10 million.

"Butt Cheek Fever"   Stern's gay parody of the movie *Jungle Fever.*

Bykofsky, Stu   A Philadelphia radio columnist who wrongly predicted that Stern ("the original freak beak himself") would not succeed in the market.

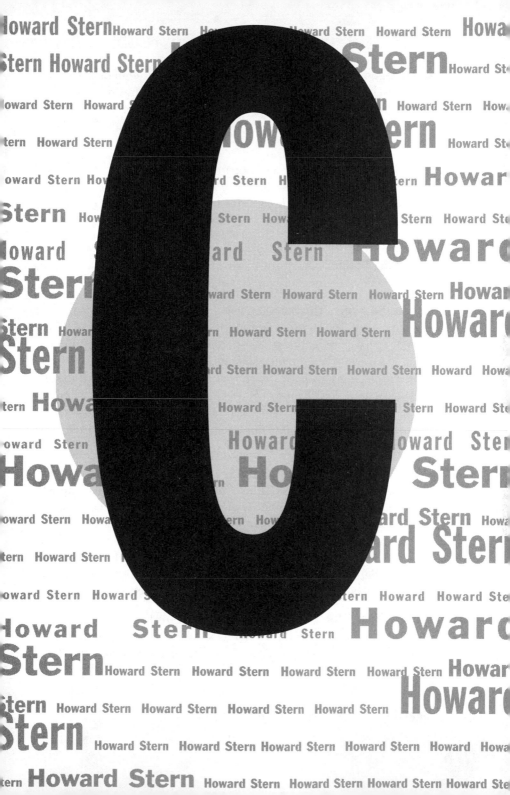

Cain, Dean   The television actor who plays Superman and Clark Kent on *Lois and Clark*, formerly one of Howard's favorite television shows. Cain was a varsity football player at Princeton University, famous for his interceptions, and was signed by the Buffalo Bills. He is the son of a movie director.

Caine, Michael   When Stern began preparing for his movie *Private Parts*, he began reading Michael Caine's popular book on acting and kidded about his advice. About Caine he said, "He's a scaly, unhealthy-looking guy and his eyes look like they're puffed out of his head . . . He looks like a frog."

Callahan, Colleen   Howard's hair dyer for the movie *Private Parts*. He (and wife, Alison) continue to use her services after production.

Callea, Samuel   The Buffalo, New York, man who threatened to kill Stern on April 16, 1996, in front of the garage ramp of 600 Madison Avenue just before 5:30 A.M. The police found a stolen shotgun in the trunk of his car. According to assistant district attorney Leemi Kahng, Callea "was angry with Mr. Stern that he went off the air in Buffalo." Curiously, he yelled, "Howard Stern is Number One" as he was led out of the Midtown North Precinct station.Callea later pled guilty to an attempted robbery charge in connection with the incident and was sentenced to five years probation.

Camp Wel-Met   The sleep-away Jewish camp that Stern attended in Narrowsburg, New York, amid the Catskill Mountains. The camp was affiliated with the *Met*ropolitan Jewish *Wel*fare Board, hence its name. He was a dishwasher at the camp during the summer after his high school graduation. In the summer of 1974, twenty-year-old Howard was a Wel-Met staff counselor who accompanied campers to Yellowstone National Park. Stern has attended at least one camp reunion (but not one high school reunion). **See Judith, Leslie, Nancy, Patty.**

Campanella, Phil   The listener from New York who did a Rodney Dangerfield imitation (talking about Jackie Martling) and won a place at a party at Scores, the nightspot where women dance naked in front of patrons. Campanella, by the way, is a patient of Dr. Lew Weinstein, Howard's longtime friend and school classmate.

Campbell, Glen   **See Hollywood Squares.**

Campbell, Jackie   The Albany Miss Howard Stern, a lesbian.

Camp Bryn Mawr   The summer camp that Debra and Emily Stern attended in the summer of 1996. Located in Pennsylvania, the all-girls camp costs about $5,500 for a fifty-two-day stay and is operated by Herb and Melanie Kutzen of Short Hills, New Jersey. The camp's address is: RR#5, Box 410, Honesdale, PA 28431. It is noteworthy that Howard did not send his daughters to a co-ed camp!

"Cancer Man, The"   A Stern song parody of "The Candy Man," one of Sammy Davis's most popular recordings, aired after Stern found out that Davis had throat cancer. (Stern is very much antismoking.) **See Kools.**

Candlewood Playhouse   A Connecticut nightclub at which Stern appeared after being fired by WNBC.

Capen, Stephen   A former deejay at WXRK radio with whom Stern liked to kid about his ex-wife.

Capricorn   Stern's birth sign. According to noted astrologer and self-help guru Naura Hayden *(Astro-Logical Love* and *How to Satisfy a Woman Every Time)*, "Howard is a triple Capricorn (Sun, Mercury, and Venus), which magnifies the Capricorn positives and negatives." She notes that he is "extremely hardworking, ambitious, determined, persistent, and very calculating."

Captain Janks   The rabid Stern fan, former shipping clerk, and part-time gas station attendant from Philadelphia who became Howard's greatest publicity man by calling television and radio shows and blurting out Stern's name, after feigning interest in the show's main theme or topic. His real name is Thomas Cipriano, and his WASPy-sounding name and voice (the nasal voice he hasn't used for a couple of years) are from his commanding officer when he was in the U.S. Army. Janks's first target: the bald "zookeeper" in Philadelphia. Howard was delighted to find out that Janks is an adopted child, making sense out of his nuttiness and misallocation of time placing "phony phone calls." Captain Janks was born on March 28, 1966. (His biological mother was only fourteen years old at the time!)

Captain Japan   A nickname that Howard has used on Prodigy, a name that he occasionally called Judge Lance Ito during the O. J. Simpson trial.

Car Cash   One of Stern's regular sponsors. While reading the commercial, Stern occasionally mentions that he ran an ad to sell a car when he was in Hartford. His wife, Alison, went for a test drive with a guy who answered the ad—making the point that one doesn't know who answers these ads, yet people put their lives in the hands of people who show up at their doorstep.

Carlin, George   The comedian and occasional guest on the Stern show who admitted that he took cocaine for five years and was once "in trouble" with the Internal Revenue Service. Carlin, by the way, was asked to replace Stern on WNBC in the fall of 1985 but declined. He also lost a 1978 Supreme Court case that forbade him to use "The Seven Dirty Words." One of Carlin's early routines highlighted the fact that he came from "White Harlem," near Columbia University. He noted that when some white guys hang out with black guys, the white guys end up talking like the black guy ("You know what I'm sayin'?"), and the black guy keeps talking the way he's always talked. **See *"The seven dirty words."***

Carlisi, Anthony   The Harley-Davidson–riding yoga instructor with whom Stern took a yoga lesson several years ago while vacationing in Scottsdale, Arizona. Carlisi joked in an on-air telephone conversation that Howard was one of his worst students.

Carlisle, Belinda   The rock singer (of the Go-Go's) who, when offered $10,000 to have sex with Stern, said she would and then corrected herself, "I said I *might* . . ." Carlisle is married to Morgan Mason, son of the late British actor James Mason.

Carradine, David   The *Kung Fu* star who told Howard that he has "an Irish organ," implying that he was well endowed. He appeared on the show to plug his book *Endless Highway.* Carradine said, "I was the first hippie and the last beatnik." Stern kidded him about naming his children Free and America, asking him, "What happens when your kid starts playing Little League?"

Carrey, Jim   About America's answer to France's Jerry Lewis, Stern said, "That bastard is the funniest bastard on the planet—he just rocks!" When Carrey first appeared on his show, Stern introduced him as "the white guy from *In Living Color.*" Ex-janitor Carrey received $20 million for starring in *The Cable Guy,* which received tepid reviews—for example, two thumbs-down from Siskel and Ebert. Carrey's father said, "Jimmy's not a ham. He's the whole pig!"

Carson, Corey   The son of talk-show host Johnny Carson, who appeared (3-20-92) on Stern's radio "Dial-a-Date." Corey handled Stern pretty well, but he would do well by not sending father Johnny an audiotape of the broadcast.

Carson, Johnny   The retired *Tonight Show* host and object of many Stern tirades. Stern calls Carson "another Hollywood phony." His main beefs with Carson are that he strongly controlled who appeared on the show and that he didn't let every comedian sit on the hallowed couch. Stern, of course, is guilty of similar practices—as is David Letterman, whom Stern has always defended. He also objects to Carson's alleged physical abuse of his first wife, Jody. Stern also has a thing against "liver spots," which Carson apparently has, and was peeved by Johnny's treatment of Jay Leno when he took over the show. He despises Carson, yet he does spoofs of Carnac routines ("Sternac") and sang "To All the Girls I've Loved Before" with Julio Iglesias, which was one of Carson's classic bits.

Carter, Dexter   The New York Jets football player who began calling the Stern show in the 1995 football season but stopped calling as the team got worse (two wins, eight losses, by November 6, 1995). Carter averaged a fumble per game and was released in early November 1995. He was immediately picked up by the San Francisco 49ers.

Carver, Daniel   The Ku Klux Klan member from Gainsville, Georgia, whose hot line ("Hello, white people . . .") Stern frequently calls on-air. In one of his recorded messages he said, "Female niggers have successfully breeded with apes and had 'porch monkeys.' " During the radio broadcast before the O. J. Simpson verdict, Carver predicted that Simpson would be found not guilty because of "ten niggers and two whites" being on the jury. He commented, "I'd let him go . . . He had killed a white slut . . . He should be turned loose . . . He's an animal." He added, "You can't punish dogs for biting." Carver told Howard that "the Jew is the lowest" and added, "I'd put a gay right under him . . . right on top of him, I guess." The Carver KKK hot line phone number is (770) 967-3479—the line is often busy, but keep trying—he's scary but funny! Carver's mailing address is P.O. Box 446, Oakwood, GA 30566.

Cash, Rosanne   The singer (and daughter of singer Johnny Cash) who told Stuttering John, "I hate Howard Stern . . . because I think he's disgusting and misogynist . . ."

Castaneda, Carlos   One of few authors whom Stern claimed to have read while a student at Boston University.

Castro, Fidel   When the Cuban dictator came to New York for the fiftieth anniversary of the United Nations, Stern commented, "My wife upside down looks like Fidel Castro," a reference to Castro's beard and wife Alison's pubic area. Castro's daughter was booked on the Stern radio show in early June 1996, but she canceled at the last minute, perhaps fearing that Stern would do some bad beard jokes.

Cates, Phoebe   The young movie actress (born Phoebe Katz) for whom Howard has lusted since he saw her topless in the movie *Fast Times at Ridgemont High*. She admitted to Howard that her bra size is 34-B.

Catholics   In a riff on presidential candidates, Stern said disparagingly, "The Catholic religion breeds guys like Pat Buchanan."

Cavett, Dick   The Iowa-born, Yale-educated television talk-show host and occasional call-in radio guest. Stern loves to kid Cavett for never having a show that achieved any significant ratings and for always getting canceled. (Cavett called in on January 22, 1996, to mention that CNBC canceled him.) Cavett's humor normally would not work on the Stern show, but Howard's constant badgering makes it work—Cavett tries the high, dry, droll approach, and Howard drags him immediately to curb, if not gutter, level. Cavett admitted to Stern that he was molested in a movie theater at age five, when an older man made him touch his "richard" during a Hopalong Cassidy movie. Stern has been disappointed that Cavett tacitly seems to approve of Woody Allen's relationship with stepdaughter Soon-Yi Previn. Cavett gave Stern some acting advice on the first day of filming: keep your buttocks tight, don't talk loud—the crew does not have to hear you—put a hand warmer in your undies, and keep your weight on the balls of your feet. Stern said that "Dick is a mental patient" and is the "only guy to use the words 'booger' and 'metamorphose' in the same sentence." Howard appeared about a foot taller than Cavett on his E! show, so Cavett cannot be much taller than five foot five.

Caviar   After his wife bought a "twenty-nine-dollar tin" of caviar and after a few first-class plane flights, Stern declared, "I love caviar." He soon ordered a tin to serve one morning during a broadcast. (Howard told his audience that his father claims that they club the sturgeon to help extract the eggs from the fish. Sturgeon, by the way, is an extremely large fish—up to twenty-four feet long and three thousand pounds! It would be a sight to see Ben Stern club one of these babies!)

Cegielski, Jim   The author of *The Howard Stern Book: An Unauthorized, Unabashed, Uncensored Fan's Guide.* Jim's loved ones listed in the book coincidentally include the names Emily and Alison. The foreword of his book was written by "Grandpa" Al Lewis of *The Munsters*. **See Lewis, "Grandpa" Al.**

Celeste   A Stern "Wack Packer," a telephone operator and occasional guest who was permanently maimed in an auto accident when she was twenty years old. She is so nutty about Stern that she has a tattoo of his face on her derriere. In the late 1980s she and her children showed up at Stern's house on Halloween night. She complained that Stern's wife, Alison, gave them only little Three Musketeers bars.

Celestine   The black woman (last name Tate) and occasional Stern guest who lacks usable arms and legs because of a rare birth defect and therefore has to move about on a mini gurney. At the "U.S. Open Sores" event, she played the "Star-Spangled Banner" with her tongue on keyboard. She wrote her autobiography *(Some Crawl and Never Walk)* by tapping a typewriter with her tongue. When Howard conjectured about what else she could do with her tongue, she told him not to worry about it because he was married. She raised two children and can also cook, sew, and swim. Financed by boxer Evander Holyfield, her book was published by Dorrance Publishing; telephone: (800) 695-9599 or (800) 788-7654; $17. When Stern found out that it cost Celestine $350 to take a taxi from Atlantic City to New York City, he coughed up $180, and Tom Chiusano produced the rest of the money. She hopes to star in a movie produced by Barbara Streisand, whom she has never met or contacted. Celestine can open a soft drink can with her tongue and pour the beverage in a glass by sucking the can and tilting it. When asked about his most memorable interviews by the Fresno, California, press, Stern was reluctant to answer but did mention his interview with Celestine.

The Celestine Prophecy   A book that Tempest, the stripper, gave to Stern to read. He started it and complained that he hated it and that it was too much like one of Carlos Castaneda's books that he read in college when he was taking drugs. *The New York Times* best-seller list, on which James Redfield's book has appeared for over two years, describes the book as follows: "An ancient manuscript, found in Peru, provides insights into achieving a fulfilling life."

Chaconas, Steve   A salesman and stand-up comedian who regularly appeared on Stern's radio show in Washington, DC, as part of the "Think Tank," a group of unpaid guests who specialized in shtick and mayhem. Chaconas did a good imitation of Curly of the Three Stooges. When Stern joined WXRK-FM in New York, he brought Chaconas aboard as a writer. He only lasted a few weeks, commuting from DC to New York, and then returned to Infinity Broadcasting's station WPGC-AM. (Stern, by the way, misspelled Steve's last name in *Private Parts*.)

Chamberlain, Wilt   The basketball great who appeared on Stern's show to plug his book. Wilt admitted that he doesn't like to sign autographs, that he once drove from Los Angeles to New York in thirty-six hours, and he lives in a thirteen-thousand-square-foot house, eight thousand more feet than Stern's house.

Chandler, Sarah   A transsexual and studio guest, who Stern said was "a Barbie doll with a hole punched in it." His/her boyfriend, Matt, accompanied her.

Chapin, Lauren   The child actress who played Kathy "Kitten" Anderson on the television series *Father Knows Best*. She said that from age nineteen to twenty-six she was addicted to heroin, spent one and a half years in a mental hospital, and served a three-year jail sentence for forging a check (in order to buy heroin). She also said she tried to commit suicide with a meat cleaver applied to her left wrist. She won Stern's "Queen for a Day" contest on his WWOR-TV show in the early 1990s, competing against child actors Billy Gray and Erin Moran.

Charity   The Scores nude dancer who "looks like Lauren Holly," comes from a broken home, and was molested as a child. She had a child at age sixteen and lived with actor Charlie Sheen for a few months. She said Sheen was five on a scale of ten in the lovemaking department ("a point for each inch"), was quick, and that she never had an orgasm with him. They made love only about four times during the relationship. He had given her about $10,000 in spending money and then had an assistant give her an additional $5,000 and ask her to move out when Sheen was smitten by another woman.

Charly   "One of the coolest movies," according to Stern. Starring Cliff Robertson, who won an Oscar for his performance, the 1968 movie is about a retarded man who becomes supersmart in a scientific experiment. It is based on the Daniel Keyes novel *Flowers for Algernon*. Robertson, by the way, appeared in the television version of the book in 1961.

Chase, Chevy   TV's *Saturday Night Live* comedian who "made one good movie," according to Stern, and is "not a funny person." A classic telephone conversation between the two confirmed that Chevy has lost his sense of humor. Howard says that Chevy is "bald, bloated, bitter, and jealous." About Stern, Chase said that he is "an ass . . . can't stand him . . . got the brain of an egg timer . . . a nothing!" When Fox TV launched the Chevy Chase show at a theater briefly named the Chevy Chase *Theatre* (not Theater!), Stern charitably predicted that the show would not last longer than six weeks. He was right—Fox canceled the show after five pathetic, agonizing weeks. Shortly thereafter, Fox wanted Howard to take over the time slot, which he turned down because his busy schedule wouldn't permit it. The network also didn't want to pay Howard $9 million, which is what they paid Chase.

Chase, Ken   The movie makeup man who taught Howard how to shave properly, using cold water and Kiehl's shaving cream.

Chazzer   Yiddish for "pig" or "hog," a name Howard called Gary Dell'Abate when he accused Boy Gary of using Stern's name to get free tickets to rock events, movie previews, etc. He also called Gary "King of the Glommers" and "The Glommeister General of the United States."

Cheating   In August of 1993 Stern committed one of the biggest sins in the male "kingdom." He announced on the air that all of his friends and co-workers cheated on their wives. All of those named denied the accusation, as did every other heterosexual man on the planet associated with Stern.

Cheating II   Stern readily admits that he often cheated in high school to get better grades. He admitted in July 1996, "I used to cheat my ass off at South Side Senior High School. I'm proud to admit it." He added, "it was the only way I was going to get through."

Chemistry   Not one of Howard's best courses at school, he admitted, "I dropped out of chemistry in high school."

Cher   The singer-actress said about Stern, "I hate him. He's just a creep." After Howard interviewed her, then boyfriend Rob Camiletti, in May 1990, Cher announced at a New York concert that Stern "really pisses me off . . . If Howard had brains in his penis, it would be the size of his pinkie." Comedienne Joan Rivers once told Howard that he looked like "Cher on steroids."

Chernoff, Mark   The former program director of K-Rock radio.

Chestnut, Mr.   Stern's gym teacher in his childhood.

Chicago   The third largest U.S. city and Stern's problem market. He is now on his third radio station, WJJD-AM. The previous station wanted him to alter his format.

Child, Julia   The French chef and speaker at Stern's commencement ceremony at Boston University in 1976. Once six feet two inches tall, the always pleasant Smith-educated cook has shrunk a few inches through the years.

Chinese   The ethnic group that Stern sometimes refers to as "Chinee." He complained that the O. J. Simpson trial had too many Chinese, including criminalists Dennis Fong and Dr. Lee, and Judge Ito—the latter, of course, being a *Japanese*-American.

Chinese food   Howard's favorite cuisine.

Chiusano, Tom   The general manager of WXRK radio, Stern's flagship station. According to Stern, Chiusano is stingy (Tom "Cheapasano") and plays a lot of golf. Stern complains about Tom every morning! His wife's name is Penelope.

Chong, Annabelle   The Chinese-American woman and Stern guest who set a record by having sex with 251 men in nine hours, including sixty minutes worth of smoking breaks. **See Saint Clair, Jasmine.**

Christopher   The CD-ROM "exec" whose phone call Howard returned to suggest titles such as "Doody Pak Man," a game about beating up illegal Mexican immigrants, "Master Stroke" (about actor Kirk Douglas recovering from a stroke), "Knock-Up" (in which blacks can have unprotected sex with as many women as possible), "The Robin Quivers Game" (about high colonics and a father molesting a daughter).

"Chubby"   One of Stern's slang words for an erection. **See "Wood."**

Chung, Connie   The former network television news anchor who, according to Stern, looks like a "wonton." She is married to television's Maury Povich.

Chwat, Sam   The New York speech therapist who worked with Elephant Boy and *Penthouse* Pet Kimberly Taylor, the latter to help her lose her Long G'islanduh accent.

Cindy and Robert   The couple who met on the book line for Stern's autograph signing at Barnes & Noble in Coral Place, Long Island. Howard said that Cindy looked like Julia Louis-Dreyfus with a 36-C bra size. Cindy and Robert immediately liked each other, and she said to herself, "I'm going to make it with this guy after this." After the book signing, they ate at a diner and then checked into the Regal Royal Hotel. She showered, he showered, and the rest is Sternomania history. She admitted, "He's the first Jewish man I've been with," clarifying that most of the guys she previously had sex with were "uncircumcised Italian guys from New Jersey." In reply to Howard's standard "three-input" question, she said, "Yes" and also said that she never wears panties. But get this: She lives in Florida and has been married for eleven years to a bodybuilder who is also more endowed than Robert.

Cipriano, Thomas   *See Captain Janks.*

Cirella, Ralph   Stern's "Man Friday"—his makeup man, hairstylist, chest-hair waxer, and clothing adviser. Stern says that he even "cuts the hair out of my nose." Stern bellyaches about Joan Rivers's having a 365-day-a-year hairdresser, yet Howard is guilty of the same indulgence. (Stern's look can be described as a "post–Louis XVI, Long Island 1970s Rock" look, in the spirit of his Long Island rock friends Dee Snider and Leslie West.) Among Ralph's other talent is his ability to do a good imitation of actor Peter Weller in the movie *RoboCop*. During one broadcast, Ralph dressed up as a woman, and prompted Howard to call him "RuRalph" and "Ralphina," noting that he looked "a little like Katie Sagal." Ralph has a nipple ring on his left nipple and a "hideous berry" or "blueberry" (as Howard calls it) on his face. Ralph admitted that around 1988, he and a friend had a black hooker perform oral sex on them for thirty dollars. (After two minutes, the hooker complained, "I don't have all day!") In late March 1996 Cirella was almost fired when he gave his assistant a list of Stern's needs for his movie trailer. On the list (Tom's of Maine toothpaste, Arm & Hammer deodorant, Q-tips, dental floss, etc.) was condoms. Laura left the list on Howard's desk in his house basement, and wife, Alison, snooping around Stern's desk, read the list and was puzzled. When Howard found out that she saw the list, he immediately confronted his wife and told her that Ralph had drawn up the list. According to Stern, "Ralphina" gets more hate mail than Daniel Carver, the Ku Klux Klan member from Georgia.

Clark, Dick   The always youthful television host *(American Bandstand)* and producer who occasionally calls the Stern show to plug one of his upcoming TV specials. Reacting to Howard's language, Clark said, "I can't say 'kiss my ass' on radio." Clark mentioned that Bob Horn and Lee Steward preceded him as hosts on *American Bandstand.* He doesn't mention that he is one of the richest men in the entertainment business.

Clark, Wally   The general manager of WWWW radio in Detroit whom Stern sent a demo tape to when he was working in Hartford. Stern was immediately offered $28,000; he asked for $30,000 and got it.

Clay, Andrew Dice   The tough-sounding, leather-jacketed comedian, born Andrew Silverstein in Brooklyn (home of Pattigan's gym). He now bills himself as Andrew Clay. A Stern favorite and regular, he periodically "disappears" from the Stern show, sometimes because he has some gripe against Howard. In his book *Private Parts,* Stern wrote five pages of glowing praise ("truly funny . . . a very nice guy . . . a very talented comic") about Clay. His movie *The Adventures of Ford Fairlane* was unanimously declared a disaster. He appeared on the CBS sitcom *Bless This House* for a year. After a long hiatus, Clay appeared on the Stern show in March 1996 to plug his HBO special *Assume the Position,* and was less than hospitable to Jackie "Jokeman" Martling, whom he called "half a fag" and said that he's been "in the business ten years and is still pressing CDs in his basement."

Clinton, Hillary Rodham   Stern pilloried Hillary, the First Lady, when he found out that she refused to autograph copies of her book *It Takes a Village* herself. (The White House maintained that an automatic signature machine would sign the books "for security reasons.") Stern has been known to sign fifteen thousand books in one day.

Club Bené   The nightclub in Sayreville, New Jersey, where Stern, some of his co-workers, and some guests have appeared. Howard made three appearances there after he was fired by WNBC-AM radio.

Club Soda Kenny   Andrew Dice Clay's personal assistant, who holds cigarettes and ashtrays for him.

Coburn, Toni   Stern's hairdresser during the *Private Parts* movie shoot, and also credited on Stern's E! show.

Cochran, Johnnie   The O. J. Simpson defense lawyer for whom Stern has no respect. Stuttering John asked Cochran embarrassing questions like "What do think about people who beat their wives?" (both Cochran and Simpson have been accused of wife beating), "Would you represent Hitler for the right price?" and "Did you send a thank-you card to Mark Fuhrman?" Stern called Cochran "the new black Jesus."

Cohen, Stephen J.   The general manager of WCAU radio in Philadelphia who came to Stern's defense when the FCC was fining him on a regular basis. Cohen said, "Stern may be distasteful to some or funny as can be to others. But he should be able to broadcast his brand of entertainment unfettered by federal control."

Cole, Harry   A communications lawyer who became one of Stern's "Think Tank" in his Washington, DC, days. A trivia expert with a sense of humor, Cole appeared on the show every couple of weeks. Cole wrote a parody of Paul Simon's "Fifty Ways to Leave Your Lover." **See Chaconas, Steve, and Kyger, Steve.**

Colford, Paul D.   The Long Island *Newsday* reporter and *Los Angeles Times* columnist who is the author of *Howard Stern, King of All Media: The Unauthorized Biography.*

"Colt 45"   Not the malt liquor but a superbosomed, high-octaned stripper in New York State who "bronskied" Libertarian (but not libertine) party leader Ludwig Vogel at Goldfinger's, a strip joint, en route to Albany for the party convention.

Combs, Ray   The host of the television quiz show *Family Feud* from 1988 to 1994. He replaced Richard Dawson. Combs was badly hurt in an auto accident and was a quadriplegic for a while but recovered through intense therapy. He committed suicide in mid-1996. Retired talk-show host Johnny Carson contributed $25,000 to help pay off Combs's existing family debts.

Comedy Tonight   The television show, hosted by Bill Boggs, on which Stern appeared on October 22, 1985, after being fired by WNBC radio. He did a comedy routine based on some S & M items (handcuffs, ankle cuff, etc.) that he bought at the Pleasure Chest.

Conlon Road   The street on which the Stern family lived in Roosevelt, Long Island.

Connelly, Dr. Scott   The head of Met-RX, a sponsor that makes nutritional candy bars, who gave Howard a $5,000 masturbation machine for his forty-second birthday.

Connick, Harry Jr.   The Louisiana singer-actor about whom Stern said, "They should cut off his trigger finger and stuff it down his throat" after Connick was arrested for carrying a gun. (Note: Stern has at least two licensed revolvers.) Connick was later ordered to tape a public service announcement to remind the public to leave guns at home before going to the airport.

"Control Freak"   *See Stern, Howard.*

Cookie Puss   The Carvel cake that Fred Norris gave his mother every Mother's Day.

Cooper, Pat   The embittered Italian-American comedian and ex-bricklayer (real name: Pasquale Caputo) whose career was revived by Stern. He left the last show in 1994 in a state of paranoia, complaining that Stern was going to "ambush" him. Cooper, judging from his on-air tirades and conversations with his family members, is an embittered and vindictive man. When his son Mike called the show, Pat said, "Mike, I love you." Mike lamented, "I never heard that before." Pat fired back, "You may never hear it again." He returned to the show on September 20, 1995, to receive his "F Emmy" award. About himself, Cooper uttered the classic line, "I am a genius of myself." He was quoted in *Stepping Out* magazine as calling Robin Quivers a "scumbag." Cooper told Stern, "I'm funny-funny-funny, you're semifunny." Cooper is a funny but alienated man who tells his family, "Kiss my fazools!" Yet one listener called to thank him for giving him fifty dollars in 1988 at the Marina Hotel for a plane ticket from Las Vegas to Los Angeles, after the listener lost all his money gambling. Cooper responded, "You try to help your fellow man." In other words, Cooper will give a stranger money but not some of his loved ones.

Coping with Alcoholic Parents   A book that Howard found in Fred Norris's bag, which he found unusual because he said that Fred's parents are not alcoholics.

Coppola, Mark   Former K-Rock deejay and brother of actor Nicholas Cage (real name Coppola), whom Stern liked to kid for being "the black sheep" of the family. The brothers are nephews of movie director Francis Ford Coppola.

Corky   The ex-husband of Miss Howard Stern (Elaine Marx), who often calls the Stern show to complain that Howard broke up his marriage. Corky was definitely a *bit* upset when Stern put Elaine on his "Fantasy Fuck List" in his book *Miss America,* and wrote that Elaine had "made it clear" that if unmarried she would "blow me, fuck me, and wash my sphincter with her tongue."

Corliss, Richard   The *Time* magazine reporter who wrote the cover article "X-Rated" (5-7-90), which mentioned Stern (and Sam Kinison, Andrew Dice Clay, Public Enemy, et al.) in the context of an overall trend toward raunchiness. The article said about Stern, "Turn him on, and odds are you can't gulp down your morning coffee before you hear him say 'penis.' "

Cornelius, Don   The emcee of television's black dance show *Soul Train.* When Stuttering John pressed him about his stand on Louis Farrakhan, Cornelius lost his deep-voiced cool, pushed John out of the way, and stormed off. Taking himself a tad too seriously, Cornelius mumbled something about being "in television for twenty-five years" as if he were a Lucille Ball, Dick Van Dyke, or some person with real talent. Howard and Robin kidded about Cornelius's interview technique with singers and bands, "Tell me about yourself"—in other words, he makes them interview themselves!

Cosby, Bill   Not one of Stern's favorite comedians. Stern called his long-running (1984–1992) comedy series "a tremendous bore." A creature of habit, Cosby gave all his children names begin with the letter E: Erika, Erinn, Ensa, Evin, and Ennis. (He told Phil Donahue, "That was my E-go!") Cosby has consistently received very high performer Q ratings (a combination of familiarity and popularity), unlike Stern. **See Q Ratings.**

Costas, Celia D.   One of the producers of Stern's movie, *Private Parts.*

Couric, Katie   NBC's *Today Show* cohost who was supposed to interview Stern about his book *Miss America* in mid-November 1995 but backed out because of "scheduling problems." About Couric he had previously remarked, "She's kind of cute . . . Maybe I'll get her dress off." Stern also complained that Couric was not afraid to interview O. J. Simpson and now is suddenly afraid to interview him. He calls Couric "Miss Perky" and predicts that she will get Epstein-Barr disease getting up early for *The Today Show* and for attending late night events.

"Courtesy flush" One of Howard's few announced laws of etiquette and a great practice in the bathroom and rest rooms: defecate and flush right away; drop another "log," flush again—to minimize obnoxious odors. **See Goodstein, Doug Z.**

Cousin Brucie **See Morrow, Brucie.**

Cousin Richie Howard's cousin, the supermarket owner in Florida. He played the saxophone in the Catskills and was destined to become the family celebrity—except that Howie was in the wings with no sax but with a flapping tongue. He says that Richie is "a nice guy . . . a good guy . . . a decent guy" whom he used to visit in Maine when he was a college student. Richie married a Cuban woman.

Crackhead Bob The man who was speech-impaired because he took too much crack cocaine. **See Harvey, Bob, and Special Kay.**

Crandall, Brad A New York radio personality whom Stern admired because he could field questions on just about any topics and "wing" the answers.

Crawford, Cindy The "supermodel" who remarked, after Howard made his Fartman appearance on the 1991 MTV awards, "I thought it was disgusting, and if my ass looked like that, I wouldn't show it on national television."

Croix The white female Stern guest who has sex only with black men but admitted she hadn't had sex at all for "five to six years." She spent almost three years in a juvenile detention home after being caught possessing marijuana while crossing the Mexico border.

Cronin, Mark The producer of the *Singled Out* television show who wanted to get on Stern's on-line bulletin board, but Howard won't let him because, according to Stern, Cronin did a lesbian television dating game rip-off a few days before. Cronin steals other material from the show, according to Stern. Cronin, a chemical engineer by training, was a writer on Stern's WWOR-TV television show.

Cronkite, Walter The retired CBS newscaster who seems to show up at a lot of social functions that Stuttering John attends. At a fundraiser for the rain forests, Stuttering John asked him if he really cared about the rain forests or was just coming to another party. Cronkite replied, "That's a dumb question . . . dumb, dumb, dumb."

Crooklyn   The Spike Lee movie that Robin Quivers didn't like because the background music was too loud. Stern refused to see the movie, complaining, "When you pay five bucks to see his movie you've been robbed."

Crucified by the FCC   The double-cassette audiotape and CD set ($29.95 plus $4.50 shipping and handling) that Stern produced, based on one of his Christmas show broadcasts.

Cruz, Brandon   The child actor who played Eddie Corbett on *The Courtship of Eddie's Father* (1969–72), and a guest on the Stern show (1-16-92). Thinking he was off-microphone, Cruz mentioned that athlete-actor Bruce Jenner had facial plastic surgery and that he "looks like a letter opener." When Cruz realized that he was on-air, he apologized, "Sorry Bruce."

Cyberqueen   One of Stern's on-line computer lovers. She said that she looked like actress Sharon Stone and sported a 36-C bra (when wearing one). (She does not look like Sharon Stone.)

Dag Hammarskjöld Plaza   The New York City location of Stern's mass protest against the Federal Communications Commission in 1987. He asked the crowd and his listeners, "Is it spelled FCC or KGB?"

Dahl, Steve   The deejay who preceded Stern at Detroit's WWWW radio, who left to go to WLUP-FM in Chicago. (His *Chicago Breakfast Club* was simultaneously aired on Detroit's WABX-FM during Stern's stint in Detroit.) Dahl's show was also simulcast on WQFM in Milwaukee. Some longtime observers of the radio scene believe that Stern adopted some of Dahl's routines but made them wilder.

Dallas   The Texas city where Stern on KEGL became number one, beating out the previously dominant Terry Dorsey.

D'Amato, Al   The U.S. senator (Republican) from New York whom Stern has supported and voted for. When Stern attended D'Amato's book signing at a New York bookstore in August 1995, Howard was given two bodyguards, only to find out later that he was being billed for them—about $500 for twenty minutes of work. One of D'Amato's lawyer friends called up and quickly solved the problem by volunteering to pay the bill himself. (The latter sounded like he didn't want the incident to flare up, for fear that it would draw attention to either D'Amato or the high cost of bodyguards.) In D'Amato's autobiography, Howard was delighted to find himself listed three times in the index.

D'Amico, Vinnie   An occasional Stern "Wack Packer" who eats live worms (in marinara sauce, of course!) and mice.

Danny   The thirty-eight-year old intern hired in 1995. An ex-bartender and waiter, he said, "You start to get sick of people."

Darden, Christopher   The O. J. Simpson prosecutor whom Stuttering John asked, "Would you ever date Arnell Simpson [Simpson's daughter]?" Darden replied, "I'd have to ask her father." Darden appeared at the studio in March 1996 to promote his book *In Contempt.* Darden admitted that he has had sex with only three women in his life. When Howard asked him to raise his right hand and swear to God, Darden raised his left hand. When Darden said, "I'm not a breast man," Howard quickly commented, "Robin's breasts will make you a breast man." He called Bob Kardashian "the skunk man," referring to the gray streak in his hair and to the fact that his socks usually have a white stripe. Darden's editor is Judith Regan, also Stern's and Quivers's editor. Regan showed up at the studio to announce that Darden's book was number one on the best-seller list.

Dare, Alexa The *Swank* magazine cover girl and former secretary who said she spent a night with talk-show host Jerry Springer. Ultimately, no hanky-panky occurred, although, according to Alexa, Jerry showed signs of wanting to quickly advance the relationship. Alexa noted that a pornographic videotape was in the VCR, but Springer removed it after briefly running it. **See Springer, Jerry.**

Darling, Bill The general manager of WNPL-TV in Naples, Florida, who canceled Stern's WWOR-TV show because advertisers and local citizen groups complained.

Darren the Foot Licker The man who was obsessed with the idea of sucking Robin Quivers's toes. He appears on Stern's *U.S. Open Sores* video. Robin beat him in a tennis match, depriving him of a chance to lick her feet.

David the Intern As a Stern Show intern for one year, David was asked to buy a slew of gay magazines and was greatly embarrassed in the process. When Froggie, the blind diabetic, visited the studio, David put a pinhole in his paper cup so that it leaked. Fred Norris's complaint about him was that he didn't provide enough butter and syrup for his French toast one morning. David said that Fred was "a genius but insane." He is now a stand-up comedian.

Davis, Don Stern's program director in Washington, DC—he replaced Denise Oliver in September 1981.

Davis, Jack The amusing artist and caricaturist who drew the WNBC radio subway posters highlighting *Imus in the Morning* and *Night Shtick* (Howard's afternoon drive-time show).

Davis, Sammy, Jr. The late entertainer who flabbergasted Stern when he found out that Davis, who wore hundreds of thousands of dollars worth of jewelry, left his wife, Altovise, not only penniless, but, in fact, in debt. Six months before Davis died, Howard called him at a New York hotel, and Sammy uttered the classic line "Man, don't you believe in preambling?" He wanted to be forewarned that he was on the air. Howard said in a Davis imitation, "Sammy, may I say, 'Cong, conga, cong'?" and then asked him, "How do you feel about Billy Crystal imitating us?"

Dead Dave   One of Stern's interns who preceded Stuttering John in asking celebrities embarrassing questions. Howard said, "His Dr. Ruth [interview] is one of my favorite interviews of all time . . . You can't beat that one for sheer entertainment."

Death penalty   Part of Stern's libertarian political platform in 1994. He later admitted that he was no longer in favor of it, having followed the O. J. Simpson case in which a rich person received one form of justice, and many others receive another form of justice—in other words, real guilt or innocence is increasingly irrelevant in trials.

De Bella, Annette   The Philadelphia zookeeper's wife, who split up with the vanquished deejay and appeared on the Stern show (for $5,000). Stern massaged her back and convinced her to play "Dial-a-Date." Her prize: a date with Captain Janks. *See De Bella, John.*

De Bella, John   The Philadelphia deejay on WMMR-FM radio whom Stern made a strong commitment to beat in the ratings. The Jerry Colonna (Bob Hope's road-show comic) look-alike eventually lost his job due to falling ratings (because of the success of the Stern show), and his wife, Annette, committed suicide. Stern later invited "Yazoo" De Bella as a guest to make him admit that Stern was number one and his master. Stern, in a surprise act of graciousness, allowed Infinity Broadcasting to hire De Bella as the afternoon drive-time deejay on their station WYSP in 1994.

Debra   The name of one of Stern's three daughters, the middle one. It is derived from the Hebrew name Deborah, which originally meant "a bee." (In the Bible, Deborah was a prophetess and judge in Israel.) Author Bruce Lansky in his book *The Baby Name Personality Survey* wrote, "Most people agree that Deborah is a good name for a willowy beauty who is dependable and intelligent. Some, though, think of Deborah as theatrical or even wild."

Dell'Abate, Gary   Gary is a graduate of Adelphi College, about which Stern kids him because Howard thinks that his alma mater, Boston University, is so much better. (Both schools share the fact that their presidents have made outrageous amounts of money!) Gary's previous jobs were at a record shop and at Houlihan's, a restaurant-bar. He also gets kidded by Stern for signing a scroll-like horizontal *H* under the *G* in the name Gary. His brother Tony is a freelance writer and commercial Realtor in Austin, Texas. His brother Steven died of AIDS in 1991. Gary is also known as "Fla Fla Flooey" and other variations.

Dellon, Vicki   One of Alison Stern's friends who has appeared on the Stern show. Her husband works in "plumbing supply," about which she interjected, "Need a toilet?"

Delsener, Ron   The producer who tried to package a *Friends of the Howard Stern Show* with Jackie Martling, Gary Dell'Abate, Elephant Boy, and others, but when Stern found out he hit the roof.

De Marco, Mrs.   Stern's second grade teacher, who, according to him had "big jugs . . . was tall . . . She was nice."

Denise   The name of Tom Chiusano's secretary.

Denver, Bob   "Gilligan" in the mid-1960s television comedy series *Gilligan's Island,* and occasional guest. Denver told Howard that one of the actresses on the series was a lesbian and a congresswoman, not making it clear if he was talking about one person or two. Gilligan's first name was never mentioned in the series, but Denver said that he and the creator/producer, Sherwood Schwartz, agreed that it should have been Willie.

De Pace, Scott   The robotic cameraman of Stern's E! show who said he met two Asian transsexuals at a club and found them sexually alluring enough to kiss. He defended his own heterosexuality and saw no aspect of homosexuality in his ardent reaction. One of them, "Bianca," said that she wanted to "lick him all over." When Stern conjectured that De Pace may not be totally straight, Scott vehemently denied the possibility. Scott's name is pronounced 'Dee Pace' because, he told Howard, the name was originally Di Pace in Italy.

Destiny   A redheaded stripper, one of the first women to strip in front of him during a "Dial-a-Date" routine on-air.

Details   A magazine about which Stern has said, "It's the coolest magazine . . . my favorite magazine."

Detroit   The city in which Stern won his second broadcasting job—at WWWW-FM, for which he was paid $28,000 in 1980. He was fired nine months later when the station went to a country and western format.

Dial-a-Date An occasional bit, a variation of television's *The Dating Game,* in which Howard tries to fix up a guest, sometimes a caller-in from previous days, with a listener. Elephant Boy has had several dates from this bit, and Fred Norris met his wife, Allison, by playing the game.

Diamond, Laurie David Letterman's assistant, whom Dave calls "Diamond" (no first name). She accompanied Letterman when he appeared on the Stern show in March 1996.

Diarrhea A word that Stern sometimes pronounces as if it were spelled dia-rear!

"Dickhead" One of Howard's favorite vulgarisms.

"Dickwad" Yet another one of Howard's favorite vulgarisms. Fortunately most listeners don't know what it means.

Dikowitz, Jerry The boy whose Bar Mitzvah Howard's band Electric Comicbook played at. Dikowitz played the drums in the trio.

Dildo *See Gabor, Zsa Zsa.*

Dinkins, David The former mayor of New York City, whom Stern did not like. After Stern found out that most Jews supported the reelection of Dinkins, he complained (10-1-93), "Is there any Jew in his right mind who would vote for Dinkins?" He added, "Someone's putting rat poison in the matzoh; there's acid in the gefilte fish; maybe the yarmulkes are too tight." Stern also made frequent fun of Dinkins's tendency to sweat. In the Dinkins-Giuliani race, Gary Dell'Abate voted for Dinkins because he felt that "blacks needed a voice." Stuttering John once asked Dinkins (and separately, critic Rex Reed), "Why do black people hoot and howl during movies?"

Disney One of the stocks that Stern admits that he owns. He frequently talks about the genius of Michael Eisner, the chairman of Disney.

Dole, Bob The U.S. senator whom Stern would not vote for because he's almost his father's age. He calls him Bob "Dull."

Donahue, Phil The former daytime talk-show host whose major sin, in Stern's mind, is that he married actress Marlo Thomas, a "shrew" who had "everything handed to her on a silver platter." Desmond Atholl, a butler for the couple, wrote a tell-all book about them—a book that Stern read with delight. When Stern reluctantly appeared on the *Donahue* show to plug his book, he scored a 7.2 rating versus the 5.7 average it achieved that month. Stern has called Donahue a "two-bit phony."

Donaldson, Sam   *See Giuliani, Rudolf (hairstyle of).*

Douche bag   One of two phrases (in addition to the other seven no-no words in broadcasting) that Stern was forbidden by contract with Infinity to use on the air. It is New York slang used as a derogatory term to describe a jerk or disagreeable person. He began using the word regularly around the same time he settled his new contract in early 1996. **See Scumbag.**

Doug   The deputy mayor of Bayville, Long Island, the town in which Jackie Martling lives. He confirmed a listener's call that Jackie was mentioned in a recent issue of the local newspaper, according to the listener, for "reneging on a deal with the Bayville mayor to raise funds for a park." Jokeman hadn't seen the article but confirmed the story. He rightfully wanted the site of a former gas station, now cemented over, changed into grass, trees, and park benches because, to him, it was an eyesore in an otherwise scenic town; but he says that the mayor, Vicky Siegel, misinterpreted the degree to which the Martlings were going to get behind this project, financially and promotionally. Doug mentioned on the air he had once met Jackie at his famous "jetty."

Douglas, Buster   The first heavyweight boxer to beat Mike Tyson, Douglas told Stern that he made less than $75,000 (Douglas actually said $7,500, but probably meant $75,000!) on a $1.3 million purse in the Tyson fight and cleared only $1 million when he grossed $25 million for his next big fight. Stern was genuinely saddened (as were many listeners) to hear that a successful boxer could make so little money on a big event and purse. Douglas further depressed Stern when he said that he appeared in a Sega commercial for only $3,000. Poor Buster came to the studio feeling good about himself and left in a despondent stupor. Stern, no doubt, will encourage reform in this area.

Douglas, Dwight   A radio consultant who almost got Howard a job in Columbus, Ohio, when he was still working in Hartford. He thought Stern's broadcasts were compelling and said that Howard sounded like "Alan Alda on acid." Douglas forwarded a tape of Stern's broadcast to WWWW in Detroit, which soon hired him, and steered him toward WWDC in Washington, DC, when the Detroit station switched from rock to a country music format.

Douglas, Eric   One of actor Kirk Douglas's sons and an occasional Stern show guest. Eric told Howard that the first time he had sex it was with actress Lesley-Anne Down in Yugoslavia in the early 1970s, on location for a movie. Eric is Kirk's youngest son but is apparently not his number-one son! Douglas was sentenced to thirty days in jail on July 16, 1996, for causing a ruckus on an airline flight from Los Angeles to Newark, New Jersey. He previously spent a night in jail for not fulfilling a court-imposed drug treatment program, and has had other scrapes with the law.

Douglas, Mike   The 1960s afternoon television talk-show host whom Stern loved to watch as a youngster when he arrived home from school. On the set of Stern's first television shows, a photo of Douglas was hanging on the wall behind him. Revisionist Stern has commented, "Mike Douglas was a puppet head who could barely read off a cue card . . . Douglas was a cardboard man."

Dove   The brand of bar soap that Howard uses.

Downey, Morton, Jr.   The irascible and pugnacious former talk-show host (born Sean Downey), who threw a punch at Stuttering John. In the late 1980s, Infinity Broadcasting offered him $500,000 plus another $500,000 in bonuses to do a one-hour radio show every weekday, and he turned down the offer. (Downey's father, by the way, was a popular tenor in the 1930s and 1940s.) He announced in mid-1996 that he had lung cancer.

Drescher, Fran   The comedic actress and star of television's *The Nanny*, and a favorite Stern guest ("She's really a hot-looking girl even though she looks like your mother"), who reluctantly discussed that she was raped earlier in her career. She and a girlfriend were raped by two black brothers, one of whom was on parole. They were sentenced to 114 years, but Stern told her, "Those guys should have had their penises chopped off." Fran, by the way, appeared in the movies *This Is Spinal Tap* and *Cadillac Man*. She has a whiny, nasal Long Island laugh, which Stern likes and uses as a "sound effect" at least once every broadcast. Before the success of *The Nanny*, Fran started a crouton business. She titillated Stern when she told him that she rarely wears panties. Regarding the possibility of engaging in lesbian sex, Drescher told Stern that it is "not to say it's not in my fantasy." When he asked her if she ever used a vibrator, she immediately said no and then added, "I think we tried one year ago." She also admitted that actor-director

Warren "Lothario" Beatty wanted to do a threesome with Fran. When Stern brought up the subject of penis size, she said, "It's not the size, it's the motion of the ocean." When Stern asked her if she ever had sex with a man other than her husband, she blinked a few extra times before Stern changed the subject. Fran mentioned that she is suing *TV Guide* for causing hot coffee to burn her during a cover shoot. *TV Guide* denied that it was negligent. The suit is pending as of this writing. She must be accident-prone. At a party her sweater caught fire and television executive Howard Stringer had to rip it off, exposing her chest but preventing burns. In late 1996, she split up with her longtime husband, a childhood sweetheart. **See Aykroyd, Dan.**

Dresner, Sy   The owner of WCCC radio in Hartford, Connecticut, where Stern worked after leaving the station in Briarcliff Manor, New York. After he fired the midday deejay, he took over and introduced records by addressing artists as "Mr. Leonard Skynyrd" and "Mr. Led Zeppelin." Sy was tight with money, to say the least. He reluctantly gave Howard sixty-five dollars to spend a week at a motel on the Berlin Turnpike. His son Ronnie is the promotion director of the station. When director Betty Thomas heard Sy on the Stern show, she decided to put his character in the movie *Private Parts.*

Drugs   Stern admits to having used marijuana and hashish in high school, as well as amphetamines, quaaludes, heroin, peyote, and LSD when he was at college. He took four "hits" of the latter (which was laced with "speed") while still under the influence of hashish and he "tripped out"—and had wild hallucinations.

Dunn, Ellen Stern   Howard's sister—she sports an effusive, gummy, and toothy smile, not unlike that of Gary Dell'Abate. Howard saw her dance nude when she was nine or ten (and he was five) and noticed that she already had "trademark Stern-woman breasts." The night before Passover in 1990, she kept telling Howard, to his dismay, "I'm glad you're not my husband."

Duva, Dan   A coproducer (with Shelly Finkle) of Stern's New Year's Eve pay-per-view special, whom Stern praised in an on-air eulogy (1-31-96), after Duva died of a brain tumor at age forty-four. Primarily a boxing promoter (e.g., the 1981 Leonard-Hearns and 1994 Holyfield-Moorer fights), Duva was a graduate of Rutgers University and Seton Hall Law School, and the son of Lou Duva, a longtime boxing trainer still.

Dworkin, Stan   Stern's lieutenant-governor running mate when he ran for governorship of New York in the 1994 election on the Libertarian ticket. Dworkin is a leather-goods manufacturer from Rockland County. Howard made Dworkin tweeze out the bushy hair in his ears during the short-lived campaign.

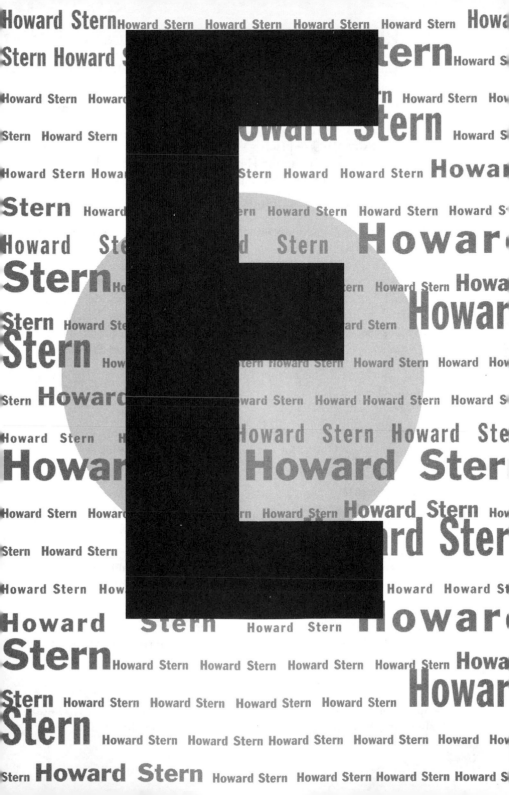

E! Network   The cable network on which Howard has had two shows: an interview show in 1992–93 (thirty-six episodes) and *Howard Stern,* a tightly edited "lift" of his radio show, which airs twelve times a week, for which Stern reportedly gets $33,000 per episode.

Earth Dog Brent   Fred Norris's predecessor at Stern's Washington, DC, radio program, prompting Howard to call him "Earth Dog Fred." Henceforth he should be known as "Earth Dog Eric."

Easterbrook, Leslie   *See Hollywood Squares.*

Ebert, Roger   The chubby movie critic and regular guest, who sometimes appears with partner Gene Siskel on Stern's radio and television shows. For several years Stern mistakenly thought Ebert was a homosexual, but Siskel convinced Howard otherwise ("He attracts a lot of women"). Now Stern likes to probe Ebert about his "forbidden" relationship—he is married to a black woman, who is a lawyer, and has two black grandchildren. Stern makes Ebert weigh himself on air, and he usually weighs over 270 pounds. ***Also see Siskel and Ebert.***

Eden, Barbara   The buxom blond star of television's *I Dream of Jeannie* (1965–70). When she appeared as a guest, Howard correctly guessed her bra size—34-C.

800-52-STERN   Stern's mail-order phone number for his videotapes and audiotapes. When Howard has no immediate product to sell, the recording instructs people to call (516) 231-5712 (Long Island, NY).

Einziger, Scott   One of Stern's three E! show producers, he has a small tattoo of a scorpion.

Electra, Carmen   A white *Playboy* playmate who has never had sex with a white male. Her first sex partner, at age seventeen, was a black rap singer. She lived with rock singer Prince for two and a half years. (Prince gave her the name Electra.) And B-Real from the Cypress Hill band paid for her saline implants.

Electric Comicbook   The name of Stern's band in his early teens. Jerry Dikowitz played drums, Robert Karger played the guitar, and Howard played keyboard.

Elephant Boy   *See Schreiber, Fred.*

Elmsford Holiday Inn   The motel in Westchester County where Howard was a deejay. He was fired because he didn't play disco music—he played songs from *Sergeant Pepper's Lonely Hearts Club Band* and other albums.

Eluction, Lance   A gay hairdresser character that Howard played opposite Fred Norris's gay Bob in their early days on WNBC in New York.

Emily   The name of Stern's oldest daughter. Stern commented that at age twelve she had in her bedroom her own telephone line, an answering machine, a big stereo, and a television set. She occasionally makes "phony phone calls" to the New York rock station Z-100 and made one to Stern sponsor Dial-A-Mattress ("Leave off the last *s* for savings"). Her Bat Mitzvah was held in May 1996. *See Bat Mitzvah.*

Enuff Z'Nuff   The rock group whose member Chip told Stern on microphone that he had sex with Madonna. This is one of Howard's favorite groups; their songs include "Fly High Michelle" and "Kiss the Clown."

Epididymitis   Howard announced on March 2, 1992, that he had this ailment, an infection, near his right testicle. His mother gave him advice and told him that she consulted his aunt Sally. Howard complained, "My aunt hasn't seen testicles in twenty-five years!"

"Equal Opportunity Offender"   What former talk-show host Arsenio Hall called Stern in his introduction when Stern appeared on his show.

Ershel, Joe   The *USA Today* editor and writer who suggested in his commentary that Stern was a more worthy political candidate than Virginia's Chuck "Give Me a Back Rub" Robb or Ollie "Stonewall" North.

Erving, Julius   The great professional basketball player, one of the famous people from Stern's hometown, Roosevelt, Long Island. Erving graduated from Roosevelt High School in 1968, when Howard was in the eighth grade.

Et cetera   The common Latin phrase which Howard pronounces "ex cetera."

"Evacuate"   The word that Howard often uses for "defecate."

Evans, Pat   The female program director at WXRK when Stern initially joined the station.

Evergreen Media   The owner of WLUP-AM and FM in Chicago, for whom Stern started broadcasting in October 1992. Ten months later

Evergreen terminated Stern. Infinity Broadcasting filed a $35 million breach of contract suit, plus $10 million in punitive damages, against Evergreen in late 1993. As of this writing, the suit is still pending.

Ewing, Patrick   The New York Knicks basketball player whom Stern calls "the missing link." He said that "they found his father in a cave."

Fabian   The name of Stern's barber (hairdresser!)—at Perfidia's Hair World in SoHo and at 10 E. Eighth Street, New York, NY.

Fabio   The Italian model-actor who told Stern that he likes American women more than French, Swedish, and Italian women. His real name is Lanzoni, and he shaves his chest once a week.

Fairleigh Dickinson University   Howard admitted (3-30-92) that he was turned down by Fairleigh Dickinson University in New Jersey.

Farentino, James   The Broadway, television, and film actor who was arrested for stalking his girlfriend Tina Sinatra, a Stern guest. Farentino pleaded no contest and was given three years' probation. He told Howard that she became hysterical when he overcooked sausage and peppers. He did admit that "it took me a long time to get off the booze."

Farley, Chris   The obese *Saturday Night Live* comic, who Stern says "is one of the funniest guys around . . . I dig that guy."

Farting   Howard's favorite pastime! His excessive gas is probably caused by his tendency to eat with his mouth open and "smack his lips." Most of his general managers and program directors have tried to get Howard to stop farting on the air, with no success. Robin Quivers, by the way, confessed one morning that she sometimes sits on the john merely to release flatulence from her royal orifice.

Fartman   A favorite Stern character who made his debut in Washington, when Howard called the Polish embassy and farted into the phone when he spoke to the ambassador. From K-Rock in New York, he called the Iranian embassy in 1988, after the United States accidentally shot down an Iranian plane, killing 290 Iranians. He phoned the Chinese consulate during the suppression of their students. He got an answering machine, blurted out his condemnation of their actions, and said that he asked F.A.O. Schwarz to boycott the sale of Chinese checkers. Stern also called the Panama Marriott Hotel in the Noriega days. When *The Satanic Verses* author Salman Rushdie was the object of a death decree declared by the Ayatollah Khomeini, he could not reach the Iranian embassy, so Gary, for reasons unknown, telephoned the Hilton Hotel in Tripoli, Libya. (He told the person who answered the phone, "Your sister circumcises camels with her eyeteeth.") Fartman's greatest exposure was at the MTV awards in 1991 when, harnessed and hitched to a cable, he "flew" onstage from the wings. His scrotumlike codpiece, exposed cellulite buttocks, and flabby belly were a sight to behold!

Fat Johnny   A grade school bully who picked on young Howard.

Father Knows Best   The prime-time television comedy series which ran from 1954 to 1963, and starred Robert Young and Jane Wyatt. Several child stars of the series have been guests on his shows. **See Gray, Billy, and Chapin, Lauren.**

FCC   The Federal Communications Commission, Stern's nemesis. In a 1990 complaint they said that Stern made "lewd and vulgar" references and dwelled on "sexual matters, including sexual intercourse, orgasms, masturbation, lesbianism, homosexuality, breasts, nudity, and male and female genitalia." Through the years, they imposed fines of $1.7 million on the Infinity-owned stations, which Infinity initially deferred paying, but ultimately agreed to pay without conceding wrongdoing. Howard loves to talk about himself as a "martyr" and continued to try to get Roger Clinton, President Clinton's stepbrother, and Senator D'Amato to come to his aid. When Infinity agreed to pay the $1.7 million in September 1995 without conceding wrongdoing, Stern objected to press reports saying that he *personally* was fined and called *New York Post* reporter Bill Hoffman to complain about his article's headline, "Stern to pay shocking $1.7M FCC fine." Yet transcripts of his daily diatribes against the FCC indicate clearly that he said that *he* was getting fined, and, in fact, he told Joan Rivers in late September 1995 that "*I* get fined by the government." In his book *Miss America* he reprints the September 3, 1995, edition of the *New York Post* featuring the headline HOWARD PAYS $1.7 M.

Feirstein, Harvey   The frog-throated drag-queen actor-writer who especially hates Stern (". . . that fucking asshole . . . I hate that fucking Howard Stern"). Stuttering John asked him, "What was the worst disaster: AIDS or *Legs Diamond* [a play starring the late Peter Allen, who had a strong gay following]?"

Feldman, Corey   The child actor *(Goonies* and *Stand By Me)* and occasional call-in guest. He told Howard that he once spent a night with singer Michael Jackson in the same hotel room, after a trip to Disneyland, but nothing sexual happened between them. Feldman said that at age fifteen he was molested by a friend and pretended that he was asleep. He lost his virginity at age fourteen and said that he had sex with actress Drew Barrymore. Stern admitted (3-30-92) that he never had sex with a virgin, including his wife! After comedian Sam Kinison

67

died, he told Howard that he and Kinison would do "Celebrity Blast-Offs" in which they would take drugs and stay awake and high for two to three days. Kinison once took Corey to an Alcoholics Anonymous meeting after a night of drinking. They parted that night in front of a liquor store. Feldman once dated disk jockey Casey Kasem's daughter.

Fellatio   The oral sex act performed on men. Out of nowhere but on a high from finishing the movie *Private Parts*, Howard treated his crew and audience to lessons on how to properly perform fellatio, proclaiming that "all women think they're good at it and they're not." Fred Norris offered his own advice—don't touch the "danglers" (testicles)!

Fiducia, Donna   A radio traffic reporter at WNBC when Stern did his stint there.

"The 50 Most Influential Baby Boomers"   A list that Howard was number forty-four on, published by *Life* magazine in mid-1996.

50 Ways to Rank Your Mother   Howard's first recording, a comedy album, produced when he was working in Washington, DC, in the early 1980s. The album cover features Howard dressed in boots and leather, and holding a whip over a motherly-looking woman. The title song lyrics were written by Harry Cole. The album was released with the title *Unclean Beaver*. **See Cole, Harry.**

Figler, Bruce   A disk jockey at WRNW radio in Briarcliff Manor, New York, when Stern worked there.

Filipinos   A group of people whom Stern detests almost as much as the French. **See Marcos, Imelda.**

Fine, Marshall   The writer who conducted the Howard Stern interview in *Playboy* magazine (April 1994).

Fink, Jimmy   A former K-Rock deejay with whom Stern talked occasionally on-air.

Finnerman, Gerard   The name of the Wall Street executive who reportedly got so drunk on a plane flight from Buenos Aires to New York that he pushed down a stewardess in the first-class section and defecated on the service cart, tracking feces all over the plane. Stern and crew took great delight in using the incident as a running gag for a week. Other passengers on the plane included the presidents of Argentina and Portugal.

Fioravanti, Dom   The general manager of WNBC radio when Stern was hired as the afternoon drive-time man. He gave Stern seven no-nos for his broadcast, only one of which (no. 7: none of the "seven dirty words") Stern has ever adhered to. Fioravanti later became senior vice president and general manager of MTV.

First Amendment   "Who do you think is going to test the First Amendment? It's guys like me. So where was Mike Wallace and Andy Rooney? Nowhere!"

Flat tax   Stern is in favor of the flat tax and joked one morning, "I'm in favor of the flat tax. Any girl that's flat gets taxed." He supported the brief presidential candidacy of U.S. Senator Arlen Specter, mostly because of his pro-choice and pro-flat-tax stances.

Fleming, Art   The quiz-show host who appeared on Howard's quiz spoof "Is This a Life?" based on the old TV show, *This Is Your Life*. It was broadcast on February 9, 1991.

Flo and Eddie   Former deejays on WXRK radio. Flo (born Mark Volman) was a member of the Turtles rock group. Flo later called in and thanked Howard for his advice on moving one's bowels, i.e., not pushing.

Florio, Jim   The former Democratic governor of New Jersey whom Stern supported before he ran against Christine Todd Whitman.

Flowers, Gennifer   President Bill Clinton's "alleged" girlfriend whom Stuttering John asked at a press conference, "Gennifer, did Governor Clinton use a condom?" She actually laughed in response to it. He also asked her, "Will you be sleeping with any other presidential candidates?"

Forbes, Steve   About the third-generation magazine publisher, Stern said that Forbes "looks too goofy to be president" and "looks like the Joker after falling into a vat of acid."

Forman, Dan   Stern's nebbishy producer at WWOR-TV, who became the producer of WNBC-TV's *Live at Five* show. In one bit about the birth of Jesus, Dan Forman's head appeared as the head of baby Jesus. Forman's wife's name is Robin. At Stern's daughter Emily's Bat Mitzvah, Forman and his wife were hugging and kissing a lot.

Fornatell, Pete   A former disk jockey on K-Rock radio, prior to the January 5, 1996, elimination of deejays at the station.

Four Seasons Hotel   The posh hotel that Stern stays at when he stays late (e.g., when taping the Letterman show late in the afternoon) in New York City. The address is 57 East Fifty-seventh Street, right around the corner from the K-Rock studios. Phone for reservations: (212) 758-5700.

Fox TV   The television network owned by Australian media mogul Rupert Murdoch, which produced five pilot Howard Stern shows but never aired them because the distributor, DIR Broadcasting, canceled the program—supposedly because it wasn't attracting enough national advertising. Joe Piscopo, Jackie Mason, Bob Goldthwait, Leslie West, David Brenner, Al Lewis, Mason Reese, Frank Zappa, and Cindy Adams were among the guests on these shows. Fred Norris and Jackie Martling barely appeared on the shows. A couple of years later Fox wanted Stern to bail them out. *See Chase, Chevy, and Salhany, Lucie.*

Foxworthy, Jeff   The "redneck" comedian (and ex–IBM salesman) about whom Stern has occasionally complained, especially after he signed a $1.75 million book deal by Hyperion Publishing. For the record, Foxworthy has generated decent sales results. His record album *Games Rednecks Play* sold 1.8 million copies, and *You Might Be a Redneck If . . .* sold 2.6 million copies. His paperbacks have sold a total of 2.2 million copies.

Fraley, Stormin'   The Cleveland listener who won the Scores/O. J. contest for his variation of the "phony phone call" to newscaster Peter Jennings ("I see O. J. . . ."). *See Maury.*

France   A country that Stern hates because of its aloofness, anti-American sentiments, and anti-Semitic acts during World War II. In *Private Parts* Stern listed the French as "my least favorite peoples." Charles De Gaulle, according to Stern, was a "pussy." The late movie director Louis Malle, husband of actress Candice Bergen, was a "creep," and the late actor Yves Montand "sucks." Howard finds the Eiffel Tower "ugly" and declared that all French clothing designers are "homos." He also derisively calls the French "snail-eaters."

Francis, Anne   The actress who played private detective Honey West on the 1965–66 television series of the same name, one of Howard's love objects as a child.

Francis, Arlene   The former panelist of the classic television show *What's My Line?* who appeared on Stern's WWOR-TV show spoof "What's My Secret?" As good as Arlene was in the old days, she didn't guess that the contestant Heather was a lesbian.

Frank, Roz   A traffic reporter at WNBC radio who was not one of Howard's big fans.

Franklin, Joe   The sunny-dispositioned longtime radio and television talk-show host and nostalgia buff, about whom Stern said, "another celebrity you have to love."

Frazier, Tyrone   The boxer who occasionally calls the Stern show and was originally introduced as "Joe Frazier's nephew." It turned out that he was not related to Frazier but used the name for promotion purposes. Tyrone plugged his fights (and usually lost) and now works at matches counting punches. Tyrone was shot in the leg in a workout gym by Joe Frazier, whose gun accidentally went off.

Freeman, Barbara   A woman who worked in the sales and traffic department of WRNW radio in Briarcliff Manor, New York when Stern worked there. She remembers that Howard won the heart of one advertiser who supplied bagels, lox, and cheeses at no cost.

Freiburg, Larry   The head of WWOR-TV when Howard had his Saturday night television show. Stern complained that he was never introduced to the executive and, at that point, didn't want to meet him.

The Fresh Prince of Bel Air   The television show on which Robin Quivers made a guest appearance. When Robin started to plug her appearance one morning, Howard was annoyed. Howard is very liberal when it comes to plugs, but *he* has to control the allocation of them.

Fred the Elephant Boy   *See Schreiber, Fred.*

Friedel, Lisa   A high school classmate who complained that Stern did not attend their twentieth reunion. She told him, "Everyone thinks you should have showed up."

Friedman, Drew   The clever illustrator who provided many of the drawings in Stern's books *Private Parts* and *Miss America*. The photograph on the back cover of *Private Parts* showing "The Author at Home"—Howard smoking a pipe and reading a book about English literature, while a well-cleavaged blond wench watches him—was based on an illustration that Friedman drew for *Spy* magazine.

71

Fuchman, Ellen   (Pronounce her last name carefully!) One of Stern's freshman-year classmates and acquaintances at Boston University, she told Stern biographer Paul Colford, "We were all screw-offs, we were all smoking pot."

Fuerst, Jeffrey B.   The *New York Observer* writer who said about Stern, "If Mr. Stern was patently unfunny, he'd be easy to ignore. Unfortunately his potshots, however cheap, hit square on target more often than expected. The viper-tongued Mr. Stern is really just an old-fashioned borscht belt comedian. Think of him as a distempered Jackie Leonard with a Louis XIV hairdo by way of Led Zeppelin, and a nose big enough to be rented out as a two-car garage."

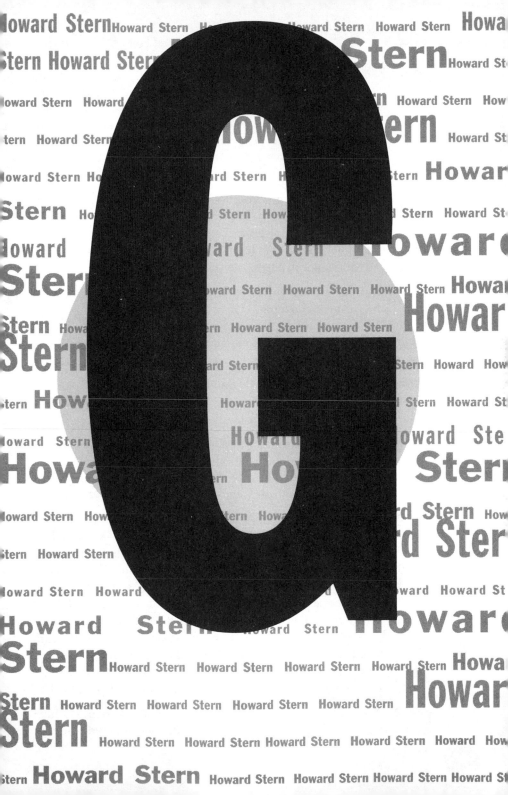

Gabor, Zsa Zsa   The Hungarian-born actress who is a perfect foil for Stern. When he showed her a dildo on-air, she said it was "too small" and did a quick segue by saying that Porfirio Rubirosa, a world-class Lothario known to sport a world-class-sized "sword," was "my greatest lover." Stern usually says that she has a large "caboose" and observed, "From the waist down, Zsa Zsa has elephantiasis." **See Hollywood Squares.**

Galina, Stacy   The actress from *Knots Landing* with an ample derriere and a padded brassiere. While appearing on Stern's television show, she came on strong to Howard, who, like a good family man, naturally resisted her advances. Her massage talents were not as good as transsexual Tula's, according to Stern.

Gallagher, Ron   Brother of the watermelon-smashing comedian Gallagher, a Stern guest who formerly sold heavy equipment. He looks like a younger (by six years) Gallagher. By contract with his brother, he is not allowed to smash watermelons on television, but he threw one at Howard—it was a Nerf watermelon, weighing only a few ounces.

Gallar, Anna   Stern's paternal grandmother, an Austro-Hungarian Jewish immigrant.

Gallin, Sandy   Singer Michael Jackson's manager, who wanted Stern to help generate mass demonstrations on behalf of Jackson when he was under fire for boy-related molestation charges. After his meeting with Gallin and Jackson, Stern said, "No guy could orchestrate major careers and be serious about this idea." **See Jackson, Michael.**

Gambling Dan   The K-Rock radio intern (last name Berkowitz) who is a compulsive gambler. Stern bet Jackie Martling that Gambling Dan would quit gambling, but in September 1995 Dan admitted that he placed football bets with Stuttering John, so Stern lost the bet. Dan thinks he has a hex on him. After a Mexican "witch" spit on him while on the beach at Cancún, he has had a lot of bad luck. He gambled and lost his college tuition one semester. He has bought stock that immediately declined in value. At Scores, the nude dancing emporium, Dan spoke to bouncer Mike Greco and asked him if anything interesting ever happened to him on the job, to which he replied no. Later that night Greco was shot to death, and a waiter was also shot, and soon died.

Gange, Mike   One of the Stern show's many bumbling interns, whom Stern has accused of having a bad attitude. He has attended Adelphi, the alma mater of Gary Dell'Abate. Gange was supposed to send a videotape of a *Seinfeld* episode to some churchgoing friends of Howard and Alison, but accidentally sent a pornographic video known as the "Japanese Surfer Enema" tape.

Gannon, Frank An occasional guest who has been a writer for both Richard M. Nixon and David Letterman. He was once engaged to broadcaster Diane Sawyer and dated Robin Quivers a few times. He was on Air Force One with Nixon after he resigned and later interviewed him for thirty-eight hours before he died. He packaged a videotape of the interviews.

Gardenia, Vince The character actor *(Bang the Drum Slowly)* whom Stern's father told Howard, as a child, that he knew. But when Howard, as an adult, finally met Gardenia in person, Vince said that he never met a Ben Stern, or at least didn't remember him.

Gardner, André The former program director of K-Rock radio, who was replaced by Sam Milkman in April 1996.

Garvey, Cyndi The former wife of baseball player Steve Garvey and former television cohost of Regis Philbin (pre–Kathie Lee Gifford). About her Stern commented, "She's a hot broad," upon hearing that she was checking into the Betty Ford Clinic in April 1996. Needless to say, Howard preferred Cyndi as Philbin's cohost over her replacement Kathie Lee Gifford.

Garyionette The puppet of Boy Gary Dell'Abate, usually operated by Fred Norris, who also does Gary's voice.

Gay Jaffe A gay comedian whom Howard has interviewed several times (e.g., September 1991, December 1995). He admitted that two days before the broadcast, he picked up a man at a Philadelphia bar, went to his hotel, bathed and showered, and "did it" two times. Howard commented, "The bathtub probably looked like egg drop soup!" Gay Jaffe called K-Rock intern Gay Rich a *"goy* toy." About Jaffe Stern said, "Gay Jaffe makes Dan Foreman look like Clark Gable."

Gay Rich The very gay K-Rock intern, famous for sitting on Fred Norris's lap when Fred got very drunk at his bachelor party at Scores, the strip club.

George The magazine edited by John F. Kennedy, Jr. Stern appeared on their April/May 1996 cover in connection with an article on virtue.

In the article Stern was quoted as saying, "Virtue is honesty, which makes me the most virtuous person in America."

George, Wally   The Los Angeles cable TV show *(Hot Seat)* host whom Stern has interviewed and dislikes. George is the father of actress Rebecca de Mornay.

Germany   Like France, Germany is not one of Howard's favorite countries.

Germs   *See Mysophobia.*

Giambelli's   The Italian restaurant where Robin Quivers dined with Chicago Bulls player Dennis Rodman. It is located at 46 E. Fiftieth Street in New York; telephone: (212) 688-2760.

Gibbons, Leeza   The talk-show host and former *Entertainment Tonight* cohost whom Stern introduced as follows: "She doesn't look like a bad girl, but she is . . . She looks all-American, but she has dirty thoughts." She told Howard that she didn't have a nose job, but coincidentally the same week the *National Enquirer* had a cover story on plastic surgery and noted that Gibbons had an excellent nose job.

Gibson, Debbie   The young singer who told Stern, with a tiny bit of sexual innuendo, "I'm a performer, I've got a lot of energy."

Gifford, Frank   A retired professional football player who became a sportscaster. His trophy wife is Kathie Lee Epstein. Giff has been known to hand out one-hundred-dollar bills to semilegal aliens in the garment district.

Gifford, Kathie Lee   The "perky" television talk-show cohost and Stern's favorite target. Howard's initial problem with her seemed to be that she was born Kathie Lee Epstein, daughter of a Jewish father (whose mother was not Jewish) and a Christian mother, but she became a zealous Christian. Stern, who is very Jewish, perhaps perceives her as a traitor, one who left the Jewish faith. Yet he's attracted to her spunkiness and is certainly ambiguous about her surprising success. Needless to say, his Jewish listeners are not happy that he calls her Kathie "Jew" Gifford. Stern complained that she is "out-Christianizing every woman." On the second page of *Miss America*, Stern called Gifford a "cunt" and then added the words "only kidding." In a *TV Guide* article, Gifford said about Stern, "If I disturb him because I'm everything he's not, it's the ultimate compliment. I wish him and his family well." Stern bellyached about her being a "phony-baloney" and "Pollyanna." He also complained about her boosting her children, Cody and Cassidy, on-air, yet it should be noted that Stern has his children on-mike or in the studio several times a year and brags about their being smart and taking piano and other lessons. During the week that the *TV Guide* article appeared, he said about Kathie Lee, "She's a vagina surrounded by an idiot." When it was discovered that her Wal-Mart line of clothing was made by children in Honduras, the ensuing flap provided Stern with enough comedic material for months.

Giglio, Chris   *See King of All Messengers.*

Gilligan's Island   The popular network television comedy series, one of Howard's favorites, which ran from 1964 to 1967, and has run ever since in syndication. Stern's television spoof ("Gag Again Island") of the show featured Bob Denver (Gilligan) and Dawn Wells (Mary Ann Summers). As a child, Howard "had the hots" for Ginger (played by Tina Louise).

Gina   One of Stern's favorite guests because of her lesbian experiences. Gina (pronounced like the second and third syllables in the word *vagina*), a nurse, went to a nudist colony with her boyfriend and immediately was attracted to a woman, despite the presence of many naked men.

Gina Man   The Stern guest who uttered the classic line, "This is Mother Teresa speaking from the bed. God don't want me yet, man. I've got more feet to taste."

Ginsberg, Ruth Bader   The Supreme Court judge, appointed by Bill Clinton, about whom Stern commented, "I dig the bitch."

Ginsberg, Scott   The chairman of Evergreen Broadcasting, owner of WLUP in Chicago where Stern aired his show. Evergreen and Stern became embroiled in a contractual dispute, and a Stern scorned is a force to be reckoned with. On his August 11, 1995, radio broadcast, Stern called the executive Scott "Jewsberg" and vowed retaliation. The suit is still pending.

Giraffe, Giraffe Head   Names that Howard calls himself when talking about his life in high school. Being very tall and gawky, he resembled a giraffe walking down the corridors of the school. He once said, in effect, he looked like a Jewish giraffe with a Cher wig on.

Giuliani, Mayor Rudolf   The mayor of New York City, who Stern says "has a hair yarmulke," a snide reference to his unusual hairstyle. **See Donaldson, Sam.**

GLH 9   The Ron Popeil hair spray for balding men that Howard sprayed on Scott the Engineer's head. It looked okay in the back, but the front looked absurd. He sprayed Steve Grillo's head, which is slightly bald in patches, and the spray looked better.

Glickenhaus, Mike   The general manager of XTRA, Stern's radio affiliate in San Diego. **See XTRA.**

Glieberman, Owen   The *Entertainment Weekly* book reviewer who proclaimed, "Howard Stern is the most brilliant—and misunderstood—comic artist in America," and gave his book *Private Parts* a B+ rating. He noted that he is "probably the only professional entertainer in the country who answers to no one but himself." He also called him "the Lenny Bruce of the information age."

Gnagy, Jon   An artist whose NBC show *You Are an Artist*, Stern liked ("a great show!"). The show aired from 1946 to 1950, yet Stern wasn't born until 1954, so how he ever got to see the show is a mystery. (Perhaps in reruns?)

"Godzilla Goes to Harlem"   The radio skit that Stern performed on his first radio appearance at the Boston University radio station WTBU. It was considered somewhat racist on campus, but Howard "hit the ground running" in the world of controversy.

Goetz, Bernhard   The New Yorker who shot four black teenage muggers on a subway train in 1984. Stern said that Goetz should have been given the Congressional Medal of Honor. Goetz served time on a weapons charge and later lost a civil suit for causing the paralysis of one of the boys.

Goldberg, Danny   The screenwriter and a producer of Stern's movie *Private Parts.* He and Len Blum also worked together on the movies *Meatballs* and *Stripes.* At the Scores "wrap" party, Goldberg spent most of his time in the men's room, staring at the floor tiles, while everyone else was ogling saline-implanted breasts and getting lap dances!

Goldberg, Whoopi   A comedienne/actress whom Stern occasionally attacks. Sidekick Robin Quivers has a lot of respect for Goldberg and has to tolerate Howard's Whoopi tirades.

Goldblum, Jeff   When Stern was asked by a reporter at the York, Pennsylvania, press conference who would play him in his movie, Stern said that one studio suggested actor Jeff Goldblum. Yet Stern would not allow another actor to play him in the movie, just as he would never have a guest host for any of his shows.

Goldman, Kevin   One of Stern's classmates at Boston University who, according to Stern biographer Paul Colford, said, "You have to understand how ugly Howard was. Take away that long, flowing hair that he has now and give him real scraggly hair and a geeky mustache. He was really unattractive, and he hung out with these grungy people who looked like the rock group Blue Oyster Cult." Goldman became a reporter for *Variety* magazine, a show-business publication.

Goldstein, Al   The publisher of *Screw* magazine who has always wanted to be on the Stern show but wanted "equal time" that Howard didn't want to give him. Howard should be fascinated by Goldstein's libertine lifestyle—Goldstein probably has run through more women than the average NBA player.

Goldthwait, Bob "Bobcat"   A former frequent guest, a comedian, whom Stern has called "Slobcat," "Blobcat," "The Blobster," "Mr. Normal," and "Bob Clit, the Big Pussy." Goldthwait accused Stern of "picking the bones of Sam Kinison" in a comedy routine, after Stern announced that he bought the rights to film a movie about the life of the late Kinison. When Stern heard, via *New York Daily News* columnist A. J. Benza, that Goldthwait entered a drug rehabilitation clinic in Tarzana, California, in September 1995, Stern was delighted and did about fifteen minutes of diatribe about "Slobcat." However, a month later Benza and therefore Stern found out that the "fact" was not true and aired the erratum. Stern commented over the air, "He [Bobcat] needs to be bent over a chair and have sex with a man. He's acting like a little girl."

Goodman, Dickie   The creator of hundreds of song parodies, using a combination of sound bites from hit records and voice-over—which Stern liked. Some of the recordings include "Flying Saucer I" and

"Mr. Jaws." (Goodman's son John, a sofa-bed salesman and Stern phone-in guest, mentioned to Howard that his father committed suicide.)

Goodstein, Doug Z.   One of the Stern E! show associate producers, he made the mistake of visiting the K-Rock men's room one morning when Howard entered. Stern said that it "reeked" in there and guessed that it was Goodstein among three male employees because of his brown shoes. He warned the producer, "A courtesy flush might be in order, man."

Goodwin, Walter   The *New York Times* television critic who wrote (11-14-93) about Howard's book *Private Parts*, "In the tradition of Jewish memoirists, Mr. Stern does a lot of *kvetching* about what he calls his dysfunctional family (Stern's Complaint), some of it funny." He ended his review by saying, "Where Lenny Bruce could be cathartic, Howard Stern is strictly laxative."

Gordon, Greg Stewart   The bisexual black man who told Stern that he wanted to strangle Ronald Wilson Reagan because he was the "antichrist." After Gordon was caught entering the Reagan house at 668 St. Cloud in Beverly Hills, California, he was arrested by Secret Service agents and institutionalized for two years ("I had a lot of sex there"). He bills himself as "King of Kings, Lord of Lords" because he believes that he is the Second Coming of Christ. The alleged graduate of Rutgers said that his mother was a schoolteacher in East Brunswick, New Jersey, for thirty years.

Gordon, Jack   LaToya Jackson's husband-manager, who seems to live quite nicely, having profitted from LaToya's success. According to Gordon, his son Aaron produced a pornographic movie *Sunset and Divine: The British Experience*, starring Hollywood hooker Divine Brown.

Gordon, Ruth   *See Rivers, Joan.*

Gossett, Louis, Jr.   The Oscar-winning actor who, after the 1996 Academy Awards ceremony, complained that he was not shown on the television broadcast, giving Howard an opportunity to have a few laughs. Gossett talked about sharing the wealth and then said, "We get the chicken wings and the necks. We need to get some of that thigh—and the big guys get the breasts." Stern complained, "Always with the chicken analogies . . . There's no other food on the planet!"

Gottfried, Gilbert   An idiosyncratic comedian and Stern regular. One female caller told listeners about an evening she spent with Gilbert, during which he awkwardly tried to seduce her. He has called in as Rabbi Gottfried for Jewish-oriented bits. One listener called Gottfried "a half a chink" because of his squinty, somewhat Oriental eyes.

Graf, Steffi   The German tennis pro of whom Stern says, "She should get a head transplant, not just a nose job."

Grand Funk Railroad   A heavy-metal rock group that Stern especially liked, going back to the early 1970s.

Grandparents   Howard's paternal grandparents were Froim and Anna (Gallar) Stern, Austro-Hungarian Jewish immigrants who settled in the South Bronx. His maternal grandparents were Sol and Esther (Reich) Schiffman, also Austro-Hungarian Jewish immigrants.

Grant, Bob   A New York–based, politically conservative radio commentator (real name Gigante) about whom Stern complains that he is "an old man with a bad hairpiece" and "his nose job is awful." He also accuses Grant of "stealing" his act. It should be noted that Grant was known for his outrageous on-air comments before Stern got out of school, and Stern's father, Ben, often listened to Grant. Stern told Larry King on CNN in 1985, "I've always admired Bob Grant, who's a local talk-show host." When Grant was fired by Disney management in April 1996, Stern came to his defense and lamented the decision as an attempt to squelch freedom of speech. (Stern had absolutely no problem with Grant's cynically commenting about the survival of Secretary of Commerce Ron Brown in the plane crash in Bosnia—"My hunch is that he is the one survivor. I just have that hunch. Maybe it's because, at heart, I'm a pessimist.") Stern spoke to him on-air and told his audience that Grant should not have been fired for his remarks. It should also be noted that Howard's father, Ben, was a longtime listener of the *Bob Grant Show,* and that Stern supports most of the political candidates that Grant supports. (Grant returned to air two weeks later on WOR radio.)

Grant, Hugh   The British actor about whom Stern guest and hooker Divine Brown said, regarding the size of his organ, "He's all right . . . he's okay," and then picked out a modest-sized cucumber when Howard asked her how big he was in an excited state.

Gray, Billy The child television actor who played "Bud" (James Anderson, Jr.) on the long-running show *Father Knows Best*. He admitted to Stern that he was jailed a couple of months for possession of marijuana.

The Grease Man A deejay (real name Doug Tracht) whom K-Rock hired for the weekday evening slot in the mid-1990s. Stern has never been a fan of The Grease Man. When Stern was fired in Washington, DC, in mid-1982, they gave The Grease Man the raise that Howard had asked for—give or take $1 million for five years. Howard has called him a "moron," among other names. He and other deejays were fired by K-Rock about a year after he started, when K-Rock changed its format and let go all of their dee-jays.

Great Sounds An early sponsor of the Stern show, headed by "Big Al."

Green, "Melrose" Larry A Stern "Wack Packer" who is headquartered at the corner of Melrose and Highland Avenues in Los Angeles. He loves to carry placards proclaiming Stern's greatness. At the O. J. Simpson trial he wore a tallis, a Jewish prayer shawl, carried placards such as "Howard Stern says guilty, I say he's guilty" and "Fry O. J.," and subsequently got into a fistfight with blacks and Mexicans and was taken to jail in handcuffs for attempting to incite a riot. He is an accountant by trade and inherited $1.6 million from his mother, which enables him to pay for his frequent flights between Los Angeles and New York. He did Andrew Dice Clay's tax returns before Clay began making big bucks. Larry says that he has an M.B.A. from Cornell University. He has self-published a 260-page book about his life and experiences with the Stern show.

Green, Petey A black UHF television host in Washington, DC, on whose show Stern appeared—in an Afro wig and in blackface.

Green, Ted *See Ted the Janitor.*

Griffin, Meg The deejay who followed Stern for a while on K-Rock. They both worked together at WRNW radio in Briarcliff Manor at the beginning of Stern's career. She remarked that back then he was "a *Beavis and Butthead* nerd kind of guy. He had thick glasses and was much heavier. His short hair was like Brillo. It was a real unfortunate look." Meg also commented on-air that her ex-husband was more talented than Howard, then clarified that they were both talented in different ways. Stern and crew did a song parody "Angry Young Meg" to the music of "Angry Young Man."

Griffin, Merv   The former talk-show host and entrepreneur whom Stern calls "a third-rate Johnny Carson." **See Terio, Denny.**

Grillo, Steve   An inept WXRK-FM radio intern affectionately called "Gorilla." Not quite a nuclear physicist, Grillo cannot spell such words as *democracy* and *separate*. Curiously, Howard dedicated his book *Miss America* to his interns, specifically singling out Grillo. He has appeared as "Tod Grossman" in the play *Grandma Sylvia's Funeral*. Howard's occasional nickname for him is "Prick."

Grodin, Charles   The film actor *(The Heartbreak Kid)* and talk-show host whom Stern dismisses as "a big zero." Almost daily he complains about his bad toupee. (He called him Charles Grow-hair one morning.) In fact, Grodin has one of the best "scalp doilies" in show business. Stern proclaimed one morning, "I will go on his show if he doesn't wear his wig." Grodin now has a Senator Joe Biden look, suggesting hair implants. Stern sometimes calls him Grodinsky, which was his original family name.

G-spot   An area of Alison Stern's vaginal terrain that Howard said he finally found during the last weekend of January 1996.

Guccione, Bob, Jr.   The publisher of *Spin* magazine and son of *Penthouse* publisher Bob Guccione, the younger Guccione has been an occasional Stern guest. When "Junior" and his "main squeeze" went out to dinner with Stern, they smooched and pawed each other like crazy. On-air Howard expressed his dislike for seeing couples "make out" in public.

"Guess Who's the Jew"   A contest that Stern features periodically— "Kurt Waldheim, Jr." (Fred Norris) names three or four famous people, and callers have to identify who's Jewish. Stern loves to bait the callers to elicit any anti-Semitic sentiments. One caller admitted that the few Jews he knew were "cheap" because "they spent a lot of time trying to figure out who owed what for lunch." Some of the famous names mentioned in past contests included broadcaster Morley Safer, actor Tony Randall (born Rosenberg), singer Cyndi Lauper, designer Mr. Blackwell, actor Charles Grodin, folksinger Peter Yarrow, Emma Samms (born Samuelson), and actor Michael Landon (born Orowitz). One segment was "Jews Who Married for Money"—the correct answer was Tom Arnold, who converted to Judaism when he married Roseanne Barr. In April 1996 the show had seven contestants, two of whom were Jewish. Only Jackie Martling guessed them right, for which Stern called him "Super Bigot." Stern missed a female Orthodox Jew, which intrigued Stern. He was fascinated by Orthodox Jews' going without sex for about twelve days, during and around the menstrual period. About the rest of the month, Stern told the woman, "You can really party up a storm and keep the marriage alive."

Gumbel, Greg   The sportscaster brother of *The Today Show*'s Bryant Gumbel, and occasional guest on the Stern show. When Greg called in the day before the O. J. Simpson jury verdict, Stern, fearing a riot, told him, "I pray that another celebrity kills someone," because things will get dull after the trial. He then asked, "How angry is Bryant? Maybe he could snap!" Howard is quick to point out that Greg is married to a white woman.

"Gunkard"   One of Howard's nicknames at South Side Senior High School in Rockville Centre, Long Island. He was also called "The Big Gunk," classmate Scott Passeser told Stern biographer Paul Colford, because "he was so big and gunky."

Gutenberg, Steve   The comedian-turned-actor *(Police Academy)* who told Stern that he graduated sixty-fifth in his class of five hundred students at Massapequa High School, which is the alma mater of Jerry Seinfeld, Jessica Hahn, Stuttering John, and the Baldwin brothers.

Guzmán, Pablo   The New York reporter who complained about Stern in his *Daily News* column, writing, "The problem with 'humor' that uses racism and sexism without making a satirical edge clear is that it reinforces, rather than reduces, sexism and racism among the audience." He noted, "I've heard the remarks of approval made by redneck listeners in cars . . . stores and bars when stuff like that comes out."

Gwynne, Fred   The six-foot-five-inch-tall Yale-educated actor-artist who played Herman Munster in television's *The Munsters* (1964–66). His publicist always asked interviewers not to ask him about *The Munsters*. Stuttering John asked the actor, "Did Van Gogh ever dress up like Frankenstein?"

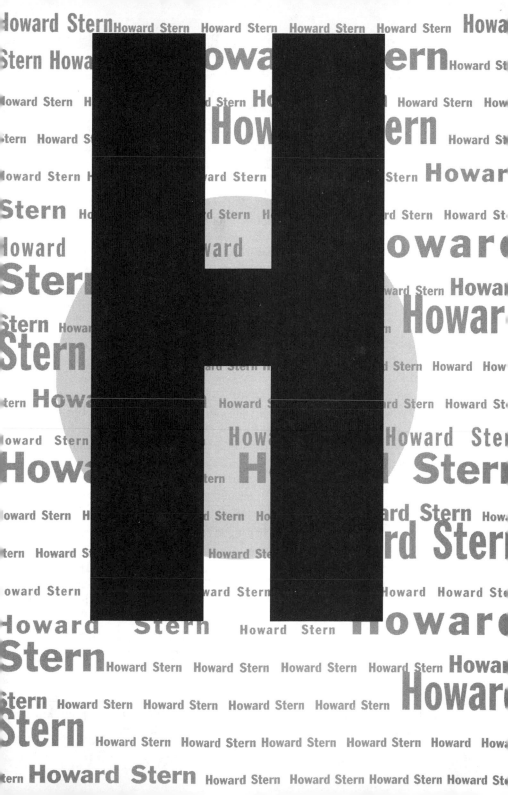

Hagar, Sammy The lead singer of the Van Halen rock group, who called Stern a "jerk." He left the group in mid-1996 because he did not want to record a "greatest hits" album.

Hagelin, John S. A political candidate whom Howard and Alison Stern each sent $250 for his 1992 presidential campaign, according to Paul Colford, author of *Howard Stern: King of All Media*. Hagelin is a member of the Natural Law party and is a believer and practitioner of Transcendental Meditation.

Hagman, Larry The television actor *(Dallas* and *I Dream of Jeannie)* and son of actress Mary Martin, whom Stern ridiculed when he was diagnosed as having liver disease from many years of boozing. After Hagman, a recovered alcoholic, received a liver transplant, Stern suggested, "We should send him a case of Jack Daniel's!" Regarding Hagman's vehement antismoking stance, Robin Quivers interjected, pretending she was Hagman, "Don't smoke in front of me, I'm busy drinking."

Hahn, Jessica A former church secretary from Massapequa, Long Island (Jerry Seinfeld's hometown), whose claim to fame was her sexual encounter with TV preacher James Bakker. She underwent some plastic surgery (breast implants, for starters) and became a celebrity of sorts, with *Playboy* spreads (November 1987 and September 1988) and a popular nude video. On a ratings victory trip in Philadelphia, she was taking a bath when Howard and Jackie Martling barged in her room and jumped in to frolic a bit. Of course, it became the subject of a Stern monologue, after which guilt-ridden Martling *over*apologized to his wife on the air, as if he had been caught in flagrante delicto. In early 1992 Hahn told Stern that she hadn't had sex for a year—she's "afraid of what's going on." **See Kinison, Sam.**

Hall, Arsenio The former television talk-show host and one of Stern's all-time hate objects. When Stern was a guest on his show, Hall introduced him as "the meanest, nastiest, dirtiest deejay in the whole wide world." Stern's favorite term for Hall is a "suck-ass," especially because of his fawning over comedic actor Eddie Murphy. He also calls Hall "a triangle-headed moron." At a press conference in July 1990, Stern said that the FCC should censor Hall's gums because they "look like private parts."

Hall, Michael **See Taxi.**

Halloween The day of the year when Stern paints orange pumpkins on the breasts of volunteers who stop by the radio studio.

Hamilton, George When movie actor George Hamilton and his ex-wife Alana Stewart aired their own talk show, they quickly became targets for Stern, who called the actor "a dummy" and "a big pussy." Howard also resented the fact that he was a good friend of Imelda Marcos, whom he hates. Hamilton said about Stern, "He's six feet five inches and nothing but a hormone." Stern called him "a tanning expert" and has done long riffs about his tanning obsession. He said, for example, pretending he was Hamilton, "I'm as dark as Sinbad [the comedian] . . . darker than Lisa Bonet . . . God, Negroes are lucky." Stern criticized the Hamilton movie version of *Dracula,* which cast a well-tanned person to play a character who can't stay in the sun.

Hammer, M.C. A rap singer whom Stern likes. He declared bankruptcy in April 1996.

Hampton, Tracy The ex–O. J. Simpson trial juror who subsequently appeared nude in *Playboy* magazine. When Tracy visited Howard in the studio, he confessed, "I'm a vagina man," as he looked at her photos in the magazine.

Harbert, Ted Howard's Boston University classmate whose father was senior exec at ABC. Son Ted became president of ABC Entertainment. When Harbert made number seventeen on the list of *Entertainment Weekly*'s one hundred most powerful people in entertainment, Stern had a fit. He regularly complains that Harbert had his success given to him by his father. Stern was delighted in early 1996 when ABC hired a woman from NBC to replace Harbert (who was retitled chairman of the division), but later reports indicated that Harbert was, in fact, promoted.

Hardin and Weaver Washington, DC, deejays who were elected to the Radio Hall of Fame in 1996. Howard complained that when his station in DC owed him money, Hardin and Weaver were on the union committee but didn't want to come to his aid because they disapproved of his "kind of broadcasting."

Harley-Davidson Cafe The West Fifty-seventh Street (New York City) site of Stern's book party for his first book *Private Parts.*

Harris, Mark The flamboyant husband of the late Martha Raye, and a favorite guest on Stern's shows. At age forty-three he married Raye, who was then seventy-five. He said that he had sex with Raye twice, but not after her legs were amputated ("that would be gauche"). Harris called himself a "producer" and said that he collected antiques. He has had a French boyfriend-lover who was about to marry a thirty-year-old woman and another male lover who later died of a heart attack. Stern especially likes to kid Harris about his various projects (e.g., the Dorian Gray play, the jogging outfit company), which never come to fruition. Harris has had a fair amount of plastic surgery, including, according to Howard, a "scrotum tuck." When Harris wore a fur coat to the studio, Howard remarked, "That leopard coat is a 'bone smuggler' magnet!" Stern calls him "the gayest guy on the planet" and says that he is "gay squared."

Harrison, Michael   The editor and publisher of *Talkers* magazine who said that Stern's "radio persona is one of the most consistent and credible in the history of the box."

Hart, Kitty Carlisle   The singer, actress, and arts advocate (real last name Conn) who appeared on Stern's WWOR-TV spoof "What's My Secret" with old television pal and actress/talk-show host Arlene Francis.

Hartford   The Connecticut city where Stern won his second deejay job, and the place where he met Fred Norris, then attending a local Hartford area college. Howard was making about $12,000 a year at his Hartford job.

Harvard Law School   The distinguished law school that invited Stern to speak on a panel. Howard turned down the offer because they didn't offer him money and because he hates the litigiousness rampant in the United States.

Harvey, Bob   The speech-impaired Stern fan who was the first in line for Stern's first book-signing event at a major New York City bookstore. "Crackhead Bob," a carpet installer, smoked a lot of crack cocaine and damaged his brain enough for him not to do simple math or know the capital of New York or the president of the United States. He has a tattoo with the names Howard Stern, Robin Quivers, *et al.*, and the K-Rock logo. Stern jokes that Bob looked like Robby Benson or Stephen Baldwin but was smarter than the latter.

Hatcher, Teri   The actress who plays Lois Lane in television's *Lois and Clark* show, one of Stern's favorite television shows. Stern has a sexual fascination with her and has corresponded with her via E-mail. In one his interviews with Hatcher, Howard learned that she was a cheerleader for the San Francisco 49'ers for a year, does not have a nose job, has no gag reflex, wears a 32-C brassiere—and she proudly announced, "I am good in bed."

Hawkins, Sophie B.   A rock singer ("Damn, I Wish I Was Your Lover") whom Stern introduced as having "these big breasts" (an exaggeration based on an album cover!) and was "into lesbian stuff and into guys." She admitted that at age fourteen she had sex with a forty-four-year-old man and eventually lived with the man for eight years. She also had sex with some of her high school teachers. Hawkins doesn't shave her legs because she likes her golden hair, but she does shave her armpits. She was twenty-two or twenty-three when she first had sexual relations with a woman.

Hayden, Chauncé   A writer for *Steppin' Out* magazine and occasional guest. In the first edition of Stern's *Private Parts,* he was erroneously listed as Chauncey Howell, the New York television reporter, formerly of WNBC's *Live at Five,* and another Stern guest in his early days in New York. Chauncé photographed the late Debbie Tay in the Bahamas and Jamaica. He has a nipple ring on his left nipple and a huge script tattoo on his back quoting philosopher Friedrich Nietzsche: "What fails to kill me only serves to make me stronger." **See Howell, Chauncey.**

Hayes, John P., Jr.   The WNBC radio executive ("The Incubus," to Howard) who replaced Randy Bongarten as general manager on October 1, 1984, and, according to Stern, "sunk the station." He later bought a station in San Francisco for $20 million. The word *incubus,* by the way, comes from the Latin word for "nightmare." It refers to an imaginary demon or evil spirit that descends on sleeping people.

Hazelden   Clinic   Where   former   Double-U-Ennnnn-Bee-Cee (WNBC) deejay Don Imus went to dry out and purge himself of certain addictive substances.

Head colds   The vague "yenta" ailment that Howard's wife Alison gets, especially when he is in an amorous mood. **See "Not tonight, Howard!"**

Heartburn   Another malady that Stern's wife has, hence her consumption of Maalox.

Heather   The guest on Stern's "What's My Secret" routine (7-13-91) and former Miss New York State. The panelists were Arlene Francis,

Kitty Carlisle Hart, and Robin Quivers. Her secret was that she was a lesbian.

Hebranko, Michael   The overweight man whom Richard Simmons occasionally helps lose weight. He made the *Guinness Book of World Records* in the Most Weight Lost category. In July 1987 he weighed 905 pounds, lost 500 in fifteen months, and by June 1989 weighed 217 pounds—he had lost 688 pounds. His weight yo-yo'ed again in 1995-1996.

Hefner, Hugh   The founder of *Playboy* magazine, who *Playboy* model and Stern guest Lillian Müller said was "a good lover . . . a nice man . . . average size." About Hefner, Playmate of the Year Shannon Tweed remarked, "He was pretty good in the sack!"

Helms, Jesse   The southern U.S. senator who, according to Howard, is preventing Infinity Broadcasting from buying a station in Atlanta in order to keep Stern off the airwaves.

Hemingway, Mariel   The model and actress (and granddaughter of writer Ernest Hemingway) who called in one morning to plug her new CBS show *Central Park West* for the 1995–96 season. When Stern kidded her about the breast implants she had for the movie *Star 69*, she remarked that she had them removed "about a year and a half ago." Her sister Margaux died in July 1996, apparently of a depression-caused suicide, which seems to run in the family.

Hemsley, Sherman   The actor who played George Jefferson on television's comedy series *The Jeffersons*, and played Whoopi Goldberg to Stern's Ted Danson on Howard's Saturday night WWOR-TV show.

Henley, Don   **See You'll Never Make Love in This Town Again.**

Herman, Pee-Wee   The campy entertainer (born Paul Rubenfeld, later Rubens) who was caught masturbating during a pornographic movie in 1991. Stern said, "He should go to every movie theater in Sarasota and scrub the theater seats where guys drop their load."

Hewitt, Don   The executive producer (real name Horowitz) of CBS-TV's *60 Minutes*, who Stern says "hates my guts. Ask him about me . . . You know what, Don? . . . You're a phony!" Stern is disgruntled because Hewitt and other news biggies would not support him in his ongoing feud with the FCC.

"Hey nanni nanni"   One of Stern's terms for women's private parts, the origins of which may have some link to William Shakespeare's *Much Ado About Nothing.*

Hickey, William   The actor whom Howard wants to play Imus, the aging deejay, in his movie *Private Parts.* Hickey appeared in *Prizzi's Honor* as Don Corrado Prizzi, for which he won an Oscar nomination.

Higgins, Robert   The pseudonym of the Stern "phony phone caller" who called ABC TV's Peter Jennings on the air and said, "I see O. J. kinda slouchin' down . . . Now lookee here . . ." *See Maury and Jennings, Peter.*

High colonics   Irrigation of the bowels with warm water, and a procedure that Robin Quivers undergoes every couple of weeks. (Robin has probably sold more garden hoses in the past twelve months than Home Depot!) Howard disapproves of the procedure, but comedic actress Mae West was a big proponent of high colonics.

Hill, Henry   The original "wise guy" and protagonist of the book *Wise Guy* (and subsequent movie *Goodfellas*), by Nicholas Pileggi, who has been on the witness protection plan since the early 1980s. He was a guest on Stern's television show (3-14-92), during which a "black woman" (played by Al Rosenberg) phoned in to say that her husband was killed during one of Hill's illegal ventures. Fred Norris also called in as WPP expert Dr. Charles and told Hill that he would be killed in three weeks. Hill kept his cool and told Fred that he'd see him in four weeks. Hill was truly upset until he found out that Stern was playing a trick on him. When he phoned the show in 1995 (9-16-95), he sounded incoherent and answered almost every question with a "pahleese." Stern is normally fast "on the trigger" to bleep profanity, but on this broadcast two "fucks" went on the air. He mentioned that he makes two hundred meatballs on Tuesday and sells them in Santa Monica. Hill called in six months later (5-1-96) and announced that he went into rehabilitation the day after his last Stern interview and temporarily cured himself of a liter-a-day vodka habit.

"Hill Street Jews"   A Stern bit that spoofs *Hill Street Blues* and features police detectives with thick Yiddish accents (once known as "Hillel Street Blues").

91

Hoffman, Jan   The *New York Magazine* writer who wrote the article "Howard Stern Just Won't Shut Up: Radio's Bad Boy Is Back" (11-18-85), which was about Stern's firing at WNBC radio and subsequent hiring at WXRK. Hoffman called him "a six-foot-five ostrich on the prowl." Hoffman wrote that Stern was "belligerent, defensive, whiny, neurotic, boastful, incisive, sophomoric, sardonic, cruel and often brilliantly hilarious."

Hollywood   The movie capital of the world, which Stern calls "a vagina farm."

Hollywood Squares   The once popular quiz show that Stern appeared on as a replacement for deejay Shadoe Stevens. Other panelists for the week included actress Edie McClurg, singer Glen Campbell, Ross Shafer *(The Match Game)*, Michael Winslow *(Police Academy)*, psychologist Dr. Joyce Brothers, Jm (no *i*) J. Bullock, Leslie Easterbrook *(Police Academy)*, and "Princess" Zsa Zsa Gabor and her big "caboose." Zsa Zsa told Howard that he was "vile" but she thought he was funny. Howard was disappointed that he was called on only three times in five shows.

"Homeless Howiewood Squares"   Howard's spoof of *Hollywood Squares* featuring celebrity panelists Gene Rayburn, Jaye P. Morgan, Ku Klux Klan member Daniel Carver (who sat next to Teresa Glover, a black woman), Underdog Lady, Martha Raye's husband Mark Harris, and a few others.

Homosexual Experience   Stern has confessed on the air to having one homosexual experience in his youth. In his book *Private Parts*, he wrote, "He [one of his friends] pulled his pants down around his ankles. I started to rub his dick up and down when he told me I was doing it all wrong." Howard said that it "was all too weird for me" and bolted out of the room. *See Belzer, Richard*

"Hooker Hollywood Squares"   A spoof of *Hollywood Squares* that Stern staged on his WWOR-TV show whose contestants were recruited on Forty-second Street. Sample questions were: "How many calories are in an average ejaculation of sperm?" (answer: five calories) and "Out of every one hundred American women, how many have had anal sex?" (answer: three to four). A black hooker said that she didn't like black johns because when they're drunk, "they can't get orgasms and they want their money back." Another hooker said that she was "tired of sex."

Hoover, J, Edgar   *See Liddy, G. Gordon.*

Hope, Bob An improbable but classic Stern show guest who has plugged his upcoming specials, the implacable comedian barely heard Howard's questions, but always had a response, even if it didn't answer Howard's playful, sometimes naughty questions. (In one of the early interviews, Hope thought that "Out-of-the-Closet Stern" was a woman interviewer and complained to NBC about "her.") He often sounded as if he was unable to hear Howard, and would throw out lines like "Ain't that something?" "What's not to like?" "Ain't she something?" "Boy, I wanna tell ya!"

Hopper, Dennis The movie actor *(Tracks)* who Stern noted had a small penis. Stern bragged, "I'm definitely bigger than Dennis Hopper." **See Keitel, Harvey.**

Hosch, Karl **See Ryder, P.I.**

Hot 97 The New York City radio station that Stern plays when he wants to make love to his wife. He says that they play "jungle music." About his musical choice, Robin Quivers said, "You can't make love to Tchaikovsky."

Hot Tub Johnny Comic Andrew Dice Clay's "gofer" and occasional Stern guest when Clay stops by the studio.

"How" One of Alison Stern's nicknames for the King of All Media.

Howard, Taneen The nut case who was caught at the governor's mansion in Richmond, Virginia, with a gun and yelling, "Howard Stern is king of all media." The man said that people pick on Stern too much.

The Howard Stern Interview Show Stern's interview show, which premiered on the E! network on November 27, 1992, and ran for a year. In these interviews Stern showed his ability to disarm his guests and extricate new information, often of a sexual nature, from them.

The Howard Stern Negligee and Underpants Party Stern's pay-TV cable special on February 27, 1988, which sixty thousand New York viewers saw for $19.95. The cast of characters included magic-meisters Penn and Teller, comedian-actor Richard Belzer, comedian Emo Phillips and his girlfriend Judy Tenuta, rocker Leslie West, singer Steve Rossi, busty Jessica Hahn, lawyer Dominic Barbara, and aspiring transsexual Siobhan. It was later sold as a $24.95 videotape.

Howard Stern's New Year's Eve Party   According to *People* magazine, one of the worst television programs of 1994. On the same list was *The Late Show with David Letterman* with Madonna as guest, the Grammy Awards ceremony, and MTV's Woodstock coverage. According to John Stossel of ABC-TV, the event grossed $27 million. The video, by the way, was plugged liberally (as all of Stern's "products" are), yet as of his March 14, 1995, broadcast, the $39.95 tape had not been shipped— he casually mentioned that the master was delivered to the videotape duping outfit on March 9.

The Howard Stern Show   According to Stern, "The World's Most Important Radio Program in the History of Man."

The Howard Stern Show   The WWOR-TV Saturday night show that debuted on July 14, 1990, and was soon nationally syndicated.

"Howch"   One of Ray Stern's nicknames for her beloved son Howard.

Howeird   The name WNBC radio used for Howard in an advertising poster headlined "Night *Shtick*" when he aired during the 4:00–8:00 P.M. time period. He was originally called Howeird by deejay Joe Piasek.

Howell, Chauncey   The cherubic television reporter at WNBC-TV, whom Stern befriended when he was at WNBC radio. Howell was one of few people at WNBC who wasn't anti-Stern. Stern noted that Howell was a big gossip and did an imitation of him, although it sounded more like Charles Nelson Reilly. **See Hayden, Chauncé.**

Howie   Short for Howard, and a name that Stern does not like to be called.

Hudson, Rock   The movie and television actor, the first famous one to die of AIDS, about whom Stern said, "His rear end became a parking lot in Hollywood for twenty years."

Hum   The rock band whose song "Stars" Stern likes ("It almost makes me cry"). When they appeared at the radio studio in April 1996, Fred Norris was worried about their ambitious amplifier needs. Said Fred, "If you have small amps, that's fine. If you're talking the Marshall halfstacks, don't even take them out of the truck." The drummer had to play in the hall outside the studio, but it worked out fine.

Humperdinck, Engelbert   Born Arnold George Dorsey in Madras, India, the British singer ("Release Me") is an occasional Stern guest, often confused with Tom Jones. Gary Dell'Abate's aunt Jean was once president of Humperdinck's fan club.

Hungate, Dick   The Detroit program director at WWWW radio who hired Stern from Hartford.

Hungerthon   The annual on-air benefit that K-Rock radio in New York has put on to raise money for the homeless. In November 1995 Howard challenged Jackie Martling to give $1,000 if Stern gave $10,000. Jackie refused to contribute, prompting Stern to do a diatribe against him. Stern humiliated Martling (who shouldn't have to give to any charity that Stern dictates), but by the end of the show, Jokeman wrote a check for $1,500.

Hygiene   Robin Quivers confessed that she wipes herself standing up, which fascinated Howard. Gary Dell'Abate mentioned that he did the same thing.

"I am thorry!"   The sound bite used frequently during the show, originally uttered by Crackhead Bob. **See Harvey, Bob.**

Ian, Janis   The singer-songwriter ("At Seventeen" and "Society's Child") and periodic guest. She admitted to Howard that she was a lesbian (first experience at age fifteen with a woman now married with children), dropped out of high school, and once tried to commit suicide. Her real name is Janis Fink—Ian is her brother's middle name. She told Howard, "I thought the name Fink wouldn't really wash with 'Society's Child.' " When she showed up at *The Tonight Show* wearing slacks, back in the 1960s, they made her wear a dress. One of her songs on her *Breaking Silence* album contains the lyrics "Hide me in the wisdom in your thighs," which greatly amused Stern. She told Howard that he "may be a lesbian trapped in a man's body." When asked if she ever participated in group sex, she disdained it, and said, "Somebody's foot always ends up in someone else's face." **See Seinfeld, "At Seventeen."**

IBM   When Stern decided to install an IBM computer system in his basement and at the studio, he became one of IBM's greatest salesmen, condemning Apple products (and Microsoft's Windows 95) at any opportunity. As of August 1995, Stern had thirty-two megabytes of RAM and one and a half gigobytes on his hard disk. His contact at IBM, whom he occasionally calls on the air, is named Jeff Schick. Stern's television shows usually showed a credit to IBM, suggesting that he gets free or discounted IBM equipment in exchange for a credit ("plug"). Stern denies that he receives anything free from IBM, which is not to say that his show or one of his production companies doesn't.

Idol, Billy   The British rock star who told Stern that he was once on heroin ("I was on everything!"). Idol has a tattoo of a woman with massive breasts on his left arm.

Ilyse   The girl at Boston University who fixed Howard up with future wife Alison Berns, Ilyse's roommate. She came from Rockville Centre, New York, and transferred to B.U. from Ohio Wesleyan.

Imus   John Donald Imus, Jr., the legendary deejay of Welsh ancestry with whom Stern hated to work at WNBC radio in New York City. According to Howard, Imus is "a drunken, over-the-hill bigot." However, some observers see similarities: They are both tall, lanky, aquiline-nosed, long-haired, big-egoed men trying to act twenty years younger than their age. Stern sometimes begins his radio show with Imus's mock-sincere early morning "Good mornin' . . ." greeting. Imus has used a lot of Stern's material. They are both former drug users, although Stern (whose experimentation with drugs ended after college) is quick to point out that Imus didn't quit soon enough. For example, because of drinking, Imus missed one hundred days of work at WNBC in 1973. Imus has four daughters, one of whom is named Ashleigh; Stern has three daughters, one of whom is named Ashley. When Howard learned in 1993 that Imus had a collapsed lung, he was in a good mood, and announced, "I can't wait until he drops dead." When Howard learned that Infinity Broadcasting, his parent company, bought WFAN-AM radio, Imus's station, he went "ballistic." Stern has called him "Grandpa Anus." As Imus ages, Stern has said, "Imus looks like a girl . . . Donna Imus . . . He looks like Beatrice Arthur, an old woman." Imus's radio show is syndicated in more than seventy markets, compared to Stern's forty markets. Imus has called Stern "a dirty-mouthed little punk." Imus has also bragged, "I'm Howard Stern with a vocabulary. I'm the man he wishes he could be." According to writer Dinitia Smith of *New York Magazine* (6-24-91), Imus was "the first of the D.J.s to fuse the top-40 format with insult humor." Imus once worked in a uranium mine in Arizona and broke his leg in an accident. He also survived a train wreck while working as a railroad worker—the engineer was drunk.

"Incest Wednesday"   On June 5, 1996, Howard received calls from a twenty-five-year old married man who had sex with his sister (also married), a man who had sex with his daughter (he was forty, she was twenty), a woman who had sex with her niece, a young man who received oral sex from his father, and a caller who "did" his stepmother. If that was not enough bad news for the broadcast, a caller named Richie said he had sex with an aunt and uncle, and the latter committed suicide shortly thereafter.

Income   *See Money.*

Infinity Broadcasting   The owner of WXRK radio, Stern's flagship station in New York City. When Infinity bought WFAN and Don Imus, among other stations and radio personalities, Stern went berserk. Infinity agreed to pay $1.7 million in fines incurred because of Stern's obscenities. O. J. Simpson was one of Infinity's board members until he was jailed after the stabbing deaths of Nicole Brown Simpson and Ron Goldman. Infinity also owns the G. Gordon Liddy talk show. On

June 20, 1996, it was announced that Westinghouse Electric Corporation was buying Infinity Broadcasting for $3.25 billion to $4 billion.

Ingram, Dan   The afternoon deejay at WXRK who was making $300,000 a year when Howard joined the station in late 1985.

Inheritances   The source of one of Stern's major tirades. He generally hates people who inherit a lot of money, yet he makes certain exceptions (e.g., Tori Spelling, Donald Trump). He announced on his radio show (7-6-92), "People who inherit money drive me crazy."

International Bartenders School   Lest you think that Stern is not, above all, a pitchman for his advertisers, here is what he has said about IBS: "We knew a guy at the Rainbow Room who made $50,000 a year nine years ago—a great job!" Other Stern IBS sound bites are: ". . . a way to meet girls . . . ninety percent job placement three years in a row . . . It's a cool profession . . . five hundred ninety-five dollars tuition . . . The classes are fun . . . Call 1-800-TOP-BARS."

Interns   Employees, usually young ones, who work for nothing. Stern's station seems to employ a lot of them. Stuttering John, for example, worked several years for nothing and incurred about $400 a month commuting costs. *See Andy, Basil, Danny, David, Dead Dave, Gambling Dan, Mike Gange, Gay Rich, Smelly James, Stuttering John, Stuttering Vic, Danny Watt, Steve Grillo, and Danny Zucker.*

IQ   Short for intelligence quotient. Stern has said that he has a 135 IQ, and Stuttering John claims a similar score. *See Melendez, John.*

Irene   Stern's very first girlfriend, whom he met at camp. At age thirteen, she was "fully developed and had a D-cup." She now lives in Cleveland.

Irene the Leather Weather Lady   One of Stern's on-air bits while at WWWW-FM in Detroit. Irene, a dominatrix, read the weather reports.

Israel   The Mexican-American caller who worked at a San Diego motel where prostitutes and their customers were the major residents.

Ito, Judge   The Los Angeles judge who presided over the O. J. Simpson trial and who listens to the Stern radio show. At the outset of the trial, Ito said, "I'm going to send Howard an autographed picture and I'm going to write on it, 'Howard: Enjoy the show, just don't get arrested in L.A.' "

Itsy Bitsy   A simple book that Stern read in the ninth grade when he was mistakenly put in a class with kids who could barely read.

Jablowme, Heywood   A person to whom Stern occasionally makes reference. A student listed with that name mischievously appeared in the Valley Stream, Long Island, 1996 high school yearbook, according to one Stern show listener. The name also appeared in the telephone book that serves the Melbourne/Pompano, Florida, area. The name apparently is a thinly disguised proposition.

Jackson, Jesse   The civil rights leader whom Stern called "an idiot" (6-23-93). He has also referred to him as Jesse Jerkson.

Jackson, Michael   The superstar singer and plastic surgery freak whom Stern often criticizes. Stern had a long, secret meeting with Jackson at singer Dolly Parton's apartment (800 Fifth Avenue), which he finally talked about in his book *Miss America.* Jackson's manager, Sandy Gallin, wanted Stern to mobilize his audience to protest the boy-molesting allegations against Jackson and then have Jackson make a "surprise" appearance on the Stern show. Michael, according to Howard, was late for the meeting and showed up in "thick white make-up . . . like Bozo . . . so thick [it could] stucco a wall." He also had bandages around his nose, except for the tip. As the meeting progressed, Jackson's makeup got smudgy and Stern thought he was melting.

Jackson, Reggie   The baseball Hall of Famer who, when asked the "fart question" by Stuttering John, answered, "Yes, and if you hang out long enough, I'll fart in *your* face." When Reggie was a "mystery guest" on the Stern radio show, he tried to fake a "white" accent but didn't fool Howard or Robin. Reggie mentioned that he has only been married one year in over thirty years of adulthood. Howard told him that he never collected baseball cards as a child—"I was a big pussy!" When Howard asked him if he would date Oprah Winfrey, Reggie said that she was "a little chunky for me."

Jackson Heights   The section of Queens, New York, where Stern was born on January 12, 1954.

Jacobs, A.J.   The *Entertainment Weekly* book reviewer (December 1, 1995) who found Stern's *Miss America* to be a B-minus effort, and less inspired than his first book.

Jacobs, Dr. Elliot   The New York plastic surgeon on the Joan Rivers television show (5-4-90) who showed Howard what he would look like with a nose job. He has threatened to get a nose job in the past but is worried that it will hurt his voice. (Jacob's address is 815 Park Avenue,

New York, NY, and phone number [212] 570-6080, for those Stern fans needing some nose work.)

Jackie "Apology"   After Howard and Jackie Martling, as a goof, frolicked in a hotel tub with a naked Jessica Hahn, Jackie the Jokeman acquired a heavy dose of guilt and made the following apology on the air: "I just want to apologize to my wife Nancy for the Jessica Hahn bathtub incident. It was stupid and I'll never do anything like that again and I love you and I'm very sorry . . . I'm very sincere."

Jackson, Leonard   The veteran stage and screen actor (*Ma Rainey's Black Bottom* and *Car Wash*) who plays a Detroit security guard in Stern's movie *Private Parts.*

James   See Smelly James.

James, Dennis   A longtime television personality and telethon participant whose career peaked in the early 1950s as a wrestling announcer and quiz-show host. When a "Kathie Lee Gifford" called James's Cerebral Palsy telethon to pledge $500,000, he and Florence Henderson were extremely thankful. However, when the caller added, "I want to make hot 'monkey love' to Howard Stern," they realized that they were victims of a classic phony phone call. The perpetrator? Gas station attendant Captain Janks, who can sound surprisingly effeminate. James lamented the ruse and referred to Janks's idol as "Harold" Stern. James, by the way, was the Richard Dawson of his era—famous for kissing female contestants and audience members.

Jameson, Jenna   The not-particularly-attractive, bleach-blond stripper-turned-pornographic film star who, at Howard's request, removed her panties so he could see her "private parts" when she crossed and uncrossed her legs. Her first sex experience was with girls at age twelve, she serviced boys orally at age thirteen, and was fifteen and a half when she first made it with a guy. She has a tattoo on her neck that Howard said was the "ugliest" he ever saw. She appeared on the twentieth-anniversary cover of *High Society* magazine. Jenna likes rough sex, "third input" sex, and "gag balls" in her mouth. She gets paid over $150,000 a year for nine porn films a year, and admitted, "I'm bisexual."

"Janet from Another Planet"   The female deejay who replaced Stern on September 30, 1985, the day that he was fired at WNBC in New York.

Janice   The girl whom Howard semi-seduced with an apricot sour. She kept her blouse on and he barely penetrated her.

Janine   Stern's date at Boston University whom he took to an erotic film festival, and a show guest. They were in bed together, but she didn't give him any sex. He started to touch her breasts ("a little bit of nip and we would've had bliss"), but she started talking about rape. She's now an art director at a Westchester ad agency.

Janks, Captain   *See Captain Janks.*

Janoff, Mr.   One of Stern's teachers at Rockville Centre's South Side High School. He was affectionately known by male students as "Mr. Jerkoff."

January 12, 1954   The birth date of Howard Stern, the FCC's incubus! He's a Capricorn. In several markets Howard tried to get a local official to declare January 12 a holiday. Stern's archenemy Rush Limbaugh was also born on January 12 three years before Stern. Other famous people born on January 12 include Kreskin (1935), once a regular guest, and actress Kirstie Alley (1955). *See Lieberman, Joseph I.*

January 11, 1976   The date on which Robin Quivers began serving active duty in the U.S. Air Force.

Jarvis, Jeff   "The Couch Critic" of *TV Guide* and founding editor of *Entertainment Weekly* who wrote a flattering review of Stern and his E! show. He wrote (7-27-96), "When you hang out with Stern for an hour a night on E! . . . you begin to see that under his bad-boy act is a brilliant comic and even a decent guy."

Jeep   A longtime sponsor of the Stern radio show. In August 1996 Stern announced that he hadn't driven his Jeep in six months, after telling his audience that his mother-in-law was bitten by a bee when she opened the door to the cobwebbed Jeep. Stern said that his wife recently bought a Land Cruiser "for the kids."

"Jelly Bean, Jelly Bean"   A song that an annoyed Stern sang annoyingly at a very young age, diligently recorded by his father, Ben.

Jennings, Peter   The ABC network TV broadcaster and frequent target of Stern's jibes. During the O. J. Simpson car chase, a Stern fan called Jennings on the air and, in an "Amos 'n' Andy" accent, said that he was across the street from Simpson's house. ("I see O. J. . . .") Jennings, a Canadian, didn't quite realize that the call was a put-on until sports broadcaster Al Michaels (and frequent Stern guest) clued him in on the joke.

Jewison, Norman   The Toronto-born movie director who Stern likes to remind his audience is not Jewish. Jewison directed the Oscar-winning movie *In the Heat of the Night,* as well as the films *Fiddler on the Roof* and *Jesus Christ Superstar.*

Jews   Stern once said, "Jews love to talk and love to sue."

Jillette, Penn   Of the Penn and Teller comedic magic act, the blustery Jillette was a frequent radio guest for a while. He also showed some romantic interest in Stern's cohost, Robin Quivers.

Jillian   The intern whose blind date ran her over in his car, hurting her left leg and arm, and breaking her ankle. She said that she was hospitalized for two hours.

Jimmy the Greek   The sports oddsmaker, born Demetrious Synodinos, from Steubenville, Ohio, who died in April 1996. Stern said, "Jimmy the Greek got a bum deal in life" and lamented the fact that CBS fired him for saying something that he and Robin agreed was true. Jimmy said, "The black is the better athalete and he practices to be the better athalete and he's bred to be the better athalete because this goes back to the Civil War when during the slave trading . . . the slave owner would breed his big black to his big woman so that he could have big black kids. I mean that's where it all started. About Jimmy, Howard said, "This guy's not a racist, he's a history professor."

Jodie   Howard's assistant on the *Private Parts* movie shoot. Jodie's main job is to carry a thermos of hot water to slake His Royal Heinie's thirst.

John, Elton   The British rock singer who rhapsodized about Stern on one broadcast: "There is a man with a small penis . . . When he was small he was beaten up by blacks and whites . . ." When Howard was about to interview him for his E! show, John's manager told Howard not to ask about his homosexuality. Stern felt this was unfair, especially since Elton had lipstick on, wore platform shoes, and had his toenails painted red.

Johnny the Retard   The guy in Akron, Ohio, whose neighbors complained because he waves to cars passing by, and the people beep their horns.

Johnson, Doug   The TV reporter who irritated Stern by doing a bad profile of him. He implied that Infinity had paid Stern's FCC fines (they hadn't at the time, but did pay later) and concluded, "Whatever he is, he cannot be denied."

Johnson, Jim "J.J."   Along with George "The Bruiser" Baier, Stern's chief disc-jockey competition in Detroit when he joined WWWW radio. (The two left WWWW to join WRIF-FM.)

Johnson, Magic   The beloved Los Angeles Lakers basketball player who has tested positive for HIV. Stern's take was that Johnson was "sex-crazed" and led a reckless lifestyle that predisposed him to sexually transmitted diseases. Stern's stand created such a controversy in Los Angeles that station manager Andy Bloom told Howard to talk about it on the air—the station received too many complaints about his anti-Magic stance. (The Stern crew's song parody contained the lyrics "It's tragic about Magic and this awful thing, Why couldn't it have happened to Larry King?") When the Lakers point guard Nick Van Exel pushed a referee toward the end of the 1995–96 season, Johnson called Van Exel "unmature," and the following week Johnson also nudged a ref.

Johnson, W. Gary   The Libertarian candidate for governor of New York, whom Stern endorsed in 1990.

Jones, James Earl   The deep-voiced actor *(Star Wars)* who read excerpts of Stern's *Miss America* (". . . make hot monkey love . . .) on the Letterman show. Stuttering John asked Jones if he was ever confused with James Earl Ray, murderer of Martin Luther King.

Jones, Quincy   When Robin Quivers read on the air that Nastassia Kinski had just given birth to a daughter (Kenya Julia Mimbi Sarah Jones) by musician-composer Quincy Jones (who has seven children), Stern went into a tirade about Jones "being into white women" from actress Peggy Lipton on. Stern had a feast when Jones gave an incoherent speech at the Rock and Roll Hall of Fame Awards ceremony. Jones rambled and was clearly under the influence.

Jones, Tom   The Welsh singer ("It's Not Unusual"), former Electrolux vacuum salesman, grandfather, and occasional Stern guest. Howard said that he heard at the Friars Club that Jones had "the biggest [penis] in Hollywood," baiting him to see if he would make any claims. He did not deny that he was well endowed. Most recently Jones lost a suit in Florida for not providing enough money to a seven-year-old illegitimate child. Howard always offers to smell Tom Jones's fingers, hoping to catch a scent of the previous night's amorous escapades.

José   The "heterosexual" Puerto Rican who told Howard in June 1996 that he had sex with an older man when he was fifteen years old while on his newspaper route. José was the "plug" and his newspaper customer was the "socket," about which Stern commented, "If some guy was bent over a chair for me and I looked at his naked buttocks, there's no way I'd stay aroused. No way, José!" José remarked that he got a good tip. Gary Dell'Abate told Howard that many Hispanics don't regard being the aggressor as being homosexual.

Judith   Howard's first girlfriend, whom he met at Camp Wel-Met when he was thirteen years old. He said that she was "a piece of ass" with "huge tits" and a "curvy body." She lived in Far Rockaway, New York.

Judy   The name of a black girl whom Howard "was in love with" when he lived in Roosevelt, Long Island.

June 4, 1978   Howard and Alison Stern's wedding date. *See Temple Ohabei Shalom.*

Just Another Dirty Joke Book   One of Jackie "The Jokeman" Martling's books, published by Pinnacle Books. Hint: It's a collector's item.

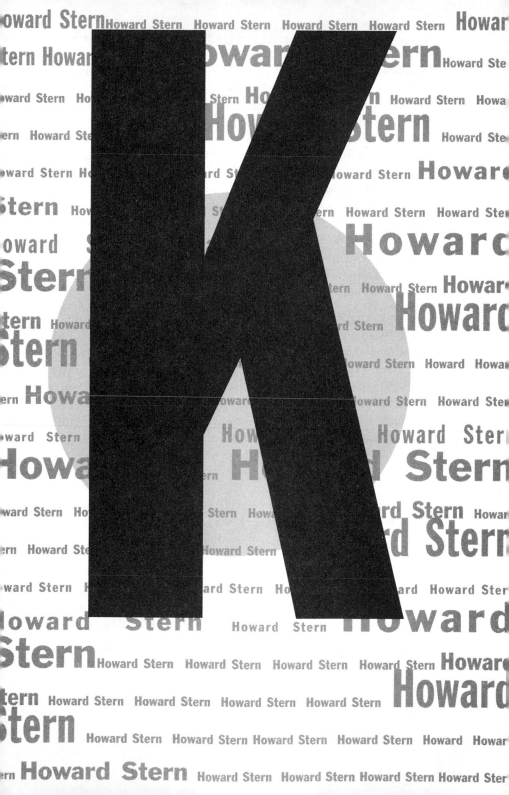

Kakutani, Michiko   The *New York Times* columnist who wrote the article "Howard Stern and the Highbrows" (1-28-96), in which she found similarities to Stern's vulgarities in more rarefied circles. For example, she pointed out that Philip Roth, winner of the National Book Award for his novel *Sabbath's Theater*, wrote about "a hero who masturbates into his best friend's daughter's underwear," and noted that *Leaving Las Vegas*, one of 1995's most popular movies, features "an alcoholic hero, who vows to drink himself to death, and his prostitute-girlfriend, who is brutally gang-raped." In conjecturing the veracity of Stern's output, she noted that it is difficult to separate fact from fiction in Oliver Stone's movie on Nixon and Joe McGinnis's book on Teddy Kennedy. Kakutani concluded that Howard is "the Dorian Gray painting we would like to hide in the attic, a telling image of what our culture is rapidly becoming."

Kallenbach, Kenneth Keith   The spaced-out Stern regular guest (and "Wack Packer") who claims that he can blow smoke through his eyes. He usually ends up crying or vomiting. About him Stern said, "He is the real Beavis and Butthead." He has put lighted firecrackers in his underwear, almost castrating himself, and in his first video, he was seen moving his bowels from the worst possible camera angle. In his next video he costarred in the pornographic movie *Pussyman 9* with porn actress Micki Lynn, who said that Kallenbach was the least endowed of all her on-screen (and off-screen!) lovers and was the second worst experience in her life, the worst being sleeping with one of her "producers." Kallenbach's girlfriend Rebecca was turned off after she found out he was to appear in the movie. His girlfriend Gina likes to French-kiss, but he wants no part of it. Keith announced that he was about to appear in a Tom Cruise movie, saying, "I'm gonna be like a psycho sports fan." About Kallenbach, Stern said, "Every time I see Keith I fear for the human race." Kallenbach will forever be remembered as the articulate politician ("I don't read the newspaper . . . I don't watch TV") who seconded Elephant Boy's nomination of Stern as Libertarian candidate for the governorship of New York in 1994. *See Lynn, Micki.*

Karasick, Rita   A Boston University classmate to whom Stern, under the influence of alcohol, confessed his love. He complained on-air that she never wanted to have sex with him.

Karger, Robert   One of Stern's band members in the Electric Comic-book trio. Karger played the guitar.

Karina   The *Playboy* "Playmate of the Year" and guest on the Stern radio show (5-6-92). Howard asked her the following questions, which she could not answer: "What is the capital of New York?" "What is the square root of one hundred forty-four?" "Who was Liza Minnelli's mother?" and "What did Mickey Mantle do?" She said that she liked to write poetry but couldn't remember any poems she had written. And she couldn't name three presidential candidates, using the excuse that she doesn't watch TV.

Karmazin, Mel   The president and chief executive officer of Infinity Broadcasting Corporation, which owns the Stern show. Stern calls Mel the "bravest broadcaster in the world" because he "believed in" Stern when, in fact, he saw the financial potential. Karmazin is one of the luckiest men in the United States—not only has he made millions off the broadcaster, but Stern's contract forbids him to talk about Mel in public. About Stern, Karmazin said in 1993, "Howard is very underpaid for what he delivers; when Howard's paycheck comes across my desk for a signature, I smile." However, on Stern's September 21, 1995, radio broadcast, he mentioned that Karmazin would not be invited to daughter Emily's Bat Mitzvah, and said, "He's just like me . . . sad." Let's not feel too sorry for Melzy—in 1995 he was paid $3.7 million in salary and bonuses, and when Infinity Broadcasting was bought by Westinghouse, his stock became worth $250 million. When Stern asked WXRK general manager Tom Chiusano the "Sophie's Choice" question (6-21-96), whether he'd push his wife, Penelope, or boss Karmazin off a cliff—only one could live—Tom hesitated a bit more than his wife wanted him to!

Kasem, Casey   The national Top 40 hits-countdown disc jockey, whom Stern hates. The recorded "intro" of Stern's radio show at 6:00 A.M. often plays Kasem's outrageous, ill-tempered recording session in which he uttered a lot of bleeped foul language and revealed himself to be a cantankerous person. ("This is fucking ponderous man, ponderous fucking ponderous!")

Kasindorf, Jeanie   The *New York Magazine* writer who wrote the "Bad Mouth: Howard Stern vs. the FCC" article (11-23-92). She wrote that Stern "has turned prepubescent humor into a multimillion-dollar business."

Kaufman, Dr. Matthew   Stern's dentist, based in Great Neck, New York. He has an office at 30 Central Park South, New York, NY; telephone: (212) 319-3999.

KEDJ-FM   The Stern radio affiliate in Phoenix, Arizona.

Keeley, Mary V.   The Philadelphia area woman who instigated the first complaint about the Stern show to the FCC in 1986. Her fifteen-year-old son was a Stern fan.

KEGL-FM   The call letters of Stern's radio affiliate in Dallas, which began broadcasting the show in September 1992.

Keillor, Garrison   According to Keillor, the host of public radio's *Prairie Home Companion,* "Howard Stern is a geek. He's the guy in the carnival who ate the live chicken . . . He stands there with blood dripping down his chin and feathers in his mouth. How could anybody do that?"

Keitel, Harvey   In an on-air discussion of actors who have exposed their private parts in movies, Stern remarked that "Harvey Keitel is twice as big as Dennis Hopper" and "I'm definitely bigger than Dennis Hopper."

Kellerman, Sally   The original "Hot Lips Houlihan" in the movie *M*A*S*H,* who told Howard, "I read your fucking book." Kellerman has big feet (10 1/2) and always wears white socks. Stern finds her voice commanding, if not sexy.

Ken   The Albany producer of the Stern radio show who often showed up late at the studio, offending listeners. During a phone conversation with Ken, Stern found out that he was an alcoholic, a pot smoker, and bisexual. He later admitted that at age seven a fifteen-year old Italian-American girl made him touch her breasts and at age twelve a male family acquaintance molested him. Stern said that Ken looks like a younger version of mass murderer John Wayne Gacy. After four weeks of rehabilitation, Ken said that he had not been drinking but, after denying it, admitted that he still smoked marijuana on "Friday or Saturday nights."

Ken the Homeless   A heavyset, "homeless" black man who made $1,500 in November 1995 selling Stern's *Miss America* "danglers" in the first few weeks of publication. Formerly Ken had his own business selling collectibles.

Kennedy, John F., Jr.   The editor in chief of *George* magazine and son of U.S. president John F. Kennedy. He appeared on the Stern radio show in mid-March 1996 to plug the issue featuring Stern on the cover of the "virtues" issue. On broadcasts Stern condemned JFK, Jr., for inheriting money, flunking the bar exam a few times, and being, in effect, a male bimbo. Having met JFK, Jr., however, Stern and Robin were favorably impressed by his presence, looks, and sense of humor. Several weeks before Kennedy's appearance, Stern said that he "spends most of his day in Central Park arguing with his girlfriends." He was also very critical of JFK, Jr., for rollerskating to his dying mother's apartment house and to the funeral service.

Kennedy, Joe   The Kennedy patriarch, whom Stern has called a "whoremeister" who "poisoned" a large part of the American population by bootlegging liquor into the United States.

Kennedy, Teddy   The U.S. senator from Massachusetts and Olympic-class swimmer—a favorite subject of Stern's bits ("a little more Chivas . . . let's do the pee pee dance"). Stern especially enjoys the gibes at Kennedy because his in-laws come from Boston and are probably pro-Kennedy Democrats.

Kerr, Jim   A deejay whom Stern hates and wishes that he would get AIDS.

Kevin the Infant   A guest on the Stern television show (8-3-91) who got his sexual kicks acting like an infant, diapers and milk bottle included, and being treated as such.

Key Club   The only high school activity listed under Howard's photo in his Rockville Centre Southside High School yearbook. Members worked on recycling projects and helped disadvantaged children. In the photo of the Key Club, Stern is nowhere to be seen.

Keyes, Roger   A cab-driver friend of rock singer Dee Snider who interviewed convicted murderer Joel Rifkin for two hundred hours.

KFBI-FM   The station in Nevada that carries Stern's show. It was fined $73,750 for indecent comments by Stern.

KFRR-FM   The Stern radio affiliate in Fresno, California.

KHOT-FM   The Stern radio affiliate located in Globe, Arizona.

Kidder, Margot   The movie actress who played Lois in the *Superman* feature movies opposite actor Christopher Reeve. She was found wandering in a Glendale, California, backyard, dazed, with two front teeth missing, after being lost for three days in the spring of 1996. She was immediately put in the psychiatric ward of a county hospital for evaluation and released seventy-two hours later. In the early 1990s Stuttering John cornered Kidder and asked, "Is the man of steel well endowed or hung like a safety pin?" She answered, "I refuse to answer that on the grounds that it may tend to incriminate me." (Note: Rumor has it that Christopher Reeve is in the top ten percent of his class, ranking with comedian Milton Berle and actor Forrest Tucker!) *See Penis.*

Kielbasa Queen   *See Miller, Denise.*

Kiker, Douglas   The late NBC television newscaster who, according to Stern, did a "negative piece that almost cost me my job . . . He lied." The report was "X-Rated Radio" for the *NBC Magazine* news show. On the air Stern later said, "Thank God [he] died of cancer."

King, Alan   The comedian/producer and hard-core tennis fan. After Stern saw him at the U.S. Open, he noted that King has his name on his seat at the stadium "in case he forgets it," and during breaks "he turns around and waves to the crowd."

King, Larry   The "King" of Stern's hatred! For starters, Howard complains that King's radio and television shows don't get decent ratings (he's right!) and that his *USA Today* column is dumb and full of nonsensical non sequiturs. Stern says he has a problem with King trying to marry any woman who will date him. Stern's "phony phone callers" love to blurt "Baba Booey" or "Howard Stern" on King's show, before the producer cuts them off. Stern has called King "the ugliest man in the world." King, who once worked as a milkman and a janitor, graduated from high school with a sixty-six average. He was a compulsive gambler, once in debt for hundreds of thousands of dollars, and he was arrested in 1972 on larceny charges pressed by financier Louis Wolfson, which were later dropped. His real last name is Zieger.

King, Dr. Marshall   A hypnotist and occasional guest, he gets women to do various sexual things such as achieving orgasm by touching their noses.

King, Rodney   According to Stern, "the world's most dangerous millionaire." He noted that King was driving one hundred miles per hour, was under the influence of alcohol and/or drugs, and strongly resisted arrest, yet was never charged for any offense, nor did he serve any time. Stern told a *Rolling Stone* interviewer, "Rodney King should have been beaten more. I think Rodney King is a blight on society." Yet he became a folk hero and, after an obvious makeover, resembled Little Richard. After the post-King riots in Los Angeles, Stern told his audience that "blacks have to solve their own problems—money and give-outs won't do any good—Koreans don't get any money."

The King of All Messengers   A messenger by trade and one of Stern's "phony phone callers." After the World Trade Center bombing, he called CNN and reported on-air, that he was on the eightieth floor, claiming that Fartman caused the explosion.

The King of All Rednecks   Yet another "phony phone caller," he uses names like Jack Marlow (as in Jackie Martling) and Kenneth Kallenbach (as in Keith).

The King of Cable   Another "phony phone caller" who has a preference for calling news programs after a disaster such as a plane crash or hurricane. He also posed as movie director Spike Lee on a call to baseball player Darryl Strawberry and told the audience, "I'd like to tell the black youth of today to listen to Howard Stern and Baba Booey . . . You know what I'm saying, brother . . ."

The King of Comedy   One of Stern's favorite movies. Directed by Martin Scorsese and starring Robert De Niro and Jerry Lewis, the 1981 movie is about a loser comic obsessed with the idea of getting on a late-night television talk show. Stern strongly identified with Rupert Pupkin, the De Niro character. Stern's chum Sandra Bernhard appeared briefly in the movie.

King of Mars   *See Norris, Fred.*

The King Schmaltz Bagel Hour   The radio show that Stern and three friends launched during his sophomore year at Boston University. It was a wild takeoff of *The King Biscuit Flour Hour.*

Kingston, Steve   The program director of K-Rock, and previously with Z-100 and WPGC in Washington, D.C. Stern says that he has a bad nose job, "looks like a girl" ("Steve Queenston"), and asked the question over the air, "Why don't you tell the world you're a Jew?" Stern commented (9-11-95), "Out of all the program directors, he was the stupidest I ever met."

Kinison, Sam   The raunchy and reckless late comedian who was Stern's quintessential guest and favorite comedian (nine pages of praise in *Private Parts*). Sam got a few good breaks from Rodney Dangerfield, who had him on his 1985 HBO special and in his movie *Back to School*. Stern says that Kinison "really changed the face of comedy," which is a slight exaggeration. Sam usually showed up at the studio after an all-night drinking binge with a bottle of champagne in one hand and two amply built women in the other hand. He had a fling with Jessica Hahn, which made the tabloids. Hahn admitted to Howard, among other things, that Kinison fell asleep once during sexual penetration and that he was so drunk one night, he defecated on the floor of his hotel room as he blindly tried to find the bathroom. He died in an auto accident on April 10, 1992, five days after he married his longtime girlfriend, Malika. He is buried in Tulsa, Oklahoma. On the broadcast following his death, Stern admitted that Kinison occasionally took cocaine while in his K-Rock office. Howard later ruminated that it would be great if they froze Kinison and thawed him out for movie appearances such as *Where's Bob III*. Stern's song parody "The Sounds of Kinison" (to the tune of "The Sound of Silence") was a tribute to the late comedian. Sam called Howard from hell on August 30, 1995, and sounded in good spirits. He said that they have booze and cocaine in hell and that Mickey Mantle just arrived. (Sam's voice was convincingly done by a Seattle comedian.) Kinison periodically calls from hell to let Howard know who has arrived. **See Malika.**

Kinkel, Max   The gray-bearded forty-nine-year old deejay who replaced Alison Steele on the 2:00 A.M. to 6:00 A.M. shift at K-Rock in New York, when she left because she was dying of cancer. Kinkel, a Vietnam war veteran, lost his job on January 5, 1996, when the station fired all of its deejays as a result of a format change.

Kinsley, Kathy   A WNBC entertainment reporter in New York who coincidentally lost her job shortly after she interviewed Stern and sat on his lap. She is now on the Fox network. She dated New York anchorman Chuck Scarborough.

Kinnear, Greg   When the Harrison Ford movie *Sabrina,* in which Kinnear appeared, was being released, Stern said about the former *Talk Soup* host, "He's a no-talent bum . . . I hope that movie bombs."

Kirkland, Sally   The busty actress and occasional guest who said about Stern, "I don't think he believes half the things he says." She said that he makes people "let the asshole in themselves come out." When she found out that Paramount was shooting Stern's movie *Private Parts,* she phoned him and gave a strong pitch, contending that she saw four or five female roles that she could play. During her audition for the movie, she freely went topless while in between costume changes, much to the delight of the crew, male and female. Sally likes to "let it all hang out" and actually made a dual-sex overture to Howard and his wife on the air. She claims to have been pronounced dead of a drug overdose as a teenager.

Kitaen, Tawny   A model-actress whom Stern finds very sexy, except for the fact that she dated O. J. Simpson several times before he was put in jail. She appeared as Mona Loveland on television's *WKRP in Cincinnati* from 1991 to 1993, and on *American's Funniest People* from 1992 to 1994. Jerry Seinfeld took her to Spago, an L.A. restaurant, but they were not allowed in.

Kitman, Marvin   The media columnist, critic, and Stern fan who wrote "Howard Stern's Small Penis" for *Penthouse* magazine.

Klein, Calvin   The designer whose underwear Sterns wears—the black version to hide any stains or, as he says, "skid marks." Stern and Jackie Martling debated one morning why underwear manufacturers didn't offer brown underwear. Jackie blurted out, "We could get rich!" Howard replied that they could call it "Jokeywear."

Klein, Robert   The hip comedian from the Bronx whose album Stern used to help produce a demo tape to help get him his first morning drive-time job at WCCC in Hartford.

Klein, Dr. Victor   The obstetrician who delivered Stern's daughter Ashley.

Klores, Dan   Stern's publicity agent, whose wedding on October 1, 1995, Stern didn't want to attend, but his wife, Alison, insisted that he attend, especially since she had bought, according to Howard, "a two-thousand-dollar dress." Dan is also the publicist for Jay Leno, Gary Shandling, Paul Simon, and Branford Marsalis. Stern showed up late at the wedding and promptly complained that there was "no food to eat," except for some shrimp and spring rolls. Stern and his wife were assigned to a dinner table next to a loud band, but lawyer Dominic Barbara quickly switched the number of another table to their table. (They were served lamb chops, which most people enjoy, but Howard complained and asked for some fish.) The biggest insult to Stern was that Klores, after dancing with his bride for a minute or two, walked up to Stern and invited him to dance with him. Stern, who hates these affairs, was livid but decided to go along with the idea. This wedding could be the last one Stern attends until his daughters get married. Klores, by the way, married Abbe Goldman, an executive at his public relations firm. His office is at 60 Madison Avenue, New York, NY, and the phone number is (212) 685-4300. Hailing from Brooklyn, Klores is the son of a furniture store owner.

KLSX-FM The Stern show radio affiliate in Los Angeles, not owned by Infinity broadcasting.

KOME-FM The call letters of Stern's radio affiliate in San Jose, California.

Kools The brand of cigarettes that Stern once smoked and a popular brand among blacks, despite the persistent rumor, according to ABC's *20/20*, that the two o's in the Kool logo represent handcuffs that the white man has put on the black man.

Korn, Sandi The busty *Penthouse* "Pet of the Month" (March 1991) who could not tell Howard which political party George Bush belonged to or what country the United States declared independence from. She has said she once dated real estate mogul Donald Trump. Trump has called her a "healthy specimen." She comes from the suburban town of Port *Chester*, New York.

Kovacs, Ernie A pioneer television comedian who Stern often says "competed with a test pattern," but whose humor was as unorthodox as Stern's. Stern's "Fartman" is as absurd a character as Kovacs's "Percy Dovetonsils," but the two are at least ninety degrees apart in subtlety and vulgarity. Curiously, Stern hired John Lollos, a producer who once worked with Kovacs, to help work on the WWOR-TV show.

Kramer, Ken The real person on which the *Seinfeld* character Kramer was based. Ken was a neighbor of Larry David, who produces and writes the show. Kramer has been a call-in guest several times and claimed that he was mistreated. Stern told him, "Kramer, you're a pushy Jew."

Kravitz, Lenny   A rock singer whom Stern likes. Half-Jewish and half-black, he is the son of the late actress Roxie Roker *(The Jeffersons)*. He was married to actress Lisa Bonet, who is also half-Jewish and half-black. Kravitz has a tattoo of a flower on his posterior.

Krise   Pronounced "Chrissie"—the girl from Brooklyn (she pronounced Stern's first name as "Howid") who did a love scene with Fred Norris. Howard said she needed a nose job and should lose thirty pounds. She is a five-foot-two-inch twenty-one-year-old hairdresser with C-cups and a belly-button ring.

Kritzer, Eddie   The pay-per-view producer who offered O. J. Simpson a $15 million advance, after his acquittal, to appear nationwide in an "interview." Stern condemned his effort but then volunteered to personally conduct the interview for free.

KROD-AM   Stern's affiliate station in El Paso, Texas.

Krone, Penny   The raspy-voiced New York television reporter who doggedly questions Stern at press conferences. A feisty, brassy woman from New York's Hell's Kitchen, she smokes Newport cigarettes and can knock down a few drinks with the best of Big Apple reporters. However, she broke down and cried during one conference when deejay John De Bella kept pointing his index finger at her. (She apparently had a phobic reaction to the gesture, saying, "I hate being pointed at.") When Stern found out that she was half-Jewish, he remarked, "No Jew would name his kid Penny, right?" Robin Quivers quickly responded, "It should be Nickel!"

Krueger, Ellie   Stern's nutritionist, whom he began consulting in August 1996.

Kruger, Barbara   The *Esquire* magazine writer whose article about Stern was entitled (subtle double entrendre!) "Prick Up Your Ears" (May 1992). She referred to Howard's "cellulite-ridden buttocks" and wrote that he was "truly enraptured by the sound of his own voice."

Krupnick, Jerry   The New Jersey reporter who, according to Stern, had the "worst toupee." In a press conference Stern told Jerry, "Excuse me, sir, can you please remove your hat?"

Kunen, James S.   The reporter who wrote the *People* magazine article (10-22-84) that quoted Stern as saying, "Yes, there is probably 10 percent of the audience that is so dumb that they really get off on this and say, 'Hey, Stern speaks our language.'"

Kuriansky, Dr. Judy   The sex psychologist who narrated movie footage of a "phallic festival" in Japan on Stern's WWOR-TV show (7-18-92). Dr. Judy dispenses sex advice to teenagers who listen to New York's rock station Z-100.

KUTZ   Stern's radio outlet (KUTZ-FM, 98.9) in Austin, Texas, as of April 1996.

KZAK-FM   Stern's Reno, Nevada, radio affiliate. Harry Reynolds in the program director, and Steve Smith is the major competition.

La Motta, Jake   The former middleweight boxing champion (1949–51) who was the referee for the Geraldo Rivera–Frank Stallone boxing match featured on Stern's WWOR-TV show (5-16-92). Howard erroneously introduced Jake as a "former heavyweight champion."

Lackner, Laura   Howard's executive administrative assistant.

Lamp, Anne Marie   Along with Doug Z. Goodstein, one of Stern's E! associate producers.

Landon, Michael   The late actor and star of television's *Little House on the Prairie,* for whom Stern had little respect because his image was that of a family man, yet he was married three times and had nine children. In *Penthouse* magazine, Marvin Kitman quoted Stern as saying, "Michael Landon was treated with this reverence, that great family man and that great family show . . . He ditched his wife, he abandoned adopted children, he married these new women . . . I am a better family man than he ever was." Landon had huge ears but instead of getting an operation to pin them back, he grew his hair excessively long. His real name was Eugene Maurice Orowitz.

LAPD   Stern proclaimed one October morning, "God bless the Los Angeles Police Department" (two weeks after the O. J. Simpson verdict and the same week of Louis Farrakhan's "Million Man March" in Washington, DC).

Larson, Jack   The actor who played Jimmy Olson on *The Adventures of Superman* television series from 1951 to 1957. Now a producer *(Bright Lights, Big City),* Larson believes that George Reeves, the actor who played Superman, did not commit suicide but was murdered. He did not get into any details.

Lawton, J. F.   From the Simon & Schuster trade catalog advertising Stern's book *Private Parts* to the book trade: "Howard's first feature film, *The Adventures of Fartman* written by J. F. Lawton *(Pretty Woman, Under Siege),* will begin filming in late spring 1993."

Lawyers   Stern has little praise for lawyers even though he surrounds himself with aggressive ones and occasionally plays poker with Long Island defense attorney Dominic Barbara. Stern has said, "Lawyers are basically guys who wanted to go to medical school but couldn't get in . . . The medical profession is being ravaged by lawyers." He also said, "These lawyers are such thieves." More recently he said, "I wish they would all drown in the ocean, every single one of them. I can't stand a one of them. I've got fifty of them working for me . . ." Stern's best anti-lawyer riff occurred on his May 20, 1996, broadcast. It was Stern in one of his finer ad lib moments. He complained, "Even the lawyers on your own side are vicious villains, but you have to hire them because they have to hire them to fight the other vicious ones." Stern's agent, Don Buchwald, by the way, is a lawyer.

Lazar, Mrs.   Howard's sixth grade teacher, whose claim to fame was that she went to school with actress Sandra Dee.

Le Beauf, Sabrina   The black actress (Sondra Huxtable on *The Cosby Show*) who appeared on Stern's "Black Folk with White Features" bit on his WWOR-TV show (1-25-92). Stern said she should work with "Phyllatio Rashad."

Le Brock, Kelly   The movie actress *(Weird Science)* who admitted to Howard that she has had a high colonic and that she and her kids walk around nude in their northern California home. When she said that she was "half-French," Howard promptly told her that he hates the French. She told Howard, "You're a nice man in spite of yourself." She said that she went to all-girls boarding schools and admitted to having sex with "quite a few" guys, starting at age sixteen. A caller who had been sexually abused by a priest said that she saved his life, explaining that after seeing her in *Weird Science*, he knew he was straight. Kelly's product line number is (800) 209-8434.

Leach, Robin   The avuncular British host of television's *Lifestyles of the Rich and Famous* is an occasional guest on the Stern show. Howard visited him once at his custom-built hideaway at Jumby Bay, Antigua, and is quite impressed with Leach's female companionship and his lifestyle.

Leather Weatherlady   *See De Cook, Irene.*

Lebhar, Godfrey "Goff"   Stern's general manager at WWDC-FM in Washington, DC, not one of Howard's favorite people. He complained that Goff was "the biggest pain in the ass I ever worked for"—until he went to WNBC in New York. On-air Stern often referred to him as "Goof Le Phoof." Goff was the son of Bertram Lebhar, Jr. (also known as Bert Lee), a sports broadcaster and national contract bridge player.

Lee, Spike   The black movie director *(Malcolm X, Crooklyn,* and *Clockers)* whom Stern detests and calls "Peanut Head."

Lennon, Julian   Beatle John Lennon's first son, who Stern said should get 50 percent of Yoko Ono's $340 million net worth. Julian received $150 a week until he reached the age of twenty-one and then received a lump sum of only $100,000.

Lenny   The 1974 movie about the legendary, foul-mouthed comic Lenny Bruce (starring Dustin Hoffman) that Howard and Alison saw on their first date.

Leno, Jay   The talk-show host and Johnny Carson heir who has been an occasional call-in guest. Stern rarely flatters people, but he called Leno "one of the nicest people in the world . . . He's like a puppy." Yet Howard told Rick Marin in a *Rolling Stone* interview, "Jay is so weak. Jay is like a deer that's been hit in the woods by a couple of bullets. He's just sort of wobbling around, waiting to be knocked out." Leno was asked to be a replacement for Stern when he was fired by WNBC but declined, not wanting to commit to a five-day-a-week job. Comic Andrew Dice Clay says that Leno's head "weighs forty pounds!" Jay's nickname as a child was "Chinzo."

Leonard   The Mexican-American who called Howard to propose to his girlfriend, Roxanne, on the air. Her parents "don't like Mexicans," but she has always dated Mexicans. He is a maintenance man at Hertz and is also a funeral escort driver.

"Lesbian Dial-a-Date"   A favorite Stern bit featuring a lesbian in his studio who talks to phone callers and picks a "winner" with whom to have a date—and later tells Howard the details on a future show.

"The Lesbian Love Connection"   The theme of one of Stern's highest-rated television shows (12-1-90) on WWOR-TV. It achieved a 10.6 rating and 21 share.

Leslie   A girl whom Stern met at Camp Wel-Met and had a lot of sex with. She stopped dating Howard because she met a boy with "a really big penis."

Letterman, David   The television talk-show host who has had Stern on his show dozens of times. Stern has had temporary "feuds" with Letterman, and in early 1992 (3-27-92) he complained to his audience that he didn't like the idea that Dave had on his show deejays like Imus and Mark and Bryan. In his interview with *Rolling Stone* in 1994, Howard said, "Dave is looking old, like an old elephant . . . It's the same show, day in, day out." Letterman finally appeared on the Stern radio show in March 1996 and, among other things, showed that he does not wear a hairpiece on his forehead, as Howard thought. Letterman admitted that he lost his virginity at age eighteen. He called Howard a "sociopath" several times during the interview and said that he was "morally bereft." One of Letterman's hobbies, besides driving fast, is listening to shortwave radio broadcasts. Letterman's current girlfriend is a television camerawoman. Stern says that Letterman should have a panel of guests and guest hosts, but "he's too insecure." (So is Howard, because he would never have a guest host on his shows.) When Howard appeared on Letterman as "Miss America," Letterman told him, "You are, without question, the single, ugliest life-form I've ever seen in my life." On separate occasions Letterman has asked both Howard and Robin during commercial breaks (when the band plays a loud segue), "Are you making a lot of money?" The Stern crew noted that Letterman likes to eat a lot of chocolate, a fact verified by several listeners who worked on the Letterman show.

Levine, Alan The deejay "Weezer" in Rochester, New York, who was Stern's main competition when his show entered the market. Levine has "more tattoos than Axl Rose," according to Howard.

Levine, Ed The program director at WJFK-FM when the Stern show began broadcasting in Washington, DC. Levine later became a radio consultant and Stern enemy, a "Sternbuster" who advised stations how to prepare for the arrival of the Stern show. Stern said, "He's nobody . . . he's a fly on a pile of crap . . . he's garbage . . . he's barely human."

Levinson, Jeff A writer and producer of in-house radio commercials at WRNW radio in Briarcliff Manor, New York, when Stern worked there.

Levy, Michael The infomercial producer and "actor" whom Stern mimicked on his December 15, 1995, E! special.

Lewis, "Grandpa" Al The "Grandpa Munster" star of TV's situation comedy *The Munsters*, which ran on CBS from 1964 to 1966, one of Stern's favorite shows in the 1960s. He is an occasional Stern guest and, for a guy in his eighties (he was born in 1910!), is energetic, funny, and still likes the company of women. At the FCC protest at Dag Hammarskjöld Plaza, Lewis yelled, "Fuck the FCC!" Grandpa Al has a Ph.D. from Columbia University and has taught black studies. Lewis wrote the foreword of the book *The Howard Stern Book*, written by Jim Ciegelski. Lewis wrote, "Our dear Howard is just full of excess, and, and a lot of other things—talent, *chutzpah*, gall, and the tenacity of a Jewish locust. Howard is a poor man's *tummeler*, a *nudnick*, and a *shtupper* . . . He is a nice Jewish boy gone astray, a terrible tennis player, a wonderful family man and father." Grandpa Al's real name is Alexander Meister.

Lewis, Jerry   Because the French have praised comedic actor/director Jerry Lewis and his films, Stern is not big on Dino's old partner and his slapstick, physical humor. Yet Lewis was in *The King of Comedy,* one of Stern's favorite movies. Also, Stern loves Jim Carrey, who has Lewis-like qualities. When Captain Janks, as a "phony phone caller," called Lewis's 1995 muscular dystrophy telethon and pretended to be talk-show interviewer Larry King, Lewis said, "You're always going to get a schmuck out there."

Lewis, Lennox   A black British boxer whom Stern likes because of his accent ("absolyootely"). He told Howard that he had sex with his first white woman before he became famous.

Lewis, Richard   The somber, whiny comedian, ex-adman, and frequent Stern guest who drones on and on, complaining about everything, including Howard. Stern keeps reassuring his audience that Lewis is very talented, when, in fact, he's annoying, paranoid, and conspicuously unmarried.

Libertarian Party   The political party ticket that Stern ran on when he ran for governor of New York. His platform consisted of getting highways and roads repaired at night when fewer people used them, reducing tolls, and instituting the death penalty. Surprisingly, his simplistic platform struck a chord beyond his audience—traffic and criminals create a lot of anxiety in most citizens' day-to-day existence.

Lichenbaum, Hal "Lich"   An overnight disc jockey at WCCC in Hartford, with whom Stern played racquetball.

Liddy, G. (George) Gordon   A favorite guest whom Stern likes because he says what it is on mind. No mincing words. When Stern kidded him about J. Edgar Hoover being gay, Liddy asserted that Hoover was heterosexual, using as proof that copies of *Playboy* were found in his home after his death. Liddy has a game on the market entitled "Hardball Politics." Stern says that Liddy is "four feet tall," and Liddy says that "Uncle Melzie" (Mel Karmazin, head of Infinity Broadcasting) is three feet nine inches tall.

Lieberman, Joseph I.   The U.S. senator from Connecticut who declared that Howard's birthday, January 12, would be an important date "for the rest of eternity." Then state senate minority leader, Lieberman soon became the Connecticut attorney general (1982) and then U.S. senator (1988).

Limbaugh, Rush   Stern constantly lambastes the equally outspoken, "sausage-fingered" conservative radio and television commentator Rush "Pumpkin Head" Limbaugh, yet, in any given day or week, any listener to both shows will immediately see that they have very similar political views. (They differ on abortion, however—Rush Hudson Limbaugh III is "pro-life," and Stern is pro-abortion.) He bellyaches that Limbaugh shills for Pizza Hut, yet Howard shills for many more advertisers of lesser renown. They also shared the same book editor, Judith Regan, at Simon & Schuster. Limbaugh's books, by the way, outsell Stern's. In a 1993 *Time*/CNN poll conducted by Yankelovich in conjunction with the article, the people surveyed thought that Limbaugh was more intelligent (71 percent vs. 49 percent), less obnoxious (66 percent vs. 81 percent), less demeaning to women (41 percent vs. 72 percent), less demeaning to blacks and other minorities (34 percent vs. 61 percent), and less irresponsible (33 percent vs. 64 percent) than Stern. Howard says Limbaugh "stole his routine," which is, of course, a delusion. Since when is there a patent on motor-mouthing? The two men also share the same birthday. They were both born on January 12—Limbaugh in 1951 and Stern in 1954. Astrologists certainly agree that they have a lot in common! Limbaugh flunked his introductory speech course at Southeast Missouri State University. He admitted on a broadcast, "I've been fired from all but two jobs I've ever had." **See Toupees.**

Lisa   The capuchin monkey guest whom Stern asked to act as a program manager for K-Rock by selecting several songs to play. Stern maintained that a monkey could program the station's recordings better than the "eighty-five- to one-hundred-thousand-dollar-a-year" program director, then named André. General manager Tom Chiusano preferred the monkey's selections (U-2, Jethro Tull, Peter Gabriel) over André's three Bruce Springsteen's tracks.

Lisa   The bikinied guest whom Stern made eat a banana on-camera. She devoured the yellow fruit so well (Jackie Martling chimed in,

"That's more than me!") that the E! show producers "prismed out" her mouth. Lisa sipped champagne during the interview to loosen up.

"Little Howard" If Elvis had "Little Elvis," Stern has his "Little Howard." He regularly comments that he has a small penis—a "nub" or "pimple." He has always been afraid to change in locker rooms lest other guys see his organ. On his June 29, 1992, broadcast he said that his organ grew to five or six inches when it had to, and essentially said the same thing in his *Playboy* interview. On the flap of his book *Private Parts*, it says that he "has been married for fifteen years, has three children, and lies about the size of his penis." Only his wife and his urologist know the truth.

Littlefield, Warren One of few senior executives at NBC whom Stern praises. Littlefield called in and admitted, "I used to be a truck driver" and "My daddy was a pickle pusher at H. J. Heinz."

Liza A hooker and coauthor of the book *You'll Never Make Love in This Town Again,* who appeared with coauthor Robin. She said she performed oral sex on Beatle George Harrison, and said that Warren Beatty was not a good lover. (She said he took two minutes, but he is famous for lasting a long time!) Liza said she met Vanna White of *Wheel of Fortune* fame at *Playboy* founder Hugh Hefner's mansion, went to Vanna's place and then agreed, "Let's party." They did *it* for a half hour, with Vanna on the receiving end.

Lloyd, Walter The director of photography of the movie *Private Parts.*

Lockhart, June The actress who played Maureen Robinson on television's *Lost in Space* (1965–68). Stuttering John asked her, "When you went to the bathroom in space, did it float in the air?" About her Stern said that she "had a set of [nice] cans."

Locklear, Heather The *Melrose Place* star whom Stern offered $10,000 to have sex with him, promising her "fifty orgasms." When he asked if she ever made love in the water, she said, "I don't remember." He said, "That's a yes!"

Lois and Clark One of Stern's favorite television shows, starring Teri Hatcher and Dean Cain, it airs opposite *Babylon 5*, another one of his favorites, in New York.

Lollos, John **See Kovacs, Ernie.**

Lombardo, Nick   Stern's plumber, about whom he said, "My plumber is Nick Lombardo and he charges me a fortune!"

Lord of the Flies   One of Stern's favorite movies (the 1963 British black-and-white production), about a group of proper English schoolboys stranded on an island, who gradually lapse into a savage state. Howard said, "I was Piggy," referring to the chubby kid with glasses ("I've got the conch . . ."). The movie is based on William Golding's novel.

Lords, Traci   The porn movie star whose father is Jewish and mother is a Gentile, according to Kurt Waldheim, Jr. (Fred Norris), in a "Guess Who's the Jew?" bit.

Loring, Lisa   The actress from television's *The Addams Family* who told Stern that she lost her virginity at age thirteen to her "childhood sweetheart" who became the father of her first child when she was sixteen.

Lowenstein, Allard   A liberal Democratic New York congressman whom Stern admired. An in-the-closet homosexual, Lowenstein was shot to death in 1980 by Dennis Sweeney, a young former employee and supporter, who was diagnosed as a chronic paranoid schizophrenic.

Lowry, Tom   The *New York Daily News* staff writer who wrote an article (1-14-96) about Howard entitled "Money Mouth." Lowry pointed out that Stern proclaimed himself "King of All Media" years ago, yet has delivered his promise. (His radio show becomes number one in most markets that he enters, his books instantly became number one on the best-seller lists, his syndicated television show often outrated *Saturday Night Live* for fractions of their budget, his pay-per-view specials are high grossers, his audiotapes and videotapes sell very well, etc.)

LSD   Lysergic acid diethylamide, known as "acid" in the drug culture. It is a drug that Howard took in his college days. He likes to say that he "took four hits and lived." It produces temporary hallucinations and a schizophrenic psychotic state.

Lugz   A footwear sponsor of the Stern show. Howard says they are "my favorite shoes."

Lutzer, Jill   One of Alison Stern's friends who appeared on the Stern show. Her husband is a lawyer.

Lynn, Amy   *See Amy Lynn Baxter.*

Lynn, Ginger   The porn star and former girlfriend of actor Charlie Sheen who "got naked" on Stern's show and let Howard spank her.

Lynn, Micki   The porn actress who costarred with Kenneth Keith Kallenbach in the pornographic movie *Pussyman 9*, for which she was paid $500 a day. She said that Kallenbach was the least endowed of all her on- and off-screen lovers. ***See Kallenbach, Kenneth Keith.***

Maccarone, Michael   The young actor who plays Howard Stern at age twelve in the movie *Private Parts.*

MacDonald, Norm   The *Saturday Night Live* comedic actor who told Howard, "I can masturbate as well as anybody." MacDonald mentioned the time that Dennis Rodman accidentally head-butted him on *SNL* and that as a result of the routine going awry Norm had to go to the emergency room that night.

MacNeil/Lehrer Report   The PBS news program featuring Robin "Robert" MacNeil and Tom Lehrer. Howard applied for a production job on the show right after college but was turned down.

Mad magazine   Stern's favorite childhood magazine. He appeared on the cover in mid-1995 and was very flattered. **See Tobiason, Arthur.**

Mad Russian   A Stuttering John "wannabe" from St. Louis, via the scenic west Ukraine, and occasional phone-in guest. Danny Hutton of Three Dog Night told Stern that the Mad Russian had bad manners and tried to hit him up for $100.

Madonna   The audacious, innovative singer, quite "full of herself," whom Stern once liked until she decided not to appear on his show in 1988, after he left a long message on her answering machine asking her to make an appearance to boost his ratings. He panned her documentary *Truth or Dare* for its egomaniacal self-indulgence and rightfully berated Madonna for not graciously accepting Kevin Costner's backstage compliment just because she didn't like the word "neat." In October 1996, she gave birth to a baby girl, whom she named Lourdes.

Maeder, Jo   Formerly the "Rock 'n' Roll Madam" at K-Rock, Maeder began working for Z-100 in early 1996, after a one-year stint announcing for the *Dr. Wally* show on WABC radio on Sunday mornings. Howard had fun with her; he "phony-phone-called" her as "Bob De Vito from *Penthouse* magazine," wanting her to "pose for a spread, so to speak." During the conversation Maeder said, "I must say that I am definitely a head turner . . . but I don't want to do anything like that." About another madam of a different sort, Xaviera Hollander, Maeder made a puzzling and provocative comment: "Her book changed my life." Maeder wrote a tribute to Alison Steele in *The New York Times* (10-29-95).

Mahesh, Maharishi Yogi   *See Transcendental Meditation.*

Mahoney, Jerry   Ventriloquist Paul Winchell's dummy, a replica of which Howard owned as a child. **See Winchell, Paul.**

Majors, Master Bill   The producer of and actor in sadomasochistic porn movies, which Stern likes. When Stern asked why he spent six months in jail, Majors said, "I got a bad movie review." Stern likes Majors's movies but says that he is "the ugliest son of a bitch you've ever seen."

Malika   Comedian Sam Kinison's girlfriend and eventual bride (4-5-92), and frequent guest on Stern's show. Malika Souiri remarried about a year after Kinison's death to producer Paul Borghese of Atlantis Productions. According to Gary Dell'Abate, Borghese provided many of the bikini-clad women who appeared on Stern's WWOR-TV show.

Malle, Louis   See France.

Malmet, Barbara   The news director of WRNW radio in Briarcliff Manor, New York, and, in effect, the predecessor of Robin Quivers. (Howie would ad-lib comments about her news items.)

Mamaroneck, New York   An affluent suburban New York community that had instances of anti-Semitism in early 1996. One house in the Pirate's Cove section was painted with the sentence "I Will Kill Howard Stern" and contained a few small swastikas.

Manchild in the Promised Land   One of few books Stern has ever admitted reading. Written by Claude Brown, the book jacket says that the story is about "a black man who made it out of the ghetto, who pulled himself up from Harlem, from the gang wars, the crime, the dope pushing to become a law student at one of America's leading universities."

Mancow   Howard's "bitch" (competitor deejay) in Chicago, Mancow Muller.

Mandela, Nelson   The black South African leader who Stern told *New York Magazine* writer Maer Roshan was his hero. Stern was kidding, of course. Just before being interviewed, his book publicist for *Miss America*, told him that she greatly admired Mandela.

"Man-pon"   A clump of tissue paper that Stern wanted to wear under his thong while shooting the Fartman segment of his movie *Private Parts*, but decided not to.

Mantle, Mickey   About the great New York Yankee center fielder, Stern said, "He was a big, drunken bum."

Marchetti, Bill   A media analyst and consultant with Paul Kagan & Associates who said, "Howard has mastered reaching a core, loyal base of fans and then pushing product through a number of media windows."

March 21, 1994   The morning on which Stern announced that he would like to run for governor of New York on the libertarian ticket.

Marco   The young Peruvian man who sported larger teeth than Gary Dell'Abate. Gary's front teeth were measured to be three quarters of an inch long, and Marco's teeth were slightly larger but didn't look like Gary's "Chiclets." Marco wants to study computer sciences but can barely spell. (He did spell the word *unemployment* right!)

Marcos, Imelda   The former first lady of the Philippines and collector of shoes whom Stuttering John asked, "If you pass gas at home in front of others, do you blame the family dog?" Stern called Imelda "the one person who raped the Filipino people." Joan Rivers told Howard that Marcos lived in her building.

Marijuana   A drug that Stern thinks should be legalized. "Head writer" Jackie Martling wholeheartedly agrees. Stern went for many years drug-free, but announced on the air in October '95 that he had smoked marijuana the previous Friday. He proclaimed, "I smoked pot on Friday. I was pretty buzzed." His favorite word for a joint is "doobie." Occasionally Fred plays Jackie's song that is a tribute to marijuana.

Marin, Rick   The writer who interviewed Howard for *Rolling Stone* (2-10-94). Marin wrote about him, "There's a chip on his shoulder the size of Long Island, all this newfound fame, cash, fandom still don't satisfy him." Howard told the writer that he loved pay-per-view as a media venue because "I can go on there and do exactly what I would love to do. I can fuck a sheep . . ."

Mark and Brian   Two Los Angeles deejays (Mark Thompson and Brian Phelps) whom Stern conquered in the ratings. Stern announced, "They ripped off my routines and now they will be my slaves." When their ratings dropped to number seventeen in Los Angeles, they sunk to a publicity stunt in which they "got naked" together with Frank Jordan, the mayor of San Francisco, and washed each other's backs. The mayor later apologized on-camera for the incident and jeopardized his political career.

"Marla"   A transsexual whose marginal claim to fame is that he/she slept with the same guy before and after having his penis surgically removed.

Marriage   In *George* magazine Stern said, "You have these playboys who run around with a lot of chippies, but I truly respect women. I made a vow to my wife when I was twenty-two—a stupid vow—but a vow. I never thought I'd be famous or have women wanting me. Now I have all these women around me and I'm still married." Stern, by the way, does not wear a wedding ring.

Marsalis, Branford   The former band leader of the Jay Leno *Tonight Show*, whom Howard likes to interview. On the broadcast of his forty-first birthday, Howard said about Branford, "He's so gentle, he's afraid of Sinbad [i.e., a laid-back black]!"

Marsh, Ali   The actress who plays the blind girl in Stern's movie *Private Parts*.

Marshall, Gary   The television and movie director *(Happy Days, Laverne and Shirley*, and *Pretty Woman)* and brother of comedic actress-turned-director Penny Marshall. Stern has always thought that Marshall was Jewish ("real name was Schwartz"), but, in fact, he was born Gary Marscharelli in the Bronx, son of an Italian industrial filmmaker.

Marshall, Leonard   The ex–New York Giants football lineman who was a regular phone-in guest for a while. On a television broadcast (2-16-91), Howard kissed Marshall's blue-jeaned posterior after losing a Super Bowl bet to him. Stern loved to kid him about his white wife and their sexual relationship. Marshall, who racked up 447 tackles in his career, is now a stockbroker in Boca Raton, Florida.

Martling, Jackie   "Jackie the Jokeman," Stern's "head writer," who has worked for him since 1986. John C. Martling is a jovial Long Island local (Bayville) who looks a bit like an overweight Don Johnson with a sunny disposition and a fondness for alcoholic beverages. Unbeknownst to radio listeners, Jackie quickly scribbles funny lines and hands them over to Stern every fifteen to thirty seconds, and Stern adds the ad libs to his motor-mouth riffs. He has also written classic songs such as "Flies" and "The Pot Song." Stern says that he uses the material more than 90 percent of the time. Jackie also helps write Stern's prepared "bits." Martling, a Michigan State alumnus (class of 1971?) and struggling stand-up comedian, always threatens to quit the show, but he knows "where his bread is buttered." His contract calls for liberal free plugs for his comedy audiotapes and CDs (e.g., *Sergeant Pecker*) and nightclub appearances, all of which earns him an extra $400,000 a year. (Boy Gary estimates that Jackie makes $6,000 a night per gig.) He began hosting a television comedy show in early 1991, which aired immediately after the Stern WWOR-TV show on Saturday nights, but didn't last long. Jackie, an admitted cheapskate, makes Jack Benny look like a philanthropist. Jackie and his wife, Nancy Sirianni, upon the birth of Ashley Jade Stern, gave them a $19.95 polyester outfit and a blue night-light. And yet he occasionally calls Howard "a cheap Jew," to which Howard usually responds, "I'm a cheap half-Jew." Of Dutch and French (Huguenot, via the Dutch West Indies, in the early 1600s) descent, on his mother's side he is a descendant of Lyman Hall, one of the signers of the Declaration of Independence. His religious upbringing was Methodist. Jackie is also called Jackie Marlow by Howard. He has no toenails because a podiatrist removed them after he came down with a severe fungus. Jackie's tape *Sergeant Pecker* contains 350 jokes in seventy-eight minutes of recording—a joke every 13.4 seconds! Jackie's phone numbers are (516) 922-WINE and (800) 323-KING. Jackie's mailing address is: P.O. Box 62, East Norwich, New York 11732. **See Sirianni, Nancy.**

Marx, Elaine   "Miss Howard Stern 1994" and shortly thereafter the future ex-wife of "Corky."

Massapequa   The Long Island, New York, hometown of Joey Buttafuoco and wife (Massapequa High School, '74), Jessica Hahn ('77), Jerry Seinfeld ('72), Alec Baldwin ('76), Billy Baldwin ('81), the other Baldwin brothers, and Stuttering John Melendez.

Masturbation   One of Stern's favorite topics. He once admitted (2-17-93) that he masturbates twenty times a month, but not on weekends. On June 24, 1991, Robin Quivers said she hadn't had sex in over a year and had masturbated the previous Thursday, using a vibrator.

Matthews, Larry   "Little Richie" on *The Dick Van Dyke Show*, Matthews told Stern that he lost his virginity at age thirteen when "[Cherokee] Indians took me out to the still and grabbed this eighteen-year-old girl" and made her have sex with him in order for him to lose his virginity.

Maury   The Jewish-Syrian "phony phone caller" from Brooklyn responsible for the classic Amos 'n' Andy–inspired "I see O. J." phone call to ABC's Peter Jennings. Jennings, a Canadian, apparently was not familiar with Amos or Andy, or Kingfish, for that matter. Maury told the screener that he was a neighbor ("Robert Higgins") of O. J. and could see O. J. in the Bronco in his driveway ("I see O. J. kindah slouchin' down . . . Now lookee here, he look very upset . . ."). Maury also called WABC-TV's Bill Beutel after Colin Ferguson opened fire on a Long Island Railroad commuter train. He used the name Dexter and feigned a Jamaican accent. Even after Maury uttered "Baba Booey" several times, Beutel was sucked in enough to ask "Dexter," "What did that mean . . . Baba Booey?"

May 8, 1986   The birth date of Howard's daughter Debra.

May 10, 1990   The date of "zookeeper" John De Bella's mock funeral in Rittenhouse Square, Philadelphia.

May 17, 1947   The wedding date of Ben and Ray Stern, Howard's parents.

"Mayberry KKK"   The Stern spoof of the television situation comedy starring Ken Berry, Sternified with Ku Klux Klan members.

Mazzeo, Vinnie   A Stern "Wack Packer" and stand-up comedian "wannabe" who, among other things, has set his genitals on fire.

McBride, Harlee   *See Belzer, Richard.*

McCartney, Linda   The wife of Beatle Paul McCartney and a favorite target for Stern. Howard was ecstatic when he received a bootlegged audiotape of Linda singing backup at one of Paul's concerts—it conspicuously demonstrated that she sings off key.

McClurg, Edie   Actress and favorite Stern guest, she has appeared in *Natural Born Killers, Carrie, Ferris Buhler's Day Off,* and many others. She said she was always called "a muttonhead" by her family. Edie appeared with Howard on *The Hollywood Squares.*

McCormack, Mary   The movie actress *(Murder One)* who plays Howard's wife, Alison, in the movie *Private Parts.* She also appeared in the remake of *Miracle on 34th Street.* Stern is quite impressed by both her acting ability and her breast size. Contrary to what some callers asserted, she did *not* appear in any of the sexy *Red Shoes Diaries* movies. After the movie was shot, Stern gave her a wedding ring.

McFarland, Spanky   The child actor from the *Our Gang* comedies of the 1930s and 1940s. Spanky turned down the invitation to appear on the Stern show.

McGinty, Judge   The Cleveland judge who presided over the WMMS *Cleveland* v. *Howard Stern* case, in which a radio station employee sabotaged Stern's broadcast to proclaim his show as being number one in the market. Although the judge did sentence the culprit who cut the cable, he made negative comments about Stern and his show—clearly not relevant to the case, whether you like Stern or not. When Stern learned that Judge McGinty had two drunk-driving charges, he repeatedly reminded his audience.

McGovern, Maureen   The popular singer ("There's got to be a morning after . . .") who admitted to Howard that she had a nose job on Halloween of 1977. She said that it didn't affect her voice but it did hurt for a while, and she had rhinitis for a year, which required occasional cauterization.

McKenna, Paul   "The World's Funniest Hypnotist" who achieved the impossible—he convinced three strippers that Howard had a large penis.

The McLaughlin Report   One of Stern's favorite television shows—a Sunday morning political commentary program that is fast-paced and features both conservative and liberal views.

McMahon, Ed   The former marine jet pilot and sidekick of talk-show host Johnny Carson. Stern calls McMahon an "ass-kisser," "a no-talent," and "a big fat jerk." His biggest sin, in Stern's estimation, was that he appeared on the Arsenio Hall show and would appear on Leno's *Tonight Show*. When McMahon appeared on *The Today Show* one morning, Captain Janks called in as comedic actor Jim Carrey and called Ed "a fat pig."

Meadows, Audrey   The *Honeymooners* actress who refused to appear on the Stern show because she didn't like him. She actually hung up the phone while talking to Gary Dell'Abate.

Meat Loaf   The occasionally overweight rock singer ("What I'd Do for Love") who is an occasional guest. His *Bat Out of Hell* album, according to his record company, sold twenty-six million copies, but he thinks it sold a lot more. Meat Loaf (real name Marvin Aday) admits that he, like Stern, has a relatively small penis.

Mein Kampf   Stern's original title for his book *Private Parts*. It was rejected by Simon & Schuster. (In German it means "My Struggle" and was the title of Adolf Hitler's manifesto.)

Medjuck, Joe   One of the producers of Stern's movie *Private Parts*.

Melendez, John   "Stuttering John" Melendez is the Stern "intern" who interviews celebrities at glitterati gatherings and asks them embarrassing and often outrageous questions. He asks every baseball great if they ever farted in the catcher's face. He baited Barbara Walters about her speech defect. He asked actress Ally Sheedy, who has had problems with bulemia, "When was the last time you threw up?" Stern calls John "Hero of the Stupid." *Rolling Stone* magazine (9-5-91) called him "M.C. Stammer." John is five feet seven inches tall (ten inches shorter than Stern), claims an IQ of 136 (one point higher than Howard claims his IQ is!), and is a graduate of New York University, which is usually ranked higher than Howard's Boston University. At the mock funeral for the Philadelphia "zookeeper" in May 1990, John played the corpse in a horse-driven carriage. Stern threatened to fire John and hire someone with Tourette's syndrome ("Stuttering is good, but Tourette's is better), but he was playing a trick on Stuttering John. When Stern found out that Stuttering John was "peddling" a book about his interviews, he killed the idea. The African dancer Uzo asked to see Stuttering John's penis when he visited her apartment, and he obliged—she said he had a "medium-size" organ, which she prefers to large or small ones. Stuttering John announced in early January 1996 that his fiancée Suzanne was three months pregnant. Stern chastised the couple for having a child so soon. His record on the Big Beat/Atlanta label received a decent review in *Rolling Stone* (6-16-94)—"Best of all is the album's good-guy underdog spirit—S.J. comes off as one swell dude." *See Uzo.*

"Melrose" Larry Green   *See Green, "Melrose" Larry.*

Melrose Place   One of Stern's favorite television shows, this Fox nighttime soap opera has featured such female talent as Heather Locklear, Josie Bissett, Daphne Zuniga, and Linda Gray.

Meltzer, Bernard   A New York radio personality whom Stern's father, Ben, enjoyed listening to years ago but whose judgment Stern questioned. Bernie gave financial and quasi-legal advice, and would field any other questions on his call-in shows on WOR and WEVD radio. When Howard found out that Meltzer was financially strapped and in a veterans' hospital, he enjoyed doing a comedy riff about self-appointed financial advisers going broke. Meltzer also wears a toupee that appears to be a few decades old and a bit off center.

Mendola, Johnny   Stern's next-door neighbor in his childhood, who appeared on Stern's "Is This a Life?" skit in early 1991. Mendola now works for Pudgie's Famous Chicken, his father-in-law's business.

Mercer, Rosko   The black deejay who was fired at Infinity Broadcasting's WKTU, now WXRK, Stern's flagship station. He was a guest on Stern's show back when he was still at WNBC.

Mercury Montego   Ben Stern's car when Howard was a senior in high school.

Mercy Hospital   The hospital where Ray Stern worked as an inhalation therapist.

Metallica   One of Howard's favorite rock bands ("the best band in the world"), about whom Robin Quivers said, "Not one of my favorites."

Metheny, Kevin   *See Pig Virus.*

Mexico   Where Howard and Alison spent their honeymoon. They flew to Mexico City, spent a few days there, and then took a long bus ride to Taxco and Acapulco. He got sick twice and hated the experience.

Miami Blues   One of Stern's favorite movies, starring Alec Baldwin and Jennifer Jason Leigh. Baldwin plays a killer stalking a cop, and Leigh is a prostitute.

Michaels, Al   The sportscaster (and Howard Stern fan) who broke the news to ABC's Peter Jennings that the "I see O. J." phone call was "a totally farcical call." The ever-effusive Al will not be playing golf with O. J., or with Jennings, for that matter, in the near future.

Michaels, Lorne   Born Lorne Lipowitz in Toronto, Canada, Michaels is the founding producer of *Saturday Night Live*, a show that Stern criticizes on a regular basis.

Micro Matt   The in-studio guest and Stanford University alumnus who said that his organ is a little larger than a thumb. When Stern and crew saw his unit, Howard said, "He's about as big as I am." Robin Quivers said that it was the smallest she ever saw on a grown-up. When he became aroused, Robin said, "He's fine . . . he can get the job done."

Microphallus   Stern's self-declared disease: a small penis ("acorn" or "turtle's head"). *Also see Penis and Shorter Wand.*

Mike the Marshmallow Guy   The Boston postal worker who declared, "I'm in love with Elaina Beastie," who appeared on Stern's *Butt Bongo Fiesta* videotape in the "Pick Your Vagina" segment and several other major Stern events. Mike was willing to eat a marshmallow from Jackie Martling's buttocks in order to win a date with Elaina. Howard described Mike as having "bad facial hair . . . zits . . . not a bad-looking guy if you lost a hundred pounds." Mike admitted that he weighted about "three bills" (three hundred pounds). He makes $13.50 an hour as a "transitional" employee at the post office. With dispatch, he ate the marshmallow ("I'm a postal worker, I can deal with it") and won his date.

"The Mike Walker Game"   The *National Enquirer* editor who began a game on the Stern show in which he reads four headlines, three of which are real headlines from the next issue of the *Enquirer* and one of which is a phony. The object is to guess the phony one. In the first game, the four stories were: (1) the word *dole* means "penis" in Iranian; (2) Rush Limbaugh flunked speech in college; (3) Candice Bergen is dating actor Tony Geary; and (4) Joan Collins commandeered Ellen De Generis's limousine at a Hollywood event. (Howard, Robin, and Jackie guessed no. 1—no. 3 was the phony story. Fred guessed right the first two times they played the game.)

Miller, Denise   The uniquely talented woman known as "The Kielbasa Queen" who was featured on Stern's WWOR-TV show. She can "deep-throat" and swallow a twelve-inch-long kielbasa or five hot dogs in a row. (Howard noted, "Honey, you must have been great at barbecues.") On a subsequent radio broadcast, movie actor Sylvester Stallone, a call-in guest, told Howard that he enjoyed the Kielbasa Queen broadcast so much that he tried to stuff "a thermos" down his girlfriend Jennifer Flavin's throat.

Miller, Dennis   A *Saturday Night Live* comedian and former talk-show host about whom Stern has mixed feelings. According to Stern, Miller can be "a great stand-up comedian," and others times is an "ar-

143

rogant asshole." In one interview, Howard probed Miller too deeply about Miller's former wife, which irritated him. Miller finds Stern's humor "unfiltered," a word he has used several times. Of course, ad-libbing is "unfiltered" by definition. Stern's other complaint about Miller is, "He has no sense of humor about himself." Miller's brother Jimmy is comedic actor Jim Carrey's manager.

Miller, Reggie   The six-foot-seven-inch-tall Indiana Pacers basket-ball star who plugged his book *I Love Being the Enemy* on Stern's show. When Stern found out that director/Knicknut/nudnick Spike Lee wrote the foreword to the book, he talked about how he hated Lee and his movies. Miller said that he lost his virginity at age eighteen, and that he had sex with an Oriental woman when he was in college.

Mills, Joshua   The *New York Times* reporter who wrote in an article (10-3-93) entitled "He Keeps Giving New Meaning to Gross Revenue" that Howard is "vibrant proof that sleaze has more commercial poten-tial in the expanding multimedia world than the philosophies of Patri-cia Ireland or Mother Teresa." Conjecturing about Stern's radio, Mills commented, "Even if Mr. Stern is paid $3 million, that's only $57,692 a week."

"Mine Shaft"   An answer on a "Sternac" routine. The correct ques-tion was "What does Arnold Schwarzenegger call his penis (as in *mein shaft*)?"

Mink, Eric   The *New York Daily News* writer who linked Stern's name with O. J. Simpson's name, which upset Stern so much that he phoned him on the air. Mink's original point, which was misstated by other media, was that pay-per-view producers had turned down an O. J. Simp-son production because it would be in bad taste, yet they have no prob-lem airing Stern's *New Years Eve* show, which was, in fact, in bad taste. Stern objected to the linkage, given what Stern thinks of Simpson.

Minnelli, Liza   The second-generation singer/entertainer about whom Stern often complains, especially because of her and mother Judy Gar-land's large gay following. Apparently Liza is a Stern fan, has handled Stuttering John's nutty questions, and thanked Stern on her album re-leased in mid-1996.

Miracle Whip   The brand name of a mayonnaise substitute that Stern's mother-in-law, Norma, uses—which drives Stern nuts. He says the product is "putrid."

Mirage   The Las Vegas hotel at which Her Royal Highness Robin Quivers stayed in a $900-a-night suite on her own money, after leaving a free room at the Riviera Hotel, which was arranged by the Stern station affiliate in Vegas.

Miss America   The title of Stern's second biographical book. On the cover he is featured "in drag." On the day of publication, November 7, 1995, it became the fastest-selling book in publishing history, a record previously held by the singer Madonna. It sold six printings in twelve hours. The Barnes & Noble store at Forty-eighth Street and Fifth Avenue in New York opened at 6:30 A.M. that morning, and about 250 people were on line to buy the book. Stern appeared in drag as Miss America on the David Letterman show on December 20, 1995. By the end of 1995, *Miss America* had sold 1,398,880 hardcover copies, making it the third best-seller of the year, according to *Publishers Weekly* (March 4, 1996), behind John Gray's *Men Are from Mars; Women Are from Venus* (2,196,935 copies) and General Colin Powell's *My American Journal* (1,538,469). The book was listed on the *New York Times* best-seller list for over four months, summarized as "anecdotes and fulminations from the radio talk show host." The *Random House Dictionary* defines *fulminations* as follows: "1. a violent denunciation or censure . . . 2. violent explosion . . ." It is from the Latin word *fulminatio,* meaning "a thundering, fuming."

Miss Howard Stern   *See Marx, Elaine.*

The Miss Howard Stern New Year's Eve Pageant   The New Year's Eve 1993 pay-per-view special that became the highest-grossing nonsports event ever. The program aired in 348,000 households (other sources say 400,000 households) and grossed $16 million, according to *Broadcasting & Cable* magazine.

Mistress Crimson   The dominatrix who got Howard to pull down his pants so that she could feel his Fartman-like buttocks. She told the audience, "He doesn't have much of a butt!"

Mitch   Another Stern intern, who replaced Dead Dave and preceded Stuttering John. Mitch's claim to fame was that he asked producer Norman Lear if he thought Fox Television, which fired Joan Rivers, was responsible for the suicide of Rivers's husband, Edgar Rosenberg.

Moir, Ed   The ad sales manager at K-Rock, a drinker and smoker, about whom Stern remarked, "He drinks until he sees Jesus." (On Ash Wednesday he arrives at the office with ash marks on his forehead.)

Monastery   Stern is no monk, but he admitted that he rented a little room ("a little, tiny closet") at a monastery for a month early in his career. He said that "there was no radio or TV allowed, and that was fun . . . it was quiet."

The Monelles   The "doo-wop" a cappella group that sang the national anthem to new lyrics in response to Sinéad O'Connor's anti-American sentiments. Their lyrics included such gems as "Frank Sinatra was right, we should kick you in your fat ass!" Stern suggested that the group be named the Sternelles and then referred to them as the "Moron Tabernacle Choir."

Money   Howard asks every male guest (and many women) how much money they are worth, but he conspicuously never gives any hint how much money *he* makes. He dropped out of the New York gubernatorial race in 1994 because he refused to disclose his financial situation. He told *New York Magazine* writer Maer Roshan, "Money is the great divide in our country. I realize it makes people uptight, so I just avoid it." But sex, race, and religion, for example, Stern's favorite topics, do not make people uptight? Do the math! A sixty-second commercial on the New York station alone costs about $2,000. His four-and-a-half-hour show grosses rock bottom $40 million in advertising revenue a year, of which Stern gets over $5 million a year or $100,000 a week, not a bad wage for about 220 days' work. Add a book ($4 million) or video a year, a cable television show, and you have close to what David Letterman earns a year ($14 million). In fact, Stern biographer Paul Colford estimated that Stern made $12.5 million in 1995.

Monkey Bar   The location of one Stern broadcast in Los Angeles in late 1995, it is owned by actor Jack Nicholson.

Montand, Yves   *See France.*

Moore, Demi   The highly paid movie actress about whom Stern said, "She's as dumb as a wall." Stern says that his wife, Alison, has "as nice a face" but needs to work out more and run more. (Demi runs six miles a day, and Alison runs one mile and walks one mile, and Alison eats "chicken with skin on it!")

Moran, Erin   The child actress who played Joanie Cunningham on television's *Happy Days* series. She appeared on Stern's spoof "Queen for Today," in which contestants told "sob stories." She admitted to Stern that she lost her virginity at age fourteen, was the first girl Scott Baio had sex with (she said he was "Quick Draw McGraw"), and was raped at age twenty-three.

Morgan, Jaye P.   A guest and contestant on a Stern *Hollywood Squares* spoof, she admitted to Howard that "Johnny Carson was an average lover," and that Warren Beatty was a good lover (and is circumcised). She admitted, "I am a size queen . . . Length has more to do with it."

Moron   One of Stern's favorite words, an old Brooklyn staple (father Ben was from Flatbush), usually used to elevate oneself by demeaning others. Ben's classic berating of young Howard ("Don't be stupid, you moron!") has been played and replayed on the show with great regularity. In fact, a moron is someone with an I.Q. of 50 to 69 or the equivalent of any eight- to twelve-year-old. So when Ben Stern was calling ten-year-old Howard a moron he was not insulting him! Morons, by the way, are smarter than idiots (the lowest I.Q. range) and imbeciles (the next lowest).

Morris, Garrett   One of the eight original cast members of television's *Saturday Night Live*, Morris refused to trash Chevy Chase, which Stern wanted very much for him to do. He pronounced Chase's name "Shevy" instead of "Chevy." Morris was shot by "a young black man" in the South Central area of Los Angeles when he was entering his Mercedes. He was a regular on the Martin Short show for two years and subsequently appeared on *The Ellen Cleghorne Show*, which debuted on September 10, 1994. He can now be seen on TV on *The Jamie Foxx Show.*

Morrow, "Cousin Brucie"   The once popular Brooklyn-born deejay whom Stern likes to badmouth, especially because of his poorly fitted toupee. Yet Stern often imitates Brucie's signature voice trick (as in "ay oogah") for the E-Vincent luggage company. Morrow's real name is Meyerowitz.

Morton, Bob   Former producer of the David Letterman show, whom Stern occasionally called on air (and awakened!) to find out where he stood with Letterman. Morton was let go from the Letterman show in March 1996 because, according to Letterman, "I wanted to make a change to get what I want: to have someone who was going to pay the most possible attention to making this the best show it can be . . . Bob wanted to do other things with his time . . ."

Mr. T   Sgt. Bosco "B.A." Baracus on television's *The A-Team*, Mr. T. was a mystery guest on March 23, 1993, and is an occasional guest. He tends to aggressively verbalize, which challenges Howard's ability to keep quiet for a couple of seconds. The son of a minister, Mr. T. has seven brothers and four sisters.

MTV Music Awards   The awards show in 1992 at which Stern made his dramatic appearance as Fartman.

Muldowney, Suzanne   *See Underdog Lady.*

Müller, Lillian   A Norwegian beauty and Stern guest who has appeared in *Playboy* magazine twenty-nine times. Author of the book *Feel Great, Be Beautiful Over 40* (she's a couple of years over forty), she likes to get naked and eats ten times a day, usually fruits, nuts, avocados, and vegetables.

Mund, Ronald   Stern's chauffeur, usually referred to as "Ronnie the Limo Driver." He admitted that he once had an attack of diarrhea while driving, and had to throw his underpants in Central Park. Stern has said that Ronnie is so hairy that he has "Chia grass on his back." He likes to remind his audience that Ronnie has a bad case of hemorrhoids from "sitting all day" in a limousine.

Muni, Scott   The gravel-throated veteran disc jockey whom Stern periodically made fun of.

The Munsters   One of Stern's favorite television shows in his youth, it ran on CBS from 1964 to 1966, when Howard was ten to twelve years old, and has been in syndication since then. The cast included Fred Gwynne, Yvonne De Carol, Al Lewis, Butch Patrick, Beverly Owen, and Pat Priest. (A new version appeared in 1988–91 with a totally new cast.)

Murdoch, Rupert   The Australian owner of Fox broadcasting, another object of Stern tirades, although Howard had some nice things to say about him ("a real down-to-earth guy") in his book *Miss America*. Fox produced several Stern pilot shows but never aired them. They underestimated the appeal of Stern's oddball skits and the magnitude of his audience. Stern's book editor, Judith Regan, by the way, was hired by Murdoch to start her own imprint at Harper Collins. **See Chase, Chevy, and Salhany, Lucie.**

Murphy, Eddie   The comedic actor and former *Saturday Night Live* star who comes from Roosevelt, Long Island, where Stern once lived. (Murphy is seven years younger.) Stern hates the fact that Murphy now has a large "posse" of friends around him and feels that Eddie's lost his comedic touch.

My Bodyguard   One of Stern's favorite movies, about a boy who hires a huge classmate as a bodyguard to protect him from the school's bullies. Having gone to school in predominantly black Roosevelt, Long Island, Stern could easily relate to the story. The movie, directed by Tony Bill, starred Chris Makepeace, Adam Baldwin, Martin Mull, Ruth Gordon, Matt Dillon, John Houseman, Joan Cusack, and Craig Richard Nelson. Look closely and you'll also see Tim Kazurinsky and George Wendt.

Mysophobia   A major phobia (a pathological fear of germs) that Stern shares with realtor Donald Trump, singer Michael Jackson, and entertainer Tiny Tim. After shaking hands with real estate mogul Donald Trump (an occasional telephone guest), Stern apologized and said, "I forgot that you have a phobia about germs." Michael Jackson wears surgical masks to keep other people's germs away from him, and he wears surgical tape on his fingertips. When staying at a hotel, Stern admits that he wears shower thongs on his feet to avoid direct contact with the tub. To ingratiate himself with model Carole Alt, he bragged that he was "the cleanest guy in America." In the same interview he announced that people with AIDS should have to have tattoos on their genitals. Stern also claims to avoid certain husbandly acts on his wife because of the "germ" factor. **See Tiny Tim.**

The Mystery of Edwin Drood   In a game of Trivial Pursuit on the air with Gary Dell'Abate, Howard answered that Edgar Allan Poe wrote *Edwin Drood.* (Charles Dickens, in fact, wrote it.)

Nachman, Jerry   A media executive who was an early supporter of Stern back in his Washington, DC, period. At the time, Nachman was general manager of WRC-AM, a news/talk station in DC. Nachman has held senior positions at the *New York Post,* WCBS radio, WCBS-TV, and others. Nachman tried to get Stern to be their early-drive-time man at WRC but was unsuccessful because another deejay arrived on the scene.

NAMBLA   The North American Man/Boy Love Association, a homosexual group that promotes sexual activity between young boys and men. Part of their phone message, played on-air by Stern, spoken by a sleazy-sounding man, is "Be safe, be brave, and above all, be proud to be a boy lover."

"Name That Tuna"   A quiz show skit that Stern featured on his WWOR-TV show (7-18-92). Two of the three women in the skit were lesbians, and the "show" was hosted by Bob *"Fish*bank." In answer to Howard's question "What's your favorite position?" the three responses were "I like to be the suffocating one," "sixty-nine," and "I just lay there."

Nancy   The first girl Howard had sex with—no, not Nancy Sirianni but a girl whom he met at Camp Wel-Met. It took him three hours to get her naked and three seconds to do the deed.

Nassau Coliseum   The Long Island location of Stern's 1989 live "U.S. Open Sores" performance, which sold out within four hours of the ticket box office opening—sixteen thousand seats at $22.50 apiece. The appearance was later packaged and sold as a videotape for $29.95.

National Endowment for the Arts (NEA)   Critical of federal support of the arts, Stern commented one morning, "It ain't art unless you pay for it." Liberal democratic actor Alec Baldwin called in one morning after a Stern tirade against the NEA to defend government support of the arts.

National Enquirer   The weekly supermarket tabloid that provides news fodder for Robin Quivers and Stern one or two days a week. Stern said, "I like the *Enquirer* . . . They have cool stuff." **See "The Mike Walker Game."**

National Stuttering Project   When Stern hired Stuttering John and made fun of him, Ira Zimmerman of the NSP complained. Stern dismisses the complaint with, "We make fun of John because he's wacky. I'm sure there are plenty of stutterers who couldn't do what John does."

Natural Born Killers   Not one of Stern's favorite movies—he complained that it was "a piece of crap." He added, "God, did that suck! The only good thing in that was Rodney [Dangerfield]." The movie, directed by Oliver Stone and written by Quentin Tarantino, was full of violence, and starred Woody Harrelson, Juliette Lewis, and Robert Downey, Jr.

Nealon, Kevin   The *Saturday Night Live* comedic actor who read the news (the Chevy Chase/Dennis Miller/Norm McDonald slot). Howard likes to comment on his hair—is it a "weave job" or something else?

Negron, Chuck   The former lead singer of the rock group Three Dog Night, who told Stern that he had so much sex at one time in his career that he had to go to the hospital because his penis "exploded . . . in midact" while having sex with a Miss Oklahoma. He was eventually banned by the band for being "unreliable" because of his twenty-three-year addiction to heroin. He admitted, "I was arrested a lot . . . and they kept throwing me in jail for four or five days. He and his twin sister lived in an orphanage when they were eight and nine years old. He squandered an estimated $50 million but still earns a lot of money from royalties—Three Dog Night had twenty-one Top 40 hits when he was lead singer and sold ninety million albums. Some of their hits included "One Is the Loneliest Number" and "Jeremiah Was a Bullfrog (Joy to the World)."

Nelson, Willie   A rare but welcomed Stern guest, Willie admitted using "peyote once a year . . . for religious observance"; he loves bee pollen, and believes in reincarnation. He told Howard that he lost his virginity at *age six!* Willie says that he comes from a family whose history includes "bootleggers and moonshiners." He picked cotton and did janitorial work at his school. He also sold encyclopedias and Kirby vacuum cleaners. He referred to himself and his first wife as the "Battling Nelsons." She was thrown in jail for hitting him over the head with a whiskey bottle.

New Jack City   After Howard heard about the riot that Mario Van Peebles's movie caused, he complained (3-4-91) about the lack of black leadership, dismissing Jesse Jackson, and told his black listeners to "stop blaming the white man every two minutes."

New Line Cinema   A feature film production company (owned by Ted Turner) that Stern signed with to make his first movie, *The Adventures of Fartman*. He crowed about the deal for weeks on a daily basis, but the agreement eventually soured, supposedly because they didn't want to give Howard the merchandising rights.

New York Knicks–Houston Rockets Bet   During the 1994 National Basketball Association finals, Howard bet Gary Dell'Abate $500 that Houston would win and, furthermore, stipulated that the loser would have to behold the flatulence of the other at close proximity—namely, smell the fart of the other guy from a couple of inches away. Gary knows a lot about pro basketball, but Howard won. Fortunately for Gary, the normally gaseous Howard, fortified with gas-producing primers and some club soda, could not produce a fart within the agreed-upon minute, so that Gary's only humiliation was losing the money.

Newman, Lee   A man who called Stern from the Santa Clara County (California) jail and confessed that in a drug stupor he killed his girlfriend. He called the show two subsequent times and essentially convicted himself. Although the county prosecutor, Lane Liroff, said that he knew that tapes of the broadcasts would have helped convict Newman, he decided not to introduce them. Newman admitted guilt to first-degree murder and was sentenced to twenty-five years to life in prison. (Liroff, by the way, was impressed by Stern's method of interrogation!)

Newman, Paul   The movie star whose salad dressing and salsa Stern likes and eats on a daily basis, usually putting the latter on rice.

Newton North High School   Alison Stern's high school in the Boston suburbs, generally considered an excellent, academic high school.

Nichols, Kim   One of Howard's black classmates in elementary and junior high school in Roosevelt, New York. He called her "one of the most dedicated students and sweetest girls on the planet." A graduate of Emerson College, she became an ad salesman at NBC and other stations. When she was knifed to death in December 1990, Stern was genuinely disturbed by the sad news.

Nikki and Janine   The two bikinied women whom Stern brought on Jay Leno's *Tonight Show* (11-30-95). They kissed, but a "cameraman" stood in front of them so the viewers didn't actually see the kiss.

Nine Inch Nails   One of Howard's favorite rock bands.

Nixon, Pat   The wife of U.S. president Richard M. Nixon. The day after she died (6-22-93), Stern said that she "always looked as skinny as a Biafran."

"No Brainer"   A phrase that Howard started using (overusing) in early 1996.

Nolin, Gena Lee   The *Baywatch* actress who told Howard that she lost her virginity at age eighteen, and doesn't wear panties (she wears panty hose).

Noone, Peter   The lead singer of Herman's Hermits, who sung the song parody "Don't You Dare Have Lunch With Jeffrey Dahmer" to the music of their big hit "Mrs. Brown, You've Got a Lovely Daughter."

Noreen   A wacky guest who admitted that she corresponded with Charles ("Charlie") Manson and "Squeaky" Fromme in prison. She stopped writing to Manson when she realized that he wanted her to try to get a recording contract for him. Noreen had her first lesbian experience at age ten (she went "halfway") and has "orgied with a couple of girls." She admitted robbing a grocery store in her teens at gunpoint with her boyfriend just for kicks, was caught, handcuffed, and spent only three days in jail—she convinced the judge that she was not serious about committing the crime. She also loves getting spanked before sex, and her husband makes her wear lots of presex uniforms ("I have a closet full of outfits"). She confessed, "I got raped when I was seventeen at the air force base at Myrtle Beach." She quickly hired men to beat the perpetrator up. She wears a 34-A push-up brassiere.

Norris, Allison Furman   The wife of Stern producer Fred Norris, a.k.a. "Princess Norris," a waitress and aspiring actress whom he met on a "Dial-a-Date" routine. She began appearing as a nun in *Tony and Tina's Wedding*, an off-off Broadway play, in August 1995. The gig became the subject of several radio broadcasts because Allison has several kissing scenes in the play. When queried by Howard, Fred Norris admitted that the kissing aspect bothered him and that three weeks after her debut, they had hardly kissed or had sex once. Stern had Allison and Patrick Buckley, the actor she kisses, in the studio (8-30-95), and things got tense. Howard wanted Allison to do her scene with Buckley, and she didn't want to, nor did Fred want to witness the event. Allison gave in, to Fred's consternation. She did the kissing scene in two minutes and thirty-nine seconds, and it was pointed out that the previous actress did it in only seven seconds. When Stuttering John wanted to do the scene with her, Fred went bonkers. **See Norris, Fred.**

Norris, Chuck The action-movie *(Missing in Action)* and television star *(Walker, Texas Ranger)*, and regular guest on the Stern show. He is one of few celebrities to be wined and dined by Stern at his Long Island home. On Stern's various radio and television shows, Norris admitted that he grew up as a "low-esteem kid," his father was an alcoholic, and his brother was killed in Vietnam. When Stern asked him if he was worth $100 million, Norris replied, "No, but my ex-wife is!" His current girlfriend, Monica Hall, is a very attractive, young blonde who is younger than any of his three children.

Norris, Eric **See Norris, Fred.**

Norris, Fred Stern's first real sidekick (and "King of Mars") who plays a good rock guitar and is Stern's creative producer/writer. They hitched up together at WCCC in Hartford, Connecticut, in 1979. (Fred was the overnight deejay and going to Western Connecticut State University during the day.) Of Latvian descent (his real last name is Nukis, which Stern quickly points out rhymes with *mucus!*), Fred was brought up in the Lutheran church. He drinks ginger tea every morning and eats lots of nuts. He has been known to wear a watch on each hand. He owns a bichon frise dog named Rosie. He plays instant sound effects, writes rock-song spoofs, lines up commercials, and performs occasional bits such as "Kurt Waldheim, Jr." and "Mr. Blackswell." About Fred, Howard has said, "I love the guy . . . He is one of the nicest, sweetest human beings on the planet." However, Howard complains about Fred "pouching" his food when he eats. Fred can disappear from the studio and no one knows where he went. To get back at his wife, Allison, who has played a steamy kissing scene in the play *Tony and Tina's Wedding,* Fred played kissing scenes with two lesbians, Lisa and Jennifer. A few months later he did another love scene with a twenty-one-year-old Brooklyn girl named Krise (pronounced "Chrissie"). Howard, who has been next to Fred at the K-Rock bathroom urinals, maintains that Fred has a large, uncircumcised Latvian penis. (On "The Stern-lywed Game," Fred's wife said he was "seven inches," and he said "six and a half"!) Fred has also been called "Frightening Fred" and Fred "Earth Dog" Norris. More recently he has been known as Eric Fred Norris because, in his words, "I always hated the name Fred." (His mother wanted to name him Eric, but his father objected because it was the name of her previous boyfriend. Fred was the name of one of his grandfathers.) Fred says that he may get a nose job ("I don't like the tip").

Nosal, Bill   The program director at WCCC radio in Hartford, Connecticut, who hired Howard from his job in Briarcliff Manor, New York. According to Stern biographer Paul Colford, Nosal observed, "If I recall correctly, his show [a thirty-minute demo tape] was quite mediocre and I wasn't interested in him. But he kept bugging me so that I had him back for a second taping. He wore me down and we hired him." However, they developed a good working relationship.

Nose job   An operation that Stern threatens to get but is afraid that it will adversely affect his voice. **See McGovern, Maureen; Spelling, Tori; Sting; and others.**

"Not for Goyim Only"   One of Stern's bits in his WNBC days, starring Rabbi Murray Kahane and his wife, Bernice, of Temple B'Nai Vegas in Atlantic City. Among the Jewish-oriented topics they discussed was pornography ("Debbie Does Yeshiva" and "The Devil and Miss Cohen").

"Not tonight, Howard"   **See Head Colds.**

Nuclear Fish   The rock band whose song parodies ("You Will Soon Be Fired" and "Stupid, Stupid Dick") are occasionally played on the Stern show.

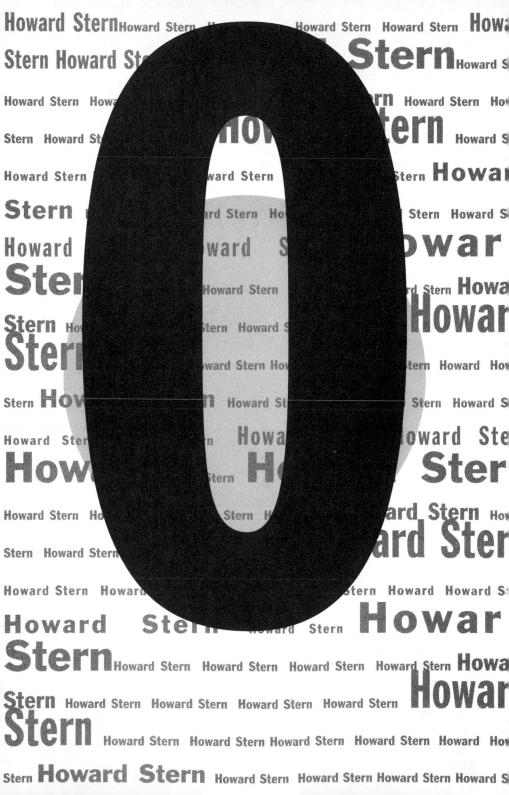

O'Brien, Conan   The former writer for David Letterman and now talk-show host. When he put his legs up on the Stern show green-room marble table, the marble broke in half. Stern badgered O'Brien by saying that he heard that his late-night show was soon going to be canceled. O'Brien is a Harvard graduate.

Obsessive-compulsive disorder   A psychological term for a mental problem Stern admits to having had. OCS is typified by ritualistic behavior.

O'Connor, Sinéad   The Irish singer whom Stern called a "skin-headed bitch."

The Odd Couple   A television series that Stern never liked. It starred Tony Randall (real name Leonard Rosenberg) and Jack Klugman. Stern remarked that Randall was "annoying" and "persnickety." He concluded that people who liked the show were "people who like going to the dentist."

O'Donnell, Rosie   A chubby comedienne high up on Stern's hate list. He says that she is "just a big fat pumpkin head who sucks." He also commented, "Her head is bigger than Rush Limbaugh's." Stern was depressed when he heard that Rosie signed a book deal in early 1996 for $3 million. *Saturday Night Live* actor Norm McDonald told Stern, "You know, Rosie O'Donnell would be good at giving really wide head." Her daytime talk show debuted to excellent reviews in mid-1996, much to Stern's dismay.

Oedipus, "Ed"   The program director (and ex–club deejay) at Stern's Boston affiliate WBCN. He says that Oedipus is his real name, "like Robin *Ophelia* Quivers."

Old Black Joe   A "dark-skinned" Stern guest who was married to a Bo Derek/Farrah Fawcett–type European woman who appeared nude in the German edition of *Playboy* magazine. (He split with the woman after ten years.) Ultimately Joe was trying to peddle a book that Howard thought was worth promoting.

"Old Black O. J."   *See Simpson, O. J.*

Old Westbury   The village on the north shore of Long Island, New York, in which Stern and his family have lived since 1988, a fact he conspicuously hides from his listeners. When he ran for governor of New York in 1994, he listed his voting address as a vacant house in

Plainview, Long Island, to avoid releasing his real address. First settled in 1658, Old Westbury has been home to such WASPy families as the Graces, Whitneys, Guests, and Phippses—pleasant polo-playing people. The average house is worth $1.1 million. (Stern bought his house for about $1.2 million and has probably done another $500,000 in renovations.) Old Westbury has one of the top median incomes per household ($162,600) in the United States. The town is about twenty miles from New York City, and its zip code is 11568.

Oliver, Denise   The new program director at WWDC ("DC-101") when Stern joined the station in Washington, DC. She was responsible for bringing Robin Quivers from a Baltimore radio station. Howard had major problems with her many format recommendations (e.g., remembering high school and street names, doing specific bits on a given day of the week).

Olsen, Susan   The actress who played Cindy Brady on television's *The Brady Bunch*. Stern's guest during the "Hooker Hollywood Squares" skit in July 1992, she confessed that she lost her virginity at age seventeen to someone involved with *The Brady Bunch*. Stern interviewed her several years later while broadcasting from Los Angeles.

104th Street and West End/Broadway   The area of New York City on the Upper West Side where Howard lived early in his career, when his wife Alison was attending nearby Columbia University in the mid-1970s. He complained that his neighbors were "lots of Puerto Ricans."

One Twelve, Inc.   One of Stern's corporations, the one that owns the copyright to his book *Private Parts*. The name is from his January 12th birthday. His book *Miss America*, by the way, is copyrighted in the name of Howard Stern.

Ono, Yoko   The widow of Beatle John Lennon and a longtime target of Stern's gibes. He suspects that she hooked Lennon because of his fame and money, and he also sees no talent in her artistic endeavors. He calls her a "home wrecker" and a "rich foreign groupie." **See Lennon, Julian; and Russell of New York.**

Ophelia   Robin Quivers's middle name. It is the name of a character in Shakespeare's *Hamlet*. Sources indicate that the name is either from the Greek word *Ophis* ("serpent") or *Ophelos* ("helpful").

Oral Sex On his May 9, 1994, radio broadcast, Stern announced that his wife performed oral sex on him that weekend and "swallowed." He made a similar announcement on October 17, 1996 ("I gave her everything . . . she loved it!"). Sidekick Quivers defensively claimed that she never did "that." When Stern announced that Ivan Reitman was producing his movie *Private Parts*, he said, "This is like getting my first oral sex!"

Osborne, Ozzy The British rock singer who once drank four bottles of Hennessy cognac and a case a beer in a day—and snorted heroin "from time to time." He calls his first wife "the Loch Ness monster," and his second wife shipped him off to rehab places to clean up his act. As he told Stern, "My wife put me in Betty Ford hoping that I would learn to drink like a gentleman." His roommate at the Ford clinic, by the way, was a mortician. Ozzy also told Howard that he takes Prozac and admitted, "I can't "bone" [get an erection] no more."

Ostrowski, James Stern's chief rival in his bid for the New York governorship as candidate of the Libertarian party in 1994. The Buffalo lawyer received only thirty-four votes versus Howard's 287.

"Out-of-the-Closet Stern" A gay bit that Stern does with Fred Norris featuring the character "Mr. Blackswell." When Howard did the bit on his television show (3-16-91), he looked like Ernie Kovacs's character Percy Dovetonsils in a zebra-skin outfit.

Oy Vay One of Howard's favorite expressions. According to Yiddish maven Leo Rosten *(The Joys of Yiddish)*, it means " 'Oh, pain,' but is used as an all-purpose ejaculation to express anything from trivial delight to abysmal woe"—more the latter than the former.

Paglia, Camille   The quick-talking feminist lesbian who wrote a favorable article about Stern in *The Advocate*, a gay newspaper. She wrote about the show as pure entertainment, not as political or sexist diatribe.

Palermo Supply   The supplier of the toilet partition used on Stern's WWOR-TV broadcast on March 21, 1992, the night of the "1992 Stern Swimsuit Issue."

Parades   Howard is against all parades in New York City because they cause traffic jams, litter the streets, and cost taxpayer dollars.

Parkinson, Dian   One of Howard's sexual attractions, Parkinson was a *The Price Is Right* model who accused emcee Bob Barker of sexual harassment (Barker denied the harassment charges.) Howard announced that he would like to eat a certain part of her anatomy, providing it is clean-shaven.

Parsons, Dale   The program director at WNBC radio when Howard was fired. He had replaced "Pig Virus" (Kevin Metheny). About Stern, Parsons commented, "People will think Howard is hilarious until he says something that affects them. Then they think he's not so funny anymore. *I* know it's all an act, but some people don't."

Passeser, Scott   One of Stern's Rockville Centre classmates who remembers Howard as having "a subtle sense of humor," according to Stern biographer Paul D. Colford.

Pataki, George   The Republican New York gubernatorial candidate whom Stern supported in the 1994 election. The Yale-educated Pataki was, among other things, in favor of the death penalty, against potholes, for nighttime construction on key highway construction work, etc.—a platform that Stern essentially won the Libertarian party nomination for. Impressed by the spunk and humor of Pataki's wife, Libby, Howard declared that she is "a real piece of ass" and is "a very sexy woman."

Patsy   The truck-driver guest who had his testicles removed because of cancer. When asked by Howard if he noticed any growth, he said, "I thought I was blessed. I had three nuts." When asked if he nevertheless could satisfy his wife, Patsy said, "I don't like fish."

Patty   A counselor at Camp Wel-Met with whom Howard claimed he had sex. Details are rarely furnished.

"Peace, Love, and Barbies"   Two months after K-Rock fired all their deejays in early 1996, Stern's daughters Emily and Debra submitted a demo tape, using the signature line "Peace, Love, and Barbies." Then program director André Gardner liked the demo and encouraged them ("You sounded real good"). Stern said proudly, "They play cocky, just like their old man."

Pearlman, Ron   The actor who played the Beast in television's *Beauty and the Beast*. Stern occasionally spoofs the actor's portrayal.

Peel, David   The street musician whose album *The Pope Smokes Dope* contains the song "Marijuana, Marijuana," which Stern occasionally plays on-air. He wrote Stern's New York gubernatorial campaign race song.

Penchina, Steve   The advertising copywriter who wrote the popular WNBC television commercial featuring both Don Imus and Howard Stern. Imus showed up at the production studio two hours late. The commercial featured the slogan "If we weren't so bad, we wouldn't be so good," with Imus reeling off the names of groups they both offend— the National Organization for Women, the Gay Men's Choir, Queen Elizabeth, etc.

Penis   A popular subject for Howard, who likes to dwell on anatomical parts. On the February 27, 1991, radio broadcast, he perused a magazine that mentioned the sizes of various celebrities. Among those reputed to be well endowed, Howard mentioned Christopher Reeve, Jim Nabors, David Letterman, Steve Martin, Eddie Murphy, Donald Sutherland, Groucho Marx, and Gary Cooper. And, of course, Howard regularly mentions Milton Berle and *F Troop*'s Forrest Tucker as having huge organs. About his own penis Howard has said at various times, "All I have is a turtle's head . . . It looks like an acorn . . . four inches erect." Stern regards his pioneer use of the word "penis" as a major accomplishment in radio. **See Vagina.**

Pentland, Bill   Roseanne's first husband and occasional Stern guest. (Stern once asked him if he got nosebleeds when he was on top of her!)

People   In reviewing Stern's book *Private Parts*, this magazine's reviewer wrote that "he has written a book that is even meaner, more tasteless and more demented than his incredibly offensive radio and TV shows, and a book that reveals him to be a human being with serious personal problems."

165

Perez, Rosie   The Puerto Rican actress who got Howard excited when she visited his trailer during the filming of *Private Parts* in mid-1996. He commented that she was "superattractive . . . her nipples and everything you could see through this little sweater she's wearing." He also noted that she had a "great ass"!

Perry, Luke   The very popular TV actor who was Fartman's copresenter at the MTV awards. He sarcastically told Howard that he had a "great ass." In a phone call to the radio show, Perry commented that he had an "average-size" penis.

Petrack, Bob   The Boston University student who played Jesus in Stern's award-winning student movie about transcendental meditation.

Phaye   The gay guest who said on the show that he has performed oral sex (with a condom, he assured Stern!) at a rendezvous off exit 49 on the Long Island Expressway. Phaye's brother Louis is straight.

Philbin, Regis   The television talk-show cohost who Stern says is "ten times more despicable" than his cohost, Kathie Lee Gifford. Stern launched into Philbin when he read in the *National Enquirer* that Philbin has a handicapped son, Danny, who is confined to a wheelchair and reportedly living on $300 a month disability. (Stern also read the statements in the *National Enquirer* of Philbin's attorney that Philbin supports Danny and has complied with and exceeded his contractual obligation regarding him.) Stern raised $5,000 for Danny during one broadcast, but Danny refused the money, suggesting that he give it to a charity—"other people need it more." Stern complained when the borough of the Bronx named a street after Philbin.

Philip Morris   One of the stocks that Stern has admitted on-air (after he dropped out of the New York gubernatorial race) that he owns. A highly successful company, it continually is barraged by negative publicity because it owns tobacco products such as Marlboro and Virginia Slims cigarettes. Howard hasn't smoked for years, but he strongly believes that tobacco should be legal (even though "everyone knows that it's not good for you"). Howard also has been critical of the CBS *60 Minutes* coverage of the tobacco industry, especially targeting founding producer Don Hewitt and correspondent Mike Wallace.

Phillips, Chynna   The attractive singer and daughter of singer-actress Michele Phillips and "Papa John" Phillips, and occasional Stern guest.

(She brought a green, filled-up water pistol in case Howard misbehaved!) Chynna commented that her mother gave her condoms at age fifteen (they were kept "under the sink") but confessed, "I didn't lose my virginity until a year later." She has a "treasure trail"—brown hair going from her belly button to her love zone ("I'm a very hairy woman"). Howard conjectured that she wore a C-cup bra, but she said "A, B . . . Are boobies that important?" About her beau, actor Billy Baldwin, she said, "I love every crevice of his body and he loves every crevice of mine." **See Baldwin, Billy.**

Phillips, Emo   Oddball comedian and former frequent guest who was a boyfriend of comedienne Judy Tenuta.

Phillips, Lou Diamond   The film *(La Bamba)* and stage *(The King and I)* actor and occasional guest whom Stern likes to kid because his first wife, Julie Cypher, left him for a relationship with singer Melissa Etheridge. Lou's second wife, Kelly, is a "knockout" from New Jersey and is in her early twenties. They had sex on the second date and now do it "three or four times a day." They honeymooned for two weeks in Bora Bora and Tahiti, and stayed naked from "sunrise to sunset." They signed no prenuptial agreement. He directed the movie *Sioux City*, in which he played an Indian raised by Jews. According to his biographies, Phillips is of Filipino, Hawaiian, Hispanic, Scottish-Irish, and Cherokee Indian descent.

"Phony phone callers"   Stern fans who call in to television and radio shows to put on the hosts. Captain Janks and The King of All Messengers are the usual culprits, and the favorite shows are Larry King's radio and television shows, CNN, and any network during a crisis when live phone-ins are accepted. Other "phony phone callers" include Ponce de la Phone, King of All Rednecks, King of Cable, King of All Messy Pants, Maury, and Stern's daughter Emily.

"The Picasso of Radio"   What Stern considers himself . . . a prolific artist, ahead of his time.

Piasek, Joe   A deejay at WRNW-FM, Briarcliff Manor, New York, originally from Chicago ("Joe from Chicago"), who encouraged Howard to get weird. Some observers suggest that Piasek's shtick gave Howard the conviction and confidence to aggressively pursue his own brand of offbeat humor.

"Pig Virus"   Stern's nickname for WNBC radio's program director Kevin Metheny, who was his archenemy. He described Howard to *Esquire* interviewer Rebecca Johnson as "basically a nice Jewish boy from Long Island," adding, "He's very clever about what his act is on and off the air. He's always reminded me of the rock 'n' roll star who, at the end of the day, takes off his leather pants, his whips, and chains, puts them in a $400 briefcase, gets in his Mercedes, and goes home to his beautiful suburban home on Long Island." In early 1984 Metheny left the station to become vice president of VH-1, the music video channel. Later reflecting about Stern, Metheny told a *New York* magazine reporter, "As time went by, his program worked in spite of everything we'd believed. We've come to recognize that some radio personalities can be compelling enough to break the rules."

Pig Vomit   Stern's band, often used for parodies of rock songs. They also backed up Sam Kinison when he sang "Wild Thing" on the *U.S. Open Sores* video.

"Pink Flute"   Howard's term for erect penis, usually used when talking to homosexuals.

Piscopo, Joe   The former *Saturday Night Live* comedic actor who is married to a beautiful young blonde named Kimberley Driscoll, who previously babysat Joe's son, Joey.

Plastic Surgery   Stern has been tempted to get a nose job, but he fears that it will hurt his voice. (Most deejays fall in love with their voices!) However, he would love wife Alison to get some breast implants. In a discussion about plastic surgery, Howard was quick to recommend Dr. Daniel Baker and Dr. Sherill Astin.

Plug   A slang term in the media business for free promotion of guests, products, services, and, in Stern's case, the nightclub and concert appearances of his staff and friends. It is surprising that there hasn't been more criticism of Stern's flagrant abuse of plugs, especially for his friends (e.g., Dee Snider, Leslie West) who don't even appear on the particular broadcast. Further, when Stern has his own book, videotape, or audiotape to sell, he spends an extraordinary amount of airtime plugging these wares and 800 numbers.

Plumbers Union   Howard's first band, established when he was ten years old.

Podell, Doug   The program manager at Stern's Cleveland radio station. When Howard found out that the station cut out some of his derogatory comments about a Cleveland Indians baseball player who died drunk in a boating accident, Podell had to explain on-air how outraged Cleveland listeners became when he first made similar comments. Podell is now working in Detroit.

"Polack girl"   Stern mentioned (10-2-90) a Polish-American girl who once tickled him where he had never been tickled before, and never since. His wife is apparently behind the curve, so to speak.

"Polacks"   Stern trashes most ethnic groups but has special hostility for the French, German, and Polish. During an interview with two German disk jockeys (after he asked them if he knew any Jews in Germany), he commented, "The Polacks got rid of all their Jews and they still complain about them." Stern seems to forget that it was Hitler who wanted to get rid of Jews, chose Poland as the major site of extermination, and was delighted to kill 2.5 million Polish Catholics in the process. Stern says that in his hometown of Roosevelt, Long Island, he was regularly beaten up by blacks and "Polacks." During the York, Pennsylvania, press conference he said, "If there are Polacks in York, there are no Jews." He has observed that "all the Polish kids love Coolio . . . They love to beat up blacks and listen to Coolio. Most Polish people think Coolio is Polish." In late 1996, he told his audience, "I'd rather be with the blacks than these Polacks!"

Poland Spring   A spring water company and regular sponsor of the Stern show. Stern had a conniption one morning when he complained that everyone at K-Rock was drinking up his cherished water and forbade everyone from drinking it anymore. Ralph Cirella and Jackie Martling were the major culprits named by Stern assistant Cathy Tobin, after which Jackie told her, "You've had your last back rub!" (Note: Poland Spring provides the water at no cost.)

Polygraph test   Howard inveigled Robin to take a lie detector test for find out if she really loved him. The findings: (1) she doesn't love him; (2) her father really molested her; (3) she did have a sex fantasy about Jackie Martling; (4) she might not be averse to fooling around with Malika Kinison, Sam Kinison's widow—which Robin, of course, thought was ridiculous.

Ponce de la Phone   An Hispanic Stern "phony phone caller" who plays convincing sound bites of Ben Stern, Jack Martling, and Robin Quivers.

He used sound bites of Howard's voice in a call to a cable show featuring singer Steve Rossi. "Howard" (Ponce) made fun of Rossi's toupee and said that he was "the worst guest ever." It was a good phony phone call, and Rossi seemed flattered that "Howard" would bother to call.

Popper, John   The heavyset lead singer of the Blues Traveler and big fan of the Stern show. Inspired by the program, he wrote the song "Fallible." Popper was offended when Stern once dismissed the group as "a bunch of old farts from the sixties." Popper and the group have subsequently appeared several times on the show, including Howard's forty-second birthday. He went to high school with Chris of the Spin Doctors. Chris said that Popper ran for vice president of the senior class and played the harmonica instead of giving a speech.

Popper, Mrs. N.   Stern's guidance counselor at Rockville Centre's South Side High School.

Poppiti, Ciro   The official of the National Italian-American Foundation who invited producer Gary Dell'Abate to attend their October 5, 1996, dinner as one of "The Brightest Italian Minds" in the United States. Other attendees included former president George Bush, Supreme Court Judge Antonio Scalia, U.S. Senator Alfonse D'Amato, and U.S. Senator Robert Dole.

Porizkova, Paulina   When the model's name was mentioned one morning, Howard called her a Polack but Robin Quivers noted that she is a Czech. Stern said, "A Czech is a Polack . . . anyone from those Slavic countries." Robin Quivers rides horses at the same West Eighty-ninth Street stable (Claremont Riding Academy) that Paulina rides at.

Porker, Bob   The "host" of Stern's spoof "The Hooker Price Is Right," obviously a play on Bob Barker's name and randy reputation.

Portnow, Richard   The movie actor who plays a convincing Ben Stern in *Private Parts*. "Shut up, sit down!" He most recently appeared in the television show *EZ Street*.

"Porto-Johnny"   The gay extra (and Stern listener) in the movie *Private Parts* who said on the show that he had sex with another guy in the Porto-San on the day the movie was being shot in Bryant Park, behind the New York Public Library in New York City.

Powell, Gen. Colin   The Desert Storm military leader whom Stern has little regard for because "the only time he opened his mouth," he advised President George Bush not to "take out" (i.e., kill) Saddam Hussein. Stern said that he "has no backbone" and is "just a big pussy." A week later he said about Powell, "He's not fit to be dog catcher." In 1995 Powell's autobiography outsold Stern's book *Miss America*. **See Miss America.**

The Presidents of the United States of America   The rock group that sang the spoof song "The Clump, the Clump" about Robin Quivers and her high colonics.

Presley, Elvis   Another guest that Stern visits "in heaven." Stern often ridicules the singer for his habituations and idiosyncrasies.

Previn, André   The pianist and conductor who told Stuttering John, "Get away from me . . . you and your jerky questions . . . you bloody fool." (John asked Previn, the adopted father of Soon Yi, "Why is everyone afraid to badmouth that cradle-robber Woody Allen?")

Prick   A previously no-no word on the airwaves that Stern started using on-air in March 1996. Around this time he gave Steve Grillo the nickname Prick, for reasons unknown. In his book *Miss America* Howard called himself "a self-centered, selfish prick who's impossible to live with."

"Prick Up Your Ears"   The title of the *Esquire* magazine article (May 1992) about Stern, written by Barbara Kruger.

Priests   Roman Catholic clergymen, who, according to Stern (4-27-92 and 10-31-95), are 99 percent gay or disturbed. (Author Truman Capote once made a similar claim and he knew!) He has said, "They're cripples . . . They couldn't make it in the outside world."

Private Parts   The title of Stern's 1993 autobiography, the fastest-selling book in Simon & Schuster history. It is believed that Stern received a $1 million advance for the book, a lot of money given that the publisher was not sure that his fans would buy a book version of his "act" or that he could deliver an acceptable manuscript. Any concerns, however, quickly evaporated. At twenty-three dollars, it sold over 1,200,000 copies in hardcover in a matter of weeks. It was a colossal success. Stern got people who hadn't bought a book in years to buy his hardback! Stern once claimed on the air he "never saw any money from the book," but his agent (after his commission) and accountant have seen a few checks totaling *at least* $3.5 million from the publisher to deposit into Stern's already large bank account.

Private Parts   Stern's movie, produced by Ivan Reitman *(Animal House)* and directed by Betty Thomas *(Hill Street Blues)*, to be released in early 1997. Howard predicted that his movie would gross at least $150 million. As with the rest of his projects, he tells his audience how great it is, whetting their appetites for months—in this case, almost a full year of on-air self-promotion. The early "buzz" is that the movie is good!

Proctologist   The doctor whom Stern visited on March 10, 1992. He announced to his audience the next day that he had his "anus checked yesterday."

"Proper Modulation"   One of Ben Stern's famous phrases, which he uttered when he was introducing young Howie Stern to the nuances of broadcasting in the recording studio that he co-owned. Ben announced, "We are now testing this out for proper modulation," and said that "the electric eye, which is a green type of tube, will open and close as we record."

Prodigy   The on-line computer service that enables Howard to become the Brad Pitt of the computer "chat" world. He was suspended for a week for abusing an Alcoholics Anonymous chat group.

"Psychedelic Bee"   A song that Stern wrote in the sixth grade, along with "Silver Nickels and Golden Dimes." Several rock groups, including Sugar Ray, have recently recorded their own arrangements of the two songs.

Public Enemy   The rap group ("Who put the Jew in jewelry?") from Stern's hometown, Roosevelt, Long Island, New York.

Puppet   One of Stern's many cyber concubines, also known as Puppetgirl, she said she looked like Teri Hatcher of *Lois and Clark*. When Puppet showed up at the studio, she looked like Ricki Lake, according to Stern.

Q Ratings   Howard may beat Imus in the Arbitron ratings but they are much closer in the Q ratings, which measure positive/negative imagery among the public. According to Marketing Evaluations, Inc. of Manhasset, Long Island, as of July 1996, both Stern and Imus have very low Positive Q ratings (7%) but Stern has a higher negative rating (69%) than Imus (53%). Rush Limbaugh, by the way, has a higher positive rating (11%) than both of them but has a negative rating (67%) closer to that of Stern.

Quaaludes   Stern has admitted that in college he usually took two quaaludes before he had sex. He certainly took some quaaludes before he had intercourse five times with one girl in an evening. He admitted on one broadcast, " 'Ludes were the only thing I could handle."

Quinn, Martha   The former MTV audio jockey who played opposite Howard in a spoof of the *From Here to Eternity* beach scene on the WWOR-TV show. When the "special effects" people tossed a bucket of water on them, the show's censor had to black out her crotch area, which apparently was overexposed. On-mike, Howard has always evinced a strong interest in Quinn for reasons not fully explained.

Quivers, Charles   The Baltimore steelworker who molested his daughter Robin, later to become Howard Stern's broadcast sidekick.

Quivers, Louise   The Baltimore housewife who often verbally and physically abused her daughter Robin.

Quivers, Robin   Robin Ophelia Quivers, Stern's black cohost and an ex-nurse who has an infectious laugh (grating to some, not unlike a "laugh track," according to a *Washington Post* reporter), reads the news in an engaging way, and is quick on her feet. She reacts to Stern's commentary, which helps keep him talking and throwing in humor. When she reads the news, they both make humorous, if not outrageous, comments. When she had a breast reduction operation in 1990, her bra size went from size 36-DD to a size 36-D. (On the March 28, 1990, broadcast she explained that they remove the nipples first, then make three incisions . . .) She studied nursing at the University of Maryland, class of 1974, and served in the U.S. Air Force, attaining the rank of captain. After she left the air force and graduated from the Broadcasting Institute of Maryland, she worked at radio stations in Carlisle and Harrisburg, Pennsylvania, and then went to Baltimore as a consumer reporter and newsreader at WFBR-AM. She joined Stern in 1981 as his newsreader at WWDC in Washington, DC. Fred Norris has been known to call Robin "Big Mouth." In addition to gaining weight, Robin has acquired an imperious attitude that some of her co-workers and interns find abrasive. Her father, Charles Quivers, a steelworker with "big ham hands," tried to sexually molest her. Robin lives like a queen in one of Trump's luxury midtown apartment houses and likes high colonics and horseback riding. She gets a massage every day of the week! She has dated Penn of Penn and Teller, Frank Gannon (formerly a writer for—get this—Richard M. Nixon and David Letterman), basketball pro Dennis Rodman, and O. J. Simpson prosecuting attorney Christopher Darden. Robin is five feet six inches tall, but her weight, no man knows. Her tattoo (on one of her breasts) is a Chinese symbol for "star," which one listener pointed out, and added the name Stern in German means "star." Howard's nickname for Robin is "Snatch." She has appeared on *The Fresh Prince of Bel Air* in November 1993 and *Deadly Web,* an NBC movie of the week (4-15-96) starring Ed Marinaro. When Fred Norris almost quit the show (4-23-96) because Howard and Robin were digging into his marital life more than he wanted, Robin reminded him that even she had to take a lot of grief for aspects of her personal life, prompting one female listener to call her "a malicious, vicious bitch." One listener called in to say that Robin is "a cackling bitch," adding, "All she knows is how to cackle and raise her nose into the air and do an eye-roll." Robin likes to leave her purse around, hence her purse has been snatched at least two times. She doesn't always buy Howard's comments about African-Americans but does her best to cope with his remarks. Robin hasn't had sex for several years but she now has a love in her life—her horse, Blaze! Like Woody and Soon-Yi, and JFK, Jr. and Carolyn Bessette-Kennedy, they can be seen frolicking together in Central Park several times a week!

Rachel the Spanker   A Stern "Wack Packer," she likes to spank Howard. She also sucked his toes during one broadcast. On the *U.S. Open Sores* video, she can be seen giving "Gina Man" a bronsky job. **See "Bronskied," To get.**

Racosi, Mike   A Stern's childhood classmate who called him "Stretch" because of Howard's height.

Radio   According to Howard, the "lowest rung" on the entertainment ladder. He told John Rivers on her television show, "There's circus clowns and then there's radio guys, and I think I'm above radio ham operators . . . so I'm just above the guy who sits in his kitchen tuning in Poland." He has also said, "Working on radio is lower than washing dishes."

Radio & Records   The trade magazine that in 1993 named Howard the most influential air personality in the two decades that the magazine had existed.

Radio Engineering Institute of Electronics   The organization that gave Howard a diploma on July 11, 1975.

Radio Flyer   A movie that Howard cried to, according to Robin Quivers, who saw the movie with him on a plane flight. The movie, released in 1992, was about child abuse—two brothers trying to cope with their mother's marriage to an abusive drunk. The actors included Lorraine Bracco, John Heard, Elijah Wood, Joseph Mazzello, Adam Baldwin, and Ben Johnson. The movie, by the way, is narrated by Tom Hanks.

Radio Shack   The electronic supply store that Stern launched into because he "always has to wait ten minutes to get help."

Radner, Gilda   The late *Saturday Night Live* comedienne whom Stern made cry when she appeared on his show.

Radzinski, Robin   The producer of Stern's E! show.

Raisins   Stern likes raisins in his yogurt, which he made clear on one broadcast (8-31-95). He also had six-foot-one-inch-tall Amy from Washington, DC, eat two Raisinettes from his navel (4-26-96).

Ramón   A black student about to start college, who showed up one morning to pitch for an intern job. He sounded in some ways like the character out of the play and movie *Six Degrees of Separation.* He said that he was about to start at Yale, that he had "1,360 SATs" (a 720 in math, and a 610 or 620 in verbal—the math doesn't agree!). Another improbable statement that Ramón made: He was going to major in "electrical engineering"—a highly unusual major at Yale.

Ramone, Joey One of Stern's favorite people, of The Ramones. After Joey quit drinking, Howard stopped having him as a guest because he became "dull." Comedic actress Roseanne once said that Stern was "uglier than Joey Ramone." Joey's real name is Jeffrey Hyman.

Raphael, Sally Jesse The television talk-show host (born Lowenthal) whom Stern calls "Satan" and a "psycho Bozo." He is very critical of her facial surgery and of her show, which strongly features the miseries of families and young people.

"Rat Show Nerd" An anagram of the name Howard Stern, mentioned by Dick Cavett on a broadcast. "Nerd Show Rat" if you prefer.

"Rat's ass" One of Howard's favorite terms, as in "I don't give a rat's ass!"

Rayburn, Gene The perennial quiz-show panelist who appeared on Stern's WWOR-TV spoof "Homeless Howiewood Squares." When Rayburn was asked to guess the word "blank-a-doodle-doo," he rightfully and mischievously answered, "Cock."

Reagan, Patti Davis U.S. president Ronald Reagan's rebellious daughter and periodic guest on the Stern radio show. She has posed nude for *Playboy* magazine. Howard says he would like to get her "messy"—his way of saying that he would like to have sex with her.

Reed, Rex A movie critic, about whom Stern commented, "I kinda dig him," after he told Stuttering John, "I think O. J. should be burned at the stake . . . the sooner the better."

Reese, Mason The former child actor, famous for his TV commercials, who is a rare Stern guest and was a judge for the "Spokesmodel of the Year Pageant" on November 16, 1991.

Regan, Judith Stern's book editor, a former *National Enquirer* reporter, and former producer of *Geraldo* and *Entertainment Tonight*. Regan is now working for Rupert Murdoch's News Corporation as head of Regan Books and her own multimedia group. Much to Stern's con*stern*ation, Regan has also been the editor of political commentator Rush Limbaugh—and of Howard's favorite hate object, Kathie Lee Gifford. Stern called Regan a "great editor" but a "cuckoo." Regan has called Stern "a slave driver . . . an extremely driven man . . . a maniac." (She has said Rush Limbaugh "is impeccable in his work, requires next to no editing." She added, "He is a gentleman, and I do mean gentle. He treated me like a queen.") Her formula for books is simple—find people who have daily talk shows and who can plug their books on an hourly and daily basis. Murdoch, by the way, is not one of Howard's favorite people because his Fox network never aired his pilot television shows. Regan says that "Ninety percent of the people [at her office] hate my guts." Regan is half-Sicilian and half-Irish, a feisty combination. She plays the viola and has been jailed and strip-searched in Utah for allegedly making an illegal left turn. What a gal!

Regina   A six-foot-tall buxom, black female guest who was accused of stalking actor Laurence Fishburne. She spent eighteen days at Rikers Island jail and had her breast implants done at Bellevue Hospital.

Reiser, Paul   When the stand-up comedian-turned-actor signed a $5 million book deal, Stern groused. (Stern probably received a similar advance for his book *Miss America*.)

Reitman, Ivan   The Czechoslovakian-born, Canadian Jewish movie producer and director who produced Stern's movie *Private Parts*. He produced *National Lampoon's Animal House* and directed *Meatballs, Stripes, Ghostbusters, Kindergarten Cop, Dave*, and *Junior*, among other movies. (Stern said that he didn't like *Junior* but lied to Ivan about it.) Ephraim Katz's *Film Encyclopedia* describes Reitman as having "a keen instinct for commercially viable, if not always tasteful, material," and pointed out that he was fined $300 and sentenced to a year's probation for his 1970 movie *Columbus of Sex*.

Renaissance Center   The hotel complex in downtown Detroit where Stern lived for three months when he became a deejay in Motown.

Renzulli, Kevin   The editor of the Howard Stern newsletter, which Stern conspicuously never publicized. On the February 24, 1992, show, Stern said that he was not going to let Renzulli "make money off my name." He reluctantly acknowledged Kevin at the beginning of his book *Private Parts*. On the August 10, 1993, radio broadcast, while discussing the progress of the book, Stern threatened to take him out of the acknowledgments section, for reasons unknown. (Howard is obsessively concerned about people making money off his "good name," yet he will routinely plug the marginal appearances of Baba Booey and the interns.) However, Renzulli is thanked in both of Stern's books, probably because his articles about the show through the years were helpful in producing essential material for the books.

Republican party   The political party that Stern votes for in most elections. (See Bush, D'Amato, Pataki, Whitman.) He is a fiscal conservative and a lapsed Eastern European–American Democrat.

Restaurant Two Two Two   A pleasant New York restaurant that Robin Quivers dined at but badmouthed several days later when a gossip column printed that she had a "low-calorie" meal there. (Some restaurants routinely send out items when celebs eat there. Robin should have been flattered that someone cared!) Located at 222 W. Seventy-ninth Street in New York City, it receives an excellent rating in the *Zagat Survey*.

Reynolds, Burt   One of Stern's favorite hate objects—first wife, actress Judy Carne, alleges that Reynolds beat her but he denies it. He wears a toupee that Howard has a problem with. Stern had a field day one morning when Robin mentioned that actress Loni Anderson announced that Burt was not a great lover. Reynolds told Jay Leno on *The Tonight Show* that Stern is "on a mission to get me."

Reynolds, Joey   The deejay who replaced Stern several months after he was fired by WNBC in September 1985.

Rhoads, B. Eric   The publisher of *Radio Ink*, a trade magazine, who wrote a pro-Stern editorial ("Are We Afraid of Howard Stern?") in late January 1996. In his "Publisher's Notes," Rhoads wrote that "Stern is a remarkable and skilled broadcaster and entertainer." He noted that the National Association of Broadcasters (NAB) featured Ben and Jerry as speakers at their big gathering (who "upset half the crowd with their political platform") and suggested having Stern (who has influenced radio) there instead. He conjectured that if Stern "spoke at a convention or received an award, it would be the industry's highest-attended event."

Rice cakes   One of Stern's favorite snacks.

Richards, Marty   The pugnacious former date of comedienne Joan Rivers who not only evicted Stuttering John from a ball at the Plaza Hotel, but actually slugged him. Lawyer Dominic Barbara called the Stern Show next day and told John to file assault charges and show the videotape to a court.

181

Rico and Jimmy   A homosexual couple who called in on Valentine's Day one morning to profess, at Stern's request, their love for each other. Rico, a Frenchman, met Jimmy, an American, at the Paris opera and have been living monogamously for nine years. Rico told Jimmy *"Je t'aime beaucoup"* on the air, and Jimmy returned the compliment.

Rieber, John   One of the three executive producers of Stern's E! show.

Rieger, George   The heavily tattooed postal worker and guest who is a Disney freak. His house is full of Disney memorabilia and he visits Disneyland several times a year. His daughter left home after he did her room in a Mickey Mouse motif.

Ringwald, Molly   The "Brat Pack" actress *(Sixteen Candles)* whose revealing smile bothers Howard because he thinks she shows too much gum. Not unlike the smile of his sister, Ellen.

Rivera, Geraldo   Talk-show host and an occasional guest, who participated in a boxing match against Sylvester Stallone's brother. Rivera, who has admitted to philandering with the likes of U.S. Senator Jacob Javits's wife, Margaret Trudeau, and singer Bette Midler. Stern loves to kid Geraldo about these odd liaisons. Rivera, in his previous incarnation as a lawyer, claimed to have won fifty cases in a row, the last being a defense of a man charged with rape. Rivera, whose first name is really Gerald (he is the son of a Jewish mother and Puerto Rican father), said about Howard on the Charles Grodin show, "He can be devilish, not in a benign way!"

Rivers, Joan   One of Stern's favorite guests. He makes fun of Rivers's late husband, Edgar, and says that "Joan has had so much plastic surgery, her eyebrows are on the side of her head." He also complained about Rivers's serving almost no food, except for "the most vile sandwiches," at one of her Christmas parties. Howard was expecting a Bar Mitzvah feast and is used to "fist food," not "finger food." She also does needlework, so her apartment, according to Howard, is full of little pillows. On Howard's show Joan has admitted that she had her nose "thinned," had an "eye job" when Melissa was born, and has confessed to Howard (5-4-92) that she had a face-lift in the late 1980s. Rivers (née Molinsky) first had sexual intercourse at age twenty-two and (as of December 1992) never had a breast job. And she's used to $1,000-a-day hairdressers coiffing her. When Howard asked her if she had a nose job, she finally commented, "There's nothing left on me that's in its original place." Stern joked that he wanted the late actress/writer Ruth Gordon to play Joan in his movie *Private Parts*. In mid-1996 she announced that she was engaged to Orin Lehman, an affluent businessman who walks with a limp due to a World War II injury.

Rivers, Melissa   The perky daughter of comedienne/jewelry hawker Joan Rivers, Melissa is a University of Pennsylvania graduate (as is actress Candice Bergen) and is on Howard's list of love objects. She's cute, according to Stern, and should inherit the "mother lode" when mother Joan dearly departs the planet.

Roast, The Howard Stern   The Friars Club–style roast of Howard, which was broadcast on WWOR-TV on January 11, 1992. Roasters included Sandra Bernhard, Pat Cooper, Richard Lewis, Maury Povich, Geraldo Rivera, Richard Simmons, Alison Stern, and the Stern crew.

Robbins, Mrs. B.   Howard's biology teacher at Rockville Centre's South Side High School.

RoboCop   A film that Stern declared to the star, Peter Weller, as "my favorite movie." Directed by Peter Verhoeven, the movie is about a cop in Detroit who is killed in the line of duty but is transformed into a cyborg and "perfect" cop, except that he still seeks revenge on his killers.

Rock, Monti, III   The hairdresser-turned-singer and television talk-show guest familiar to viewers in the late 1960s and early 1970s, especially on the Merv Griffin show. Monti said, "I was born gay . . . My mother wanted a girl, my father wanted a boy." His parents threw him out of the house at age fourteen. He played a deejay in the movie *Saturday Night Fever* and owns half a point in the movie. He now lives in Miami, still has a nightclub act, but also cuts hair for $100 a pop.

Rockville Centre   The Long Island town that the Stern family moved to when Howard was about to enter the tenth grade.

Rodman, Dennis   The Chicago Bulls basketball player whom Stern calls "rod man" because he boasted that he is well endowed. Rodman admitted that he had his penis pierced and had spent a week in jail for stealing watches when he was a janitor. Rodman didn't have sex until he was twenty-two, and previously did "Monique and Judy," slang for masturbation. He told Howard that he had sex with Madonna on their first date—"She did something to me and I did something to her." He and Robin Quivers went out to dinner one night (1-22-96). He was a perfect gentleman—he didn't have sex with her and he didn't head-butt her. He brought her long-stem roses. Rodman, by the way, admitted that he was once married for eighty days and is the father of one child.

Roker, Al   The jovial, avuncular NBC weatherman who is an occasional Stern guest. About Roker, Stern commented that he was "the kind of black guy you'd want to live next to you . . . He makes Sinbad [the laid-back rap singer] look like a missionary cooker [one who cooks missionaries in cartoon strips of yore]."

Ronnie the Limo Driver   See Mund, Ronald.

Ronstadt, Linda   The half-Mexican, half–German-American singer whom Stern calls "Piggy" because of her weight gain. Ronstadt appeared on *The Tonight Show* (3-27-95) with Robin Quivers, and the two of them quarreled when Ronstadt attacked Stern and his show, especially after his comments about Selena Quintanilla, the singer who had recently been murdered. When Leno asked Quivers if she felt she should defend women and blacks, she responded, "I'm supposed to, but I don't find it necessary." That statement incensed Ronstadt, who said, "As a woman and a Mexican-American, I feel he [Howard] is very offensive and extremely irresponsible."

Rooney, Andy   The CBS *60 Minutes* commentator about whom Stern often complains and parodies. He says that Rooney "looks like a woman—he looks like Liz Smith." He also has said, "Andy Rooney's a pussy." Stern does a very good imitation of Rooney and has done several ad-lib comedy riffs about him, notably one about Andy's not having solid bowel movements, and another one about the different types of bread sticks.

Roosevelt, Long Island, New York   The predominantly black town (with "three Polish kids") in Nassau County, New York, where the Stern family lived in a $14,000 house before they moved farther east on Long Island to Rockville Centre. Originally named Greenwich Point, the town was renamed in honor of Theodore Roosevelt. **See Murphy, Eddie, and Public Enemy.**

Roosevelt Junior-Senior High School   The high school that Stern attended in 1968–69. If you check Stern's Roosevelt yearbook, you'll see that about 33 percent of his classmates were white. Stern said he had a 98 grade average at this school.

Rose Lane   The street on which the Stern family lived when they moved to Rockville Centre, Long Island. Although many of the people in town were Roman Catholics, many of the Sterns' neighbors on Rose Lane were Jewish.

Roseanne   The chunky comedienne and television star whom Stern has called both "talented" and "a fat slob." Regarding Stern, she said that he was "a racist, sexist, homophobic fucking pig" and added that "his fans are plumbers masturbating in their trucks on the way to work." She said that Howard was "an ugly son of a bitch . . . uglier than Joey Ramone." Their icy relationship thawed and she appeared on his radio show in 1994, during which she confessed that she was a prostitute earlier in her life and charged "the going rate . . . about forty bucks." Robin Quivers does a decent imitation of a kvetchy Rosanne. *See Tag Heuer; Ramone, Joey.*

Rosenberg, Al   A former co-worker, ex–municipal bond salesman, and writer at WNBC radio, one of few NBC people Stern speaks well of. He later cohosted a morning radio show on WNEW-AM with the late veteran announcer Bob Fitzsimmons.

Rosenberg, Howard   The *Los Angeles Times* TV critic, a Pulitzer prizewinner who wrote that Stern's WWOR-TV show was "at once incredibly funny and incredibly vile." The critic especially liked *The Howard Stern Interview Show* on the E! cable network, asserting that "there may not be a better half hour on television."

Rosenstein, Dr. Melvin   The urologist who did penis enlargements and worked on rehabbing John Wayne Bobbitt's reattached organ. *See Bobbitt, John Wayne.*

Roshan, Maer   The *New York* magazine writer who wrote a relatively neutral cover article (actually, an interview) about Stern in the November 20, 1995, issue in conjunction with the publication of his book *Miss America.*

Rossi, Steve   The singer in the Allen and Rossi team, which often appeared on television's *The Ed Sullivan Show* in the 1960s. Rossi was a regular Stern guest for a while. He usually called in to plug an upcoming Las Vegas or Atlantic City appearance.

Roth, David Lee   A regular and fun Stern guest, formerly of the Van Halen rock group, who said, "My mind's like a steel trap. Nothing gets in!"

Rubberbaby   Stern's "cyber-sex" girlfriend Karen, whom he picked up on Prodigy. She claimed to be a Janine Turner *(Northern Exposure)* look-alike, with a 34-C bra size. When she showed up at the studio one morning (on crutches with a broken ankle), Howard was quite underwhelmed. Despite the cyber-fact that she "gave him oral sex in a parking lot" and performed other cyber-illicit acts on him, he said that in person she looked like "a housewife!"

Ruesch, Robert   One of Howard's English teachers at South Side Senior High School in Rockville Centre, Long Island, who told Stern biographer Paul Colford that "Howard basically slept through my class."

Russell of New York   When Yoko Ono was interviewed on a K-Rock show, Stern called in as "Russell of New York" and told her how much he appreciated her as an artist, asked her about her success as an investor, and asked if she would marry again ("That is not in my thoughts").

Russo, René   The model-turned-actress *(Outbreak* and *In the Line of Fire)* whom Stuttering John asked if she douched before filming love scenes. That question would have chased away 99 percent of the female population, but the poised actress handled it and said, "I don't douche."

Russo, Sean   The twenty-four-year-old listener who died of an aneurysm. His mother called Stern to say that her son was a big fan: "He loved you very much." The woman and her daughter cried, but Boy Gary and some listeners felt that it was a "phony phone call."

Ryan, Meg   The movie actress who ranked the same as Howard on *Entertainment Weekly*'s list of the most powerful people in Hollywood in late 1995.

Ryder P.I.   The 1986 low-budget movie, a detective spoof, in which Howard played a wacky television newscaster named Ben Wah. He was paid $1,000 for his brief appearance. The producer and codirector was Karl Hosch. The movie starred Dave Hawthorne. Listen closely and you will hear Jackie Martling doing a voice-over. **See Wah, Ben.**

Rysher Entertainment   The TV and film production company that almost produced Stern's first movie.

Sabo, Walter   One of few media observers who have zeroed in on Stern's major talent and worth. The radio consultant calls Stern "a modern-day Arthur Godfrey." Stern gets little credit for "his great relationship with stations and advertisers."

Sabrina   Sister of Malika Souri, comedian Sam Kinison's girlfriend and eventual wife, and frequent guest on Stern's show. Unbeknownst to Malika, Sam was having sex with Sabrina.

Saint Clair, Jasmine   A former Wall Street "investment banker," Jasmine attended a private school (McBurney) and Columbia University in New York City and appeared on the Stern show just before her attempt to set the "world record" by having sex with 300 men in a movie shot on April 28, 1996, to break the record of 251 set by Annabelle Chong. Part French and Italian, Jasmine lost her virginity at age eighteen. Originally an A-cup, she had implants to take her to a D-cup. She claimed to have had sex with actor Corey Feldman and commented that he was "small . . . Minute is the word," adding the lament, "Usually when guys are that small, they make up for it."

St. Croix   The Caribbean island that Stern has called "St. Crime" because "a few years ago" some American tourists were killed on a golf course. In fact, that incident occurred over twenty years ago, but a caller, who lived on the island for five years, told Stern that the first time she drove to a restaurant on the island, she returned to her car in the parking lot and discovered that her tires had been stolen. Howard announced to all Caribbean natives: "Service is not an insult . . . just serve the man!"

St. Patrick's Day   The Irish–Roman Catholic holiday celebrated in New York every March—a special time when Stern has the urge to get Kelly green paint and adorn the breasts of select female studio visitors who usually have C-cup and larger bra sizes.

Salem, Scott   "Scott the Engineer," the heavy-smoking, huffing and puffing bald guy. His toupee was featured in one segment in which Howard controlled the front flap with a fishing rod as it "talked" to the "Garyionette" puppet. Stern complained when Scott the Engineer was selling candy at the K-Rock studios to help raise funds for his children's school. Dressed in a sailor's cap, a Hawaiian shirt, and huge "walrus" mustache, Salem played the deceased "zookeeper" John De Bella at his Philadelphia funeral in May 1990. Stern made Scott take a lung test ("he has the lungs of a mummy"), and the tests indicated that he had the lungs of an old man (79 years old in two tests and 105 years old in another one). On Stern's October 6, 1995, broadcast, he debuted the *Brown Fingers* video, which featured Scott as a huge cigarette, based on a spoof song that Fred Norris and Stern wrote. A listener said that Scott looked like Uncle Fester Frump (played by Jackie Coogan) in *The Addams Family* sitcom.

Sales, Soupy   A radio personality whom Stern idolized as a child but grew to hate as an adult when he worked with him at WNBC in 1985. Hints: Soupy had a limousine, and Stern and Norris had a "Fugazy fleet car." When Soupy left the leftovers of Beanstalk restaurant lunches strewn all over the studio every afternoon, Stern complained and pretended to cut some wires on Soupy's studio piano. On Stern's last broadcast at WNBC, he moaned and ranted on about a rumor that Soupy was given a nationally syndicated radio show. According to a caller who worked at a Sixth Avenue delicatessen, Soupy does not like mustard on his sandwiches and gets hysterical when mustard is used. Stern, by the way, does a very good imitation of Soupy.

Salhany, Lucie   The Fox TV executive who "green-lighted" (approved the production of) the Chevy Chase show, which lasted only five weeks. Had she hired Stern, she would be known today as the "Judith Regan of Broadcasting"!

Salk, Dr. Jonas   For reasons not elaborated upon, in *George* magazine Stern called the codiscoverer of polio vaccine "the biggest prick around."

"Sal the Stockbroker"   The Stern show fan who calls Gary Dell'Abate a "horse tooth jackass."

Sam   The man who attended a *Private Parts* book signing in Washington, DC, and had Howard autograph his arm. Sam proceeded to get the autograph permanently tattooed into his arm. Stern was favorably impressed by the tattoo but remarked that "Holocaust tattoos were more attractive."

Samatier, Dr. Ricardo   The cosmetic surgeon who injects fat into men's penises to make them larger. He was featured on Stern's television show (2-8-92). As a visual aid, Howard showed a regular hot dog and a larger sausage.

Sambora, Richie   *See Bon Jovi.*

Sanches, Stacy   The *Playboy* Miss March 1995 and 1996 Playmate of the Year, for which she received $100,000 and a Jeep Wrangler. A former Hooters waitress, she is five feet ten inches tall, thirty-four-twenty-four-thirty-six, has green eyes, and is part Spanish, Irish, and Native American. Having started shooting his movie *Private Parts*, Howard was full of vim and vigor and joked to her off the bat, "Do you wanna ball?"—show-biz lingo for "Do me or you won't be in my movie!" Later in the interview, he told her he had a role ("Ms. Fellatio") for her.

Sarah Louise   The transsexual (real name Jeffrey Dwight Luiz) who appeared on Stern's mid-1990s "The Slice Is Right" bit. He/she has appeared eleven times on Sally Jesse Raphael's show.

Sarandon, Susan   Stern said he used to confuse film actress Sarandon with June Lockhart and said, "For years I thought she [Sarandon] was Lassie's mom."

Saresky, Ethan David   The fourteen-year old comedian with braces and baggy pants who competed with intern "Smelly James" for stand-up ability and won hands down. Howard praised the ninth grade student, son of a lawyer, for his "gumption and moxie."

Sarno, Dr. John   The doctor who cured Howard's back problems. In *Private Parts,* before Stern thanks his parents and his wife, he thanks Dr. Sarno "for ridding me of back pain and obsessive-compulsive disorder." His practice is located at the Rusk Institute of Rehabilitation Medicine, 400 E. Thirty-fourth Street, New York, NY. His office phone number is (212) 263-6035.

SATs   The Scholastic Aptitude Test, the key pre-college test. Stern scored, by his account, 1,200 on the test, quite decent for a six-foot-five-inch guy from Roosevelt, Long Island, but second-tier for a Rockville Centre South Side Senior High School student.

Savannah   One of Stern's favorite porno stars, who is no longer with us.

Schick, Jeff   Stern's computer adviser at IBM. Stern said on-air, "Two things I love—my satellite [dish] and Jeff Schick at IBM." **See *IBM.***

Schiffman, Sol and Esther   Howard's maternal grandparents, both Austro-Hungarian Jewish immigrants.

"Schfincter"   Another Stern Yiddishism for sphincter muscle, usually referring to the anal muscle.

Schifoso   Stern claims to be "half Italian," but this is one of few Italian words that he ever uses, a word that he learned from comedian Pat Cooper. It means "a loathsome person."

"Schmega-dildos"   Stern's version of Rush Limbaugh's listeners' "mega-dittos," acknowledging admiration of and agreement with the host on the part of the caller.

Schmidt, Clark   A radio consultant who predicted that Stern's presence in the Boston market would fragment the market, as opposed to dominate the market. Schmidt was working at WCOZ in Boston when Stern applied for a job there after college.

"Schnot"   Stern tends to "Yiddify" any word that begins with *sn* or *sph* by adding a *ch*. Thus he pronounces "snot" as "schnot."

Schreiber, Fred   Also known as "Fred the Elephant Boy"—a Stern "Wack Packer" with an obvious speech impediment. He occasionally plugs professional wrestling matches and goes out on blind dates with female callers. Stern said that deaf actress Marlee Maitlin was Fred's speech coach. When Howard asked one of Fred's girlfriend's if he was well endowed, she said, "He's got a trunk down there." At the Libertarian party convention in Albany, it was Fred who nominated Stern as the party's candidate for governor.

Schreier, Fred   One of the owners of WRNW radio in Briarcliff Manor, New York, where Stern worked. Schreier commented that Howard was "very pleasant and always very cooperative."

Schulz, Robert L.   The Libertarian who replaced Howard on the ballot for governor of New York when he dropped out of the race.

Schwartz, Georgia Bedford   The former cheerleader for the New Jersey Generals football team, who plugged Bioline, a weight-loss product, on Stern's show. When asked if she was married, she bragged, "I hit the jackpot—[I married] a Jewish lawyer!"

Schwartz, Steve   The line producer of Stern's ill-fated Fox TV venture. He thought that the five shows already taped were "pretty good" and "very funny."

Schwarz, F.A.O.   The children's toy store at 767 Fifth Avenue in New York City, which is opposite the K-Rock studios at Madison Avenue and Fifty-eighth Street. (Scenes in Tom Hanks's movie *Big* were shot in the store, the memorable one being the dance number on the oversize piano keyboard.)

Schwarzenegger, Arnold   The bodybuilder-turned-movie-action-hero *(True Lies)* and a regular guest on the Stern show to plug his latest movie. Stern likes to kid him about marrying into the Kennedy family. Unlike the Kennedys, Arnold is a fervent Republican. He has a good sense of humor and handles Stern's embarrassing questions (e.g., whether he fools around with other women) quite well. He admitted to Howard that when he first met Maria Shriver, his future wife, he was awestruck not by the Kennedy family connection but by her attractive derriere. Stern kidded Arnold that the name Schwarzenegger meant "black penis" in German.

"Schween"   A term that Howard occasionally uses to describe his penis—it's a combination of the Yiddish word *schwantz* (penis) and the slang word *weenie*.

Scientology   According to Stern, Scientology is a "voodoo" religion founded by L. Ron Hubbard and practiced by John Travolta, Tom Cruise, Kirstie Alley of television's *Cheers,* and a few other Hollywood types.

Scores   The nude dancing club in New York where Stern and his crew party on special occasions. Busty, topless women writhe in front of the horny crew while they toss "funny money" twenty-dollar bills around as if they were confetti. The first Stern party spent $10,000; one of the most recent forays (10-27-95) cost $20,000. At Fred Norris's own bachelor party at Scores, he got "plastered," let Gay Rich sit on his limp lap, and then fell, injuring himself badly enough to be rushed to the emergency room at a nearby hospital. At another time, actor David Hasselhoff was seen there getting special lap-dance treatment from a statuesque, buxom, blond Pamela Anderson look-alike named Athena. A Scores dancer called from Albany and complained that Howard was almost as cheap as Jackie Martling. The address is 333 E. Sixtieth Street, New York, NY (adjacent to the Fifty-ninth Street Bridge). The phone numbers are (212) 431-3600 and (212) 421-3763. Though it's normally a quiet place, a bouncer and waiter were shot to death at Scores in mid-June 1996.

Scott the Engineer   *See Salem, Scott.*

"Scrapple in the Apple"   The three-round charity boxing match in May 1992 between television personality Geraldo Rivera and singer Frank Stallone, brother of actor Sylvester Stallone. The fight was introduced by Michael Buffer, refereed by Arthur Mercante, Sr., and announced by NBC sportscaster Len Berman. Stallone won by a unanimous decision. (Stern, Robin, Michael Spinks, and Tyrone Frazier predicted that Stallone would win. Fred, Jackie, Ralph, Gary, and Jessica Hahn thought that Geraldo would win.) The $10,000 raised was given to a charity for the mentally retarded, one of Rivera's pet charities.

Scumbag   One of several words (in addition to the other seven no-no's) that Stern was forbidden by contract to use on the air, but when his contract ran out in late 1995, he began using them. It is New York slang for a condom (new or used, usually the latter), and is most often used as a derogatory term to describe a disagreeable person. **See "The seven dirty words."**

Sebastian, John   The singer-songwriter who wrote the theme song to *Welcome Back Kotter*, "What a Day for a Daydream," and "Did You Ever Have to Make Up Your Mind?" He mentioned to Stern that he doesn't own the rights to his songs.

Seavey, Neal   The WNBC radio reporter who read the news during Stern's early broadcasts at the station.

The Second Coming   Stern's first choice for the title of his second book. The cover photograph was Howard as Jesus Christ, wearing a crown of thorns. His publisher vetoed the title and the cover. His alternate titles, not quite "upmarket," mentioned on his September 13, 1995, broadcast, were *Sloppy Seconds, SternFeld, Stern Language, Howard Stern's Number Two,* and *Howard Stern's Anus.* The final title selected was *Miss America.*

Sega   The popular computer game that Gary Dell'Abate had installed at Stern's house on the basis that they were going to be a sponsor. Stern bragged to his children that they were "the first kids on Long Island to play the game," but soon found out that the company wanted Stern to sign a contract with them—riling Howard, who, in turn, chewed out Gary.

Seinfeld, Jerry   The popular stand-up comedian and comedic television actor about whom Stern has had mixed feelings. Jerry was a regular guest (plugging his appearances at Governor's and other small venues) until his TV show really took off. Stern envied his lifestyle, namely his dating a different model every week. Seinfeld really drove Stern crazy when he began dating a large-breasted, seventeen-year-old New York prep school senior named Shoshanna Lonstein. Stern's spoof song (based on Janis Ian's "At Seventeen" and sung by her and Stern) about his relationship with the young preppie (". . . can't he get an older girl . . .") irritated Seinfeld enough for him to stop appearing on Stern's show, especially after Stern kept playing the parody every hour. Stern also complained that Seinfeld's book was a "rip-off to the reader" because it was "thrown together in a day," and contained a lot of his stand-up comedy material rather than revealing biographical details. Howard told Rick Marin of *Rolling Stone*, "Jerry has a sense of humor about everyone but himself. Jerry dating a seventeen-year old is very funny." When asked before an audience at Caesars Atlantic City what he thought of Stern, according to a reporter, Jerry said, "He's a funny [he later used the word *entertaining*] jerk and an amusing idiot!" Stern's response, "He's a dick. I always knew it." When Seinfeld visited the studio the next (and last?) time, Howard asked who else was an "entertaining jerk," to which Jerry responded, "The Three Stooges" and "Cheech and Chong." Stern chided him for launching a greeting card line and for being in American Express commercials instead of feature films. He has also called Seinfeld "a pompous ass," "too arrogant for me," and "full of himself." Jerry, by the way, sold stolen umbrellas and jewelry on New York City street corners after graduating college.

Selena   The popular Mexican-American singer (full name: Selena Quintanilla) whom Stern ridiculed after she was killed. Stern attracted a lot of criticism from the Hispanic community, and later apologized (*"Como ustedes saben, soy una persona satírico"*—"As you know, I am a satirist"), which he rarely does. **See Ronstadt, Linda.**

Sennett, Hank   Stern's first boss—at the Boston University closed-circuit radio station. Hank fired Stern while he was on the air. Sennett said that Howard stole records. (Howard admitted stealing only one record.) He also went down to the "Combat Zone," a strip-joint area, and interviewed Chesty Morgan, later airing the interview. Hank, a B.U. senior, also had his own radio show, which he opened with, "Hey, campers, I'm here."

September 12, 1949   The date of Howard's sister Ellen's birth.

September 27, 1985   The rainy, stormy Friday on which Stern was supposed to get fired but was not because the threat of Hurricane Gloria prevented two key executives, Randy Bongarten and Dale Parsons, from reaching NBC headquarters in New York (although Howard and his crew did show up!). It was the date of Howard's last broadcast on WNBC radio. He was officially fired on September 30, 1985, for "conceptual differences" between him and NBC radio management. By contract WNBC owed him about $800,000 for the last two years of his contract, according to Stern biographer, Paul Colford.

Sgt. Pecker   The title of one of Jackie "The Jokeman" Martling's more recent audiotapes—"seventy-eight minutes of filthy jokes."

Serrano, José E.   The New York congressman (sixteenth district) who called in to thank Howard for his act of heroism when he talked a man out of jumping off the George Washington Bridge. Congressman Serrano assured Stern that his act of valor would be entered in the *Congressional Record.*

Seth   The man from West Hartford, Connecticut, who drinks his own urine for "health reasons." Stern asked him if he was Jewish and he said yes. (From his WCCC days, Stern remembered that West Hartford has a large Jewish population.)

"The seven dirty words"   Stern has managed to get the words *prick, douche bag,* and *scumbag* on the airwaves, but thanks to the U.S. Supreme Court, he cannot use the words *shit, piss, fuck, cunt, cocksucker, motherfucker,* and *tit.*

"Shades of Blue"   Stern's nickname at camp. ("I always wore sunglasses to make my nose look smaller!")

Shafer, Ross   *See Hollywood Squares.*

Shandling, Gary   One of Stern's favorite comedians. Stern has said that *The Larry Sanders Show* on HBO is "the best show on television," flattering to Shandling but a slight to Jerry Seinfeld. Stern taped a segment of the show in mid-August 1993. In May 1992 Stern conjectured that Shandling, who had just appeared on *The Tonight Show,* "looks like he's dying his hair."

Shannon, Scott   One of Stern's least favorite deejays, on whom he wishes cancer.

Shark Bar   Producer Gary Dell'Abate's favorite bar—at 307 Amsterdam Avenue between Seventy-fourth and Seventy-fifth Streets—when he lived on the Upper West Side of New York. They also serve "soul food." Gary was quoted as saying, "It's a great place to hang out with cool music and a cool atmosphere." Their phone number is (212) 874-8500. A waiter called the show to say that Robin Quivers went there several times and was a poor tipper.

Shark Tank   Howard casually mentioned one morning that he went to shop for a shark tank in Greenwich, Connecticut—a curious statement, not elaborated upon at the time. (He quickly mentioned that he and his wife also shopped for a new Swedish bed with three layers of springs—another interesting statement, since Howard says on-air that he always calls Dial-A-Mattress for his bedding needs!) He subsequently installed the tank in his basement and apparently has at least one shark to keep him company—a real swell pet!

Sharpton, Rev. Al   The New York black activist whom Stern visited in a hospital after he was stabbed. Stern said that the wound was so long that Sharpton would have been circumcised if it were longer.

Shatner, William   The Canadian-born actor who played Captain James T. Kirk on the *Star Trek* television series, and has been an occasional guest on the Stern show. Howard likes to make fun of Shatner's recordings and his toupee. However, Stern enjoys talking to him and says, "He's a good dude, that Bill Shatner. I dig that man!" (And Howard hasn't complained about Shatner's toupee much lately!) During a broadcast in April 1996, Howard took Shatner into the coveted "Homo Room," reserved for special male guests of the Stern show.

Shea, Fran   One of the three executive producers of Stern's E! show. Her real claim to Stern fame is that she is the person who told Howard that his severe back pain was all "in his head."

Sheedy, Ally   The bulimic "Brat Pack" actress *(St. Elmo's Fire)* whom Stuttering John asked if she had puked lately.

Shepherd, Cybill   The movie and television actress about whom Stern said, "She's annoying. She thinks she can do everything."

Sheridan, Nicolette   The television actress *(Knots Landing)* who Stern conjectured was "icy" and "high maintenance" in a conversation with actor Scott Baio, who responded, "It's a very good observation!" (Baio dated Sheridan for a while.)

Sherman, Robert B.   The executive vice president of NBC radio stations who was instrumental in hiring Stern to work the afternoon drive-time shift at WNBC radio in New York. However, it should be noted that Sherman also was responsible for bringing Don Imus back to New York from Cleveland. Sherman did not want Robin Quivers and Fred Norris to be part of Stern's deal with WNBC radio.

Shields, Brooke   When Stern had Bob Hope on his television show, he commented to Bob, "I hear there's a family living in Brooke Shields's eyebrow."

Shoe Size   Howard wears a size fourteen shoe, the same size as film actor Billy Baldwin's shoe.

Shore, Pauly   The comedian who Stern thinks is unfunny but gets television and movie gigs because his mother (Mitzi) owns the Comedy Store in Los Angeles. Shore's original shtick was to pronounce one syllable as two (e.g., "Hey-ey!").

Shore, Sammy   A comedian who often opened for Elvis Presley in his Las Vegas appearances. Shore appeared on one of Stern's Fox TV shows that never aired.

"Shorter wand"   Another anagram of the name Howard Stern, perhaps a coincidental reference to the alleged size of his alleged penis.

Shower cap   Something Howard wears a couple of times a week when he doesn't shampoo his 1970s-looking hair. (He says that shampooing every day is not good for his hair!) What a sight to behold! A Long Island giraffe with size fourteen feet and wearing an Esther Williams skullcap! Oy!

Shredded wheat   One of Stern's favorite breakfast foods.

Silber, John   The former autocratic president of Boston University, Stern's alma mater. Silber has a severely withered right arm (which ends at the elbow) and tends to be a right-winger politically. Formerly a professor of philosophy at the University of Texas, he was strongly influenced by the writings of Immanuel Kant. About the influence of Kant, Silber said, "It changed my virtue from an impure act of contrition to a pure act of contrition." He built his ethical life on reason rather than religious guilt. President of Boston University since 1970, he has been the highest-paid university president ($564,000 a year versus $278,000 for the president of Harvard University). Silber ran for governor of Massachusetts as a conservative Democrat in 1990, and lost by a narrow margin to William F. Weld. His son David, an actor, died of AIDS in 1994 at the age of forty-one. When Stern made his radio debut in Boston, he said that Silber "whipped out the stump when he ran for governor . . . I hope John Silber's good arm falls off."

Silva, Lisa   Stuttering John's eleven-year-old niece who won a trivia quiz, playing against *Playboy* playmate Stacy Sanches and thirty-two-year-old intern Smelly James.

"Silver Nickels and Golden Dimes"   One of two songs that Stern wrote when he was twelve years old. *See "Psychedelic Bee."*

Simmons, Richard   The swishy fitness guru and former frequent guest on Stern's radio show, about whom Stern asked, "What kind of man collects Barbie dolls?" (He owns at least three hundred of them!) It was Simmons, an occasional dinner guest (e.g., on April 12, 1992) at the Stern household, who suggested the name Ashley for their third daughter. When Stern asked Simmons how many times he has seen female private parts, Simmons asked, "Do you count Barbie dolls?" About Stern, Simmons told *Esquire* interviewer Rebecca Johnson, "Howard is almost like Sybil—the Howard Stern you hear on the radio is not what he's really like." Simmons clarified his statement, "He's a very sensitive, brilliant, compassionate man, but . . . very calculated. Everything he does is planned out." Simmons invited Howard to see Barbra Streisand's movie *Prince of Tides,* which Howard had absolutely no desire to see. After the birth of Ashley, Simmons's limousine driver stopped by the WXRK studio to deliver a present for the newborn, but Stern refused to accept it.

Simmons, Sue   The attractive, light-skinned black WNBC-TV newscaster whom Stern likes to taunt. For example, he pointed out how many mistakes she makes in a given sixty seconds on-air. (Her strength is that she covers up the mistakes in a pleasant way!) However, when he appeared on her *Live at Five* show (7-12-90) to plug his new television show, he brought her flowers, kissed her—then darted his tongue on her lips—not quite the way to Sue's heart. (Comedic actor Bill Murray and Governor Mario Cuomo appeared on the same show.)

Simpson, O. J.   The former football star whom Stern met at the Trump wedding. Stern found him personable and engaging, and noted that he liked to talk about women. Simpson made a quick appearance on the radio show on April 29, 1993, when he was there to attend an Infinity Broadcasting board of directors meeting. Ironically, one of O. J.'s last comments during the brief interview was, "I plead the Fifth"! Stern devoted his entire October 3, 1995, broadcast, the morning of the jury verdict, to Simpson. He played the spoof song "Old Black O. J." ("Old Black O. J. had a white wife, lookee, lookee here . . . with a nip nip here and a nip nip there . . ."). Expecting riots in Los Angeles after a Simpson conviction, Stern said, "If we picked our own cotton, none of this would happen." The day before the Simpson verdict, Stern announced, "If O. J. is innocent, I'll shave my head and pubic region." He never shaved. When Stern was about to publish his second book, he wanted to include a doctored photo of Simpson teaching him how to slash a wife's throat (using wife Alison in the photo), but his editor, Judith Regan, nixed the photo on the grounds that it was "beyond tasteless." He did include a photo of him and O. J. at the Donald Trump–Marla Maples wedding on the back cover of the book.

Sinatra, Nancy   The singer and daughter of Frank Sinatra. Stern called her the "chairman of the broads." She posed nude in *Playboy* in 1994, which delighted Howard and prompted him to ask if she had any surgery. Nancy responded, "I did have a lift." Stern asked her, "Have you ever seen Sammy Davis, Jr., nude?"—which she hadn't. She told Stern that she would date broadcaster Larry King because "he's adorable and sexy." After the interview, she said about Stern, "I love that man . . . He's funny and adorable."

Sinbad   The comedian and occasional Stern guest. He is the son of a preacher.

Sing Sing   A prison in Ossining, New York, from which Stern received a letter from an inmate announcing that *Private Parts* was the best-selling book of all time at the prison.

Siobhan   Pronounced "shiv-VAHN"—the gay male, transsexual "wannabe" guest on the Stern show in the late 1980s and early 1990s who dressed in women's clothing and was always about to have a transsexual operation. He has "Archie" and "Veronica" tattooed on his left forearm.

Sir Mix a Lot   The black rap singer who told Howard that "all record companies are run by Jews . . . Goldstein and Frankenstein." He also told Stern that his nose was so large from telling lies and that "Jewish guys like to look like they're still in the sixties."

Sirianni, Nancy   The wife of Stern's "head writer," Jackie Martling, and a singer. She has a good voice, but according to Howard, should run her own career, and not meddle in Jackie's career. She looks somewhat like a dark-haired Susan Sarandon.

Siskel and Ebert   The television movie critics and occasional Stern guests who lamented that they were not mentioned in Stern's book *Private Parts*. Gene Siskel, the skinny, balding one, mentioned once that he bought the white suit that John Travolta wore in *Saturday Night Fever* for $2,000 and sold it for $145,000 at a Christie's auction. Siskel and Ebert were on the Jay Leno *Tonight Show* when Stern was accompanied by two bikini-clad lesbians (11-20-95). **See Ebert, Roger.**

"Six Degrees of Kevin Bacon"   A game in which a person names an actor and the contestants try to connect other actors and movies to the actor Kevin Bacon. The game was devised by three former college classmates, Mike Gianelli, Brian Turtle, and Craig Fass, who were guests on the Stern show in mid-1996.

Slash   The Guns N' Roses rock star who called the show from Hawaii and insisted on using the word *fuck,* one instance of which was not "bleeped." When Sam Kinison's girlfriend, Malika, called to say that Slash was drunk, Slash asked, "Is she drunk or am I drunk?" He said he has had sex with three women at a time.

"The Slice Is Right"   A mid-1996 Stern bit that he promised would be one of his best, but was one of his lamest. In this supposed spoof of *The Price Is Right*, three panelists were supposed to guess, based on the exposed genitalia of three "women," which one was a transsexual.

Sliders   A Fox television show, which mentioned that Howard Stern was leading a revolutionary movement.

Sloman, Larry "Ratso"   A Runyonesque editor at Regan Books (formerly at Simon & Schuster) who worked with Howard on his bestselling books *Private Parts* and *Miss America*. Ratso left in more *fucks* and *shits* than most editors would have tolerated, which is probably why Howard likes him. Sloman is a former executive editor of *National Lampoon* magazine, and has hobnobbed with the likes of Bob Dylan, Abbie Hoffman, Kinky Friedman, and a few of the New York Rangers hockey team.

Small penis syndrome   **See Microphallus.**

Smasher, Adam Born Asher Benrubi, a Greek-American disc jockey who took an afternoon job at DC-101 around the time that Stern decided to leave the radio station.

Smelly James The thirty-two-year-old K-Rock intern and Jersey City State student who thinks he is a stand-up comedian but is dangerously, pathetically, and naturally unfunny. One listener phoned in, "He sucks gerbil urine!" When Howard made a "phony phone call" to James as "Paul Drayton," a Los Angeles talent agent, he got James to say that Steve Grillo looks like an elf, and that he "allows himself to like some of" Jackie's humor. Howard told him that his assistant, "John Beshevis . . . the son of Isaac Beshevis Singer," would call back with the plane ticket and hotel arrangements. He thinks that he is "cutting edge" and looks like Chris Isaacs. He admitted taking a lot of LSD (three hundred "hits" in the summer of 1995!). He has been in and out of colleges since 1983. He has had "crabs" four times (and used gasoline to get rid of them), drinks everything in hotel minibars and then fills the bottles with water, and can fart on cue after drinking milk.

Smith, Amber The *Playboy* centerfold model who appears in a lesbian fantasy in the movie *Private Parts.*

Smith & Wesson .38 A revolver that Stern has a permit to carry. He also owns a .32-caliber gun. On the air he revealed a fairly specific knowledge of weapons and ammunition, although he did not admit to owning any.

Smith, Anna Nicole The lusty-lipped and superbusty *Playboy* centerfold girl who married a senile multimillionaire who "kicked the bucket" soon after she married him! In a discussion about sex, Anna Nicole told Stern, "I like it like a dog every now and then . . . I howl!"

Smith, Beaver A black basketball player with whom Howard attended Rockville Center South Side Senior High School.

Smith, Chris The New Jersey politician who incurred Stern's wrath by taking a strong antiabortion stand. Stern said that if Smith's two daughters were raped, he would change his mind about abortion. The *Trentonian* newspaper then reported Stern's pro-choice comments in an article by Kim Haber, further upsetting Stern enough to call her on the air and chew her out.

Smith, Howard K. The late journalist and broadcaster whom Stern correctly guessed, in an on-air Trivial Pursuit game with Gary Dell' Abate, was the moderator of the 1960 Kennedy-Nixon debates

Smith, Liz   The jovial newspaper and television gossip columnist whom Stern doesn't like. When Stuttering John ran into Liz one night, he asked her, "Why are you such a fat cow?" Liz, an old pro, was unruffled.

"Smoothie"   Stern's latest snack drink: Blend one cup of skim milk, one banana, a tablespoon of peanut butter (he likes Smucker's, which he mispronounces "Schmuckers"!), one half-cup of ice, and one-fourth cup of orange juice.

Smyth, Patty   The throaty singer ("Sometimes Love Just Ain't Enough") and regular guest of the Stern show. When she was a guest on his E! television show, she admitted that she hadn't had sex for a long time and that Howard was the first guy she'd kissed in two months. She thereafter became pregnant with former tennis pro John McEnroe's child.

Snapple   A former longtime Stern show soft-drink sponsor. When Stern found out that Snapple, which he helped in their launch period, signed up the "robotic" tennis player Ivan Lendl to be a national spokesman, he was rightfully enraged. At the Howard Stern television roast (1-19-95), the Snapple spokesmodel admitted that one of her breast implants had exploded, which probably didn't please Snapple executives. After Quaker Oats bought Snapple for $1.7 billion, they canceled Snapple advertising on the Stern show (and other radio shows such as the Rush Limbaugh show), and Stern put Snapple on his already long hate list.

Snegaroff, Gary   The coordinating producer of Stern's E! cable television show.

Snider, Dee   Stern's heavy-metal rock pal, originally from Baldwin, Long Island—formerly of Twisted Sister. Born Daniel Dee Snider, he is the son of a state police officer and oldest of six children. He attended the New York Institute of Technology. His wife's name is Suzette Guilot. The names of his previous bands included Quivering Thigh, Garbage, Peacock, Harlequin, and Heather. Snider has two tattoos: a horse's head on his right arm, and flowers and a heart on the left arm. Even when Snider is not a guest on his show, Stern plugs his nightclub appearances on a regular basis.

Snow, Phoebe   A regular Stern guest and singer (née Laub) who really can belt out a song, and usually shows up for his birthday parties.

Snyder, Tom   The late-night talk-show host on CBS whom Stern calls "a zero . . . an old man . . . a horrible interviewer . . . a no-talent jack-off."

Somers, Suzanne   The *Three's Company* actress who seems to drive up Howard's testosterone level. She told him that she hadn't wet her bed since 1975. To help her eliminate the habit, she used a machine made by the Night Dry Company—urine on the mattress would turn on a light and bell to awaken her. (When she married at age seventeen, she still wet her bed and sucked her thumb. Bruce Somers, her first husband, subsequently married and divorced Nora Hope, daughter of comedian Bob Hope.) Suzanne commented that her honeymoon night was not remarkable. In response to her plugging the Buttmaster ([800] 803-8855) buttocks shaper, Stern gratuitously offered, "I'll give you a hundred bucks if you let me tongue your butt." Somers admits that she has one fetish—she buys lots of expensive bed sheets.

Soto, Euler Bill   The Hispanic freelance designer from Yonkers who won the Robin Quivers song parody contest ("Robin, wake up! This is your daddy . . ."). He has been in a wheelchair for eight years since an auto accident on a rainy day. About Soto's intense look, Stern said, "He's scarier than De Niro." He won a Jet Ski, which he obviously couldn't use, so lawyer Dominic Barbara bought it for $3,800.

South Side Senior High School   Stern's high school in Rockville Centre, Long Island. He said that no one at South Side would ever talk to him, and he complained, "High school was prison!" Stern's grades were not as good at this school as they were in Roosevelt, New York. For example, he received a D in a business course. He graduated in 1972—he did not attend the graduation ceremony because he left for Camp Wel-Met to be a dishwasher. In a class of over three hundred students at South Side, there were just fourteen blacks.

Southmayd, Jeffrey   A lawyer whom Stern hired when he was renegotiating a contract with his Washington, DC, radio station when his contract was due to expire on July 31, 1982.

Spacey, Kevin   The Oscar-winning actor *(The Usual Suspects)* who admitted, "I wake up every morning to that [Stern] show."

Spade, David   The *Saturday Night Live* regular who, as a Stern guest, admitted that he and some high school friends got drunk and stole a car and drove out to the desert and got lost. He also said that after he made fun of Eddie Murphy on *SNL*, Murphy called him and complained, "I kept that show going for years. Don't attack my whole career instead of one movie." Of course, Murphy made fun of Bill Cosby, Stevie Wonder, Mr. Rogers, and others all the time.

Special Kay   According to her story, the fiftyish woman discovered that her husband was cheating on her, so she logically (?) vowed to perform oral sex on one hundred men each month for the rest of her life—we're talking a rare form of logic that ancient and wise Greeks never envisioned! For reasons not fully explained, the Staten Island resident prefers men who work on "the stock exchange" or "at NYNEX," all of which makes sense in her unusual way of thinking. She performed her special act 117 times in April 1996. Perhaps an indication of her pulchritude, or lack of it, when Stern offered Crackhead Bob, Marshmallow Mike, and Captain Janks a chance to be orally serviced by her on a humid June morning in New York, Janks bowed out, apparently on visual grounds. Even Janks, who sported a boil on the side of his neck that resembled, according to Robin Quivers, a second head, has some standards! A few days later, Special Kay announced that she'd consummated the act with Crackhead Bob in a hotel on Fifty-ninth Street. The act took two minutes and she admitted that she had performed oral sex on six other guys that day. What a gal!

Specter, Arlen   The U.S. Republican senator from Pennsylvania whom Stern supported during his brief 1996 presidential candidacy, mostly because of his pro-choice and pro-flat-tax stances. Specter dropped out of the race relatively early because he could not gather enough support outside his state.

Spector, Jack   The New York rock 'n' roll deejay who once had a sports call-in show that Howard often called as a "goof." Stern said that Spector knew almost nothing about sports.

Spelling, Tori   TV producer Aaron Spelling's daughter, whom Stern finds attractive. Tori is on the hit show *Beverly Hills 90210* (not so coincidentally, a Spelling production) and will inherit hundreds of millions of dollars when her father dies. When Stern quizzed her, she was unable to name the capital of New York. After seeing her on the Jay Leno show the night before, Howard told her that her jiggling breasts were "like two puppies fighting in her blouse." He also said, "You have such a tiny ass, how do you make doody?" Her nose job is the finest that money could buy but still needs a little more chiseling. After hearing Howard kiss Tori's *tuchis* one morning, a disgruntled listener told Howard that she was a "bug-eyed, homely-looking Jew on *90-Jew-10.*"

"Sperm," Howard A name that Stern was called as a teenager, to his dismay.

"Sphincter Awards" First held on Stern's television show in 1992 (5-23-92). Among the winners have been KKK promoter Daniel Carver ("Niggers are stockpiling guns . . . going to take over . . . Jews are destroying this country . . .") and Imelda Marcos.

Spin Doctors The popular rock group that recorded the song "Miss America," inspired by Stern and his book *Miss America.* Chris went to high school with John Popper of Blues Traveler.

Spotlight Cafe The short-lived television show that Jackie Martling hosted on WWOR-TV, after Howard Stern's show.

Springer, Jerry The television talk-show host, former politician—and occasional target of Stern's barbs. It was revealed and he admitted that he visited a brothel in nearby Newport, Kentucky, when he was a Cincinnati, Ohio, councilman. In his 1982 gubernatorial commercial, Springer admitted, "Some nine years ago, I spent time with a woman I shouldn't have. And I paid her with a check." **See Dare, Alexa.**

SPS Stands for small penis syndrome, an affliction that writer Marvin Kitman said that Stern has set up a foundation for.

Stacy Stern's cousin (a guy!), the party planner.

Stallone, Frank, Jr. The singer brother of actor Sylvester Stallone, Frank croons a decent tune and fought a decent three-round boxing match against Geraldo Rivera on Stern's May 16, 1992, television broadcast. Stallone was unanimously declared the winner. Rivera said that Stallone was "a very gracious winner." About Stallone's perfumed lotions, Geraldo quipped, "I didn't know whether to hit him or kiss him." **See "Scrapple in the Apple."**

Stallone, Jackie The mother of actor Sylvester Stallone, astrology nut, and occasional Stern guest. Having a foul tongue and given to hyperbole, she talked to her ex-husband (Sly's father) on one broadcast and called him a "pig," a "prick," a "slob," a "son of a bitch," an "old bastard," and a "goddamn half-ass hairdresser." She also claimed that he often beat her and almost choked her to death. She told Howard and his audience that Jesse Jackson wanted her as his running mate in the 1988 election, but never quite explained why. For those fans who think Sly's unusual mouth configuration was the result of an accident, as his early news clippings suggest, check out the shape of Jackie Stallone's mouth! Her psychic hot-line number is (900) 370-4441. Her maiden name is Labefish.

Stallone, Sylvester   *See Kielbasa Queen.*

Stamos, John   *Full House* actor and occasional Stern guest, last seen dating swimsuit model Rebecca Romaine. Stamos played a character named Blackie on a soap opera and had previously dated dancer-singer Paula Abdul.

Stanton, Bill   A private investigator with whom Stern has played cards—he occasionally works for lawyer Dominic Barbara. Stanton has worked with and pals around with the likes of Bruce Willis, Sly Stallone, and Robert De Niro. When Stanton met President Clinton, through artist Peter Max, he shook hands with Clinton and said, "Howard Stern told me to mention the FCC." A bit dazed, Clinton said, "Tell Howard hello."

Star Trek   One of Howard's favorite television shows, it ran on NBC from 1966 to 1969. In its first season, it ranked only fifty-two among network shows—in other words, fifty-one shows got higher ratings! Three years later it was canceled because not enough adults watched the prime-time program. In syndication since then, it is an enormous success. *See Shatner, William.*

Steele, Alison   The late deejay at K-Rock radio and longtime fixture on the New York radio scene. Billed as "The Night Bird," she worked the 2:00 A.M. to 6:00 A.M. shift, preceding the Stern show. After she died of cancer at the age of fifty-eight in late 1995, Howard lamented her passing away, and mentioned that he was one of few people to visit her after she began chemotherapy. She is a member of the Rock and Roll Hall of Fame. The Stern show sent $350 worth of flowers to her wake. Jo Maeder, the "Rock 'n' Roll Madam," wrote a tribute to Steele in the *New York Times* (10-29-95) saying that she was a strong influence on her.

Steinem, Gloria   After seeing Stuttering John try to interview feminist Steinem at a women's lib gathering, Stern remarked that "she looks like Dyan Cannon's mother."

Stern, Ben   Howard's father (and sound-bite-meister: "Shut up, sit down!" and "I told you not to be stupid, you moron!"), who was a producer in a studio that recorded voice-overs for commercials. The first time Howard played baseball with his father, he "hit him in the nuts." He says that his father is "badgered" and "pussy-whipped." Ben has been known to call in to New York radio shows and share his political wisdom. Son Howard has said, "My dad . . . he's a smart, miserable guy." However, Howard laments periodically, "My father never tells me he loves me. He always says, 'Okay, son.' " And then hangs up the phone.

Stern, Froim   Howard's paternal grandfather, an Austro-Hungarian Jewish immigrant.

Stern, Howard   Stern described himself as looking like "a cross between Big Bird and Joey Ramone." Regarding his heritage, he said "I come from a long line of garbagemen, pants pressers, and butchers."

Stern, Ray   Howard's mother, who has always worn large bloomers, according to him, and never has had sex with husband Ben, Stern jokes. She also used an anal thermometer on Howard until he was fifteen years old. Ray took up transcendental meditation when Howard was eighteen years old and became, in Stern's words, an "Indian guru." Like Stern or not, he is one of few media personalities who has said on the air that he loves his mother, and he has said it dozens of times. When Howard asked if she read his book *Miss America*, she replied, "I read the first chapter . . . It's not my style." Her rendition of "Daisy, Daisy, give me your answer true . . ." needs a bit a work.

"Sternac"   Stern's comedy routine based on Johnny Carson's "Carnac" routine in which three answers are given and Sternac/Carnac gives a humorous question. During one "Sternac" bit, the answers were "Coretta King, Mrs. Arthur Ashe, and a spider." Howard's response: "Name three black widows." During a "Sternac the Improbable" television routine (5-9-92), Howard, as Carson, slapped his wife and said, "Shut up, you bitch." He hit her with pots and pans, and threw her (a dummy) off the stage.

"The Sternlywed Game"   A Stern show game during which Howard and Alison agreed that he was six inches erect and that after sex he rolls over and goes to sleep.

Sterns, Howard   Until recently, talk-show host David Letterman sometimes referred to Howard's last name as Sterns.

Stevens, Shadoe   *See Hollywood Squares.*

207

Stewart, Alana   The spunky ex-wife of actor George Hamilton called in one morning to make nice with Howard, who immediately said that Hamilton was "inane and vapid." She met George when she was twenty years old and had sex with him on their second date. They were together for nine or ten years. Stewart was given a copy of Stern's first book by actress Farrah Fawcett. The ex-couple's son Ashley married actress Shannon Doherty.

Stewart, Jon   The television talk-show host whom Stern called "the new Letterman" and told him, "Don't leave MTV." When Howard said that he was short, Stewart said that he was "almost five seven." Stewart, like Jerry Seinfeld and unlike Howard, has dated actress Tawny Kitaen "a few times."

Stewart, Rod   See You'll Never Make Love in This Town Again.

Stiller, Ben   The young actor and director *(Reality Bites)* about whom Howard complained, "He's no director. He had it handed to him on a silver platter." He thought *Reality Bites* was "unwatchable" and couldn't understand what anyone said in the first half of the movie. Stiller also directed Jim Carrey's *The Cable Guy,* which was a major box-office disappointment. He is the son of the comedy duo Stiller and Meara of *The Ed Sullivan Show* fame.

Sting   The British rock singer (born Gordon Matthew Sumner), worth about $90 million, is a favorite guest of the Stern show—as is his wife, Trudy Styler. Sting, a former schoolteacher, plays the bass jazz style. He does yoga exercises every morning and is in excellent physical condition for a rocker. Sting had some minor plastic surgery on his nose, and it certainly didn't hurt his voice.

Stomach cancer   A disease that Stern once claimed he had.

Stommel, Anne M.   The retired Red Bank, New Jersey, technical writer and editor who initiated an FCC action against Stern after she accidentally tuned in to his show announcing the 1988 "Christmas Party." She taped the show and sent cassettes and transcripts to the FCC, which began an inquiry on October 26, 1989. She appeared on one of Stern's television shows (12-9-90) to debate him. The debate was moderated by television talk-show interviewer Dick Cavett. Stern flashed a black brassiere and an S & M leather mask at her and said, "Miss Stommel, probably you would object to these." On the broadcast, she complained about Stern's "shenanigans," saying that she had thought it was going to be a reasonable debate. Stommel later ran for political office in Red Bank, New Jersey.

Stone, Sharon   The film actress who lit up the screen in *Basic Instinct* by flashing some flesh and uncrossing her legs. She's not high on Stern's list because they appeared on David Letterman's show the same night, and he apparently spooked her. She called Stern "a loser." He calls her "a stupid bimbo" and "a dumb twit" who should keep her "legs open" and her "mouth shut." **See Zappa, Dweezil.**

Stossel, John   ABC's *20/20* reporter who produced a segment on Stern in conjunction with the publication of *Miss America* in early November 1995. Stossel admitted that he had never listened to the show. Stern bragged to him that he was "the Picasso of radio" and noted, "I have to belittle others to make a living." Stossel was a bit dazzled by Stern's aggressiveness and refused to talk about himself and his family, although he parenthetically mentioned that he was a rehabilitated stutterer. After watching the *20/20* segment (11-10-95), Stern remarked, "Stossel was not the right guy" to produce the segment, and it was "a bland piece," even though Stern initially had good vibrations about him. Stossel said that Howard is the "King of Morning Crude" and that his humor is "crude and vulgar." He admitted, "Frankly, I wasn't too pleased about getting this assignment."

Streep, Meryl   The Oscar-winning movie actress who Stern thinks has had a nose job. Coming from Long Island, a center of rhinoplasty rivaled only by Beverly Hills, California, he observed, "You can't have a nose that thin without a nose job."

Stringer, Howard   The senior CBS television executive who offered Stern a chance to have his own program opposite *Saturday Night Live.*

"Stump the Jokeman"   A rare Stern show bit in which callers tell a joke and see if Jackie Martling knows the punch line. (A recent example: "What does a woman have in common with a bowl of spaghetti?" Jackie: "They both wiggle when you eat 'em.")

Stuttering John   *See Melendez, John.*

Stuttering Vic   A stuttering Indian intern hired by Stern's assistant, Cathy Tobin. Howard playfully threatened to have Vic replace Stuttering John to "yank his chain." Vic's best moment was when he met Kathie Lee Gifford, hawking a cookbook, and asked, her, "Don't you think it's strange that someone who has a c-c-c-c-cook writes a c-c-c-c-cookbook?" Vic, unfortunately, did not stutter enough to replace Stuttering John Melendez.

Suicides   Stern is a magnet for suicidal people. A topless dancer, was going to commit suicide until she heard him say something funny. She was pregnant by a deejay who told her to get an abortion two days after Valentine's Day, and was living with a homosexual. Stern receives calls from suicidal listeners on a regular basis. **See Bonilla, Emilio.**

Sunset Marquis   One of Stern's favorite hotels in Los Angeles, where he has seen the likes of Ozzy Osborne, Little Richard, and Kevin Bacon coming out of the lobby.

"Superman Curse"   After movie actress Margot Kidder *(Superman)* was found disheveled and disoriented in a Glendale, California, back-yard in April 1996, Howard offered his theory that there is a Super-man curse and she is another victim of it. George Reeves, star of the 1950s *Superman* television series, shot himself to death in 1959, Christopher Reeve is now paralyzed from a horseback-riding accident, Richard Pryor *(Superman III)* has multiple sclerosis, and Marlon Brando . . . well, Howard has no regard for Marlon (whose daughter Cheyenne hanged herself in 1995). The newspapers picked up the story the next day (4-25-96) and *New York Post* reporter Bill Hoffman elab-orated on the curse. He maintained that "the dreaded curse began in 1938 when Superman's creators, seventeen-year-old cartoonists Jerry Siegel and Joe Shuster, sold their rights to the character for an as-tounding [-ly low] $165 in cash." Hoffman stretched the theory a bit too much, noting that Kirk Alyn, who played Superman in 1940s seri-als, contracted Alzheimer's disease. Hoffman also cited John Haymes Newton, who played Clark Kent/Superboy for "one reason," never had much of a career, and was last seen as the corpse of a soccer player being eaten by teammates in the movie *Alive.* In fact, the syndicated *Superboy* series lasted three years (1988–91). Newton also appeared as agent Tony Pagano in *The Untouchables* series (1992–94). And New-ton played Mark Warren in the 1994–95 television series *Models, Inc.,* starring Linda Gray. Someone should tell Bill Hoffman that appearing in over 140 episodes in seven years is not quite a curse—it's the life of a busy actor!

Swan, Michael   The television soap opera actor whom Robin Quiv-ers dated briefly. A caller told Stern that he saw Swan and Quivers at a Grateful Dead concert and they were kissing a lot and "getting to second base." The license plates on his Porsche are a shortened version of the word SWASHBUCKLER.

Swedish Massager   *See Vibrator.*

Switzerland   A country that Stern dislikes, saying, "They look like Nazis . . . Don't you love guys who are proud of themselves 'cause they were neutral." He added, "The stupid scumbags, we should nuke that country . . . blow up the goddamn Alps! I hate the Swiss!"

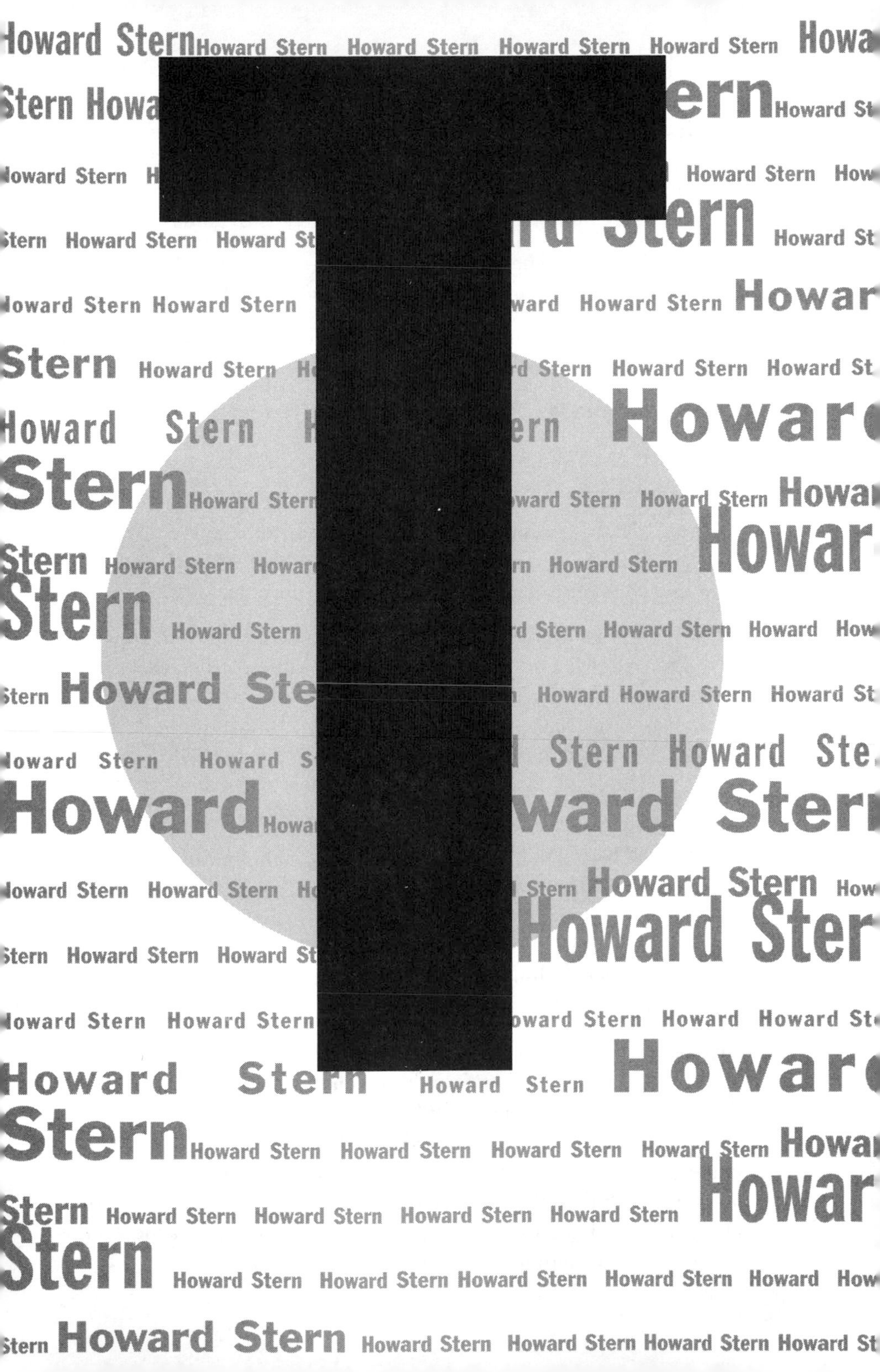

Tag Heuer   A brand of wristwatch and a Stern sponsor. To help make a claim that the watch is excellent for skin divers, Stern claimed to be Roseanne's gynecologist on a "dive" into and up her private zone (". . . we're six hundred feet in and the watch is still going!").

Tanger, Howard   The president and CEO of Marlin Broadcasting who launched a campaign to get Stern off the air in the early 1990s.

Tarantella   The Italian music that Fred Norris once played as Gary Dell'Abate's "theme music" when Gary makes on-mike appearances.

Tartikoff, Brandon   The television executive who called Stern "the future of TV."

Tate, Celestine   *See Celestine.*

Tattoos   Howard wants to get a tattoo of a ram but keeps delaying the decision. Robin has a tattoo of a Chinese symbol for "star" above her right breast. Scott Einziger has a tattoo of a scorpion.

"Taxi"   A black transvestite (real name Michael Hall) who appeared on the Stern television show (3-21-92) in a bikini, with his male organs clearly present under the bikini bottom. He told Stern, "I want you, Howard . . . You make enough bucks for me. I have the best of both worlds." Stern told him: "You have a better ass than my wife." Taxi admitted that he once slashed a "john" (customer) with a nine-inch knife.

Tay, Debbie   A "wired" and wild Stern guest who was a heroin addict. She confessed that she had sex with space aliens. Stern called her a "space alien" and commented that she was a "gorgeous girl," "wild," and "into lesbianism" (when she first masturbated, she fantasized about a woman). Writer Chauncé Hayden, who accompanied her to Jamaica and other Caribbean islands, brought an urn of her ashes to the show after she died.

Tay-Sachs   A hereditary disease that kills young Jewish children. It is one of few charities that Stern has admitted supporting on-air—he donated his black lacquer, stainless steel pool table to their auction. (They hoped to get at least $20,000 for it.) When Robin asked, "Isn't that a Jewish disease?" Stern replied, "I think so. I don't know much about it." And then he added, "Actually it's a pretty serious disease." Of course, he knows exactly what the disease is but curiously was afraid to tell his audience that he really knew about it.

Taylor, Elizabeth   The eight-times married movie actress whom Stern sarcastically calls a "pillar of stability."

Taylor, Kimberly   One of Stern's *Penthouse* Pet guests. Kimberly, according to Stern, has "huge implants and a beautiful hourglass figure." (Photos of her appear on page sixteen of *Miss America.*) Stern suggests that despite a lack of intelligence, an annoying "yenta" voice, and a compulsive need to not make sense, she understands the needs of men. She received a modest amount of voice coaching from Sam Chwat but still has a long way to go. One listener said that she is so stupid that it takes her two hours to make Minute Rice. Another listener said that "when Kimberly talks, my wallpaper falls out." Stern said that she "has a voice that can ruin an erection." She thinks that she is "very, very intelligent." Kimberly is perfectly willing to show her labia majora and minora and anus to *Penthouse* readers but won't get naked for poor old Howie.

Technoweenie   One of Stern's nicknames on Prodigy.

Ted the Janitor   The janitor, now deceased, at WXRK radio who was an occasional guest. He lusted after Robin Quivers and said that he wanted to play "road" with her—he wanted her to lie down naked, on her back, and he then would "blacktop" her! A colorful character, he used funny phrases like "wiggle the tiggle" for having sex. Stern paid great tribute to Ted, and Fred Norris sung the song parody "Ted the Janitor" to the music of "Desperado." A listener called in mid-April 1996 to say that he attended Ted's funeral, that Ted was a Buddhist, and that his real name was Ted Green.

Television   Dissatisfied with his progress in the medium of television as of early 1993, Howard noted: "TV is for chumps—you never see Jack Nicholson on TV."

Tempest   The sexy stripper who, with *Penthouse* pet Amy Lynn, posed with a seminaked Howard for the cover of his book *Private Parts* but was left on the "cutting room floor." Sternophiles, of course, know that the promise of sharing the cover with Howard was probably just a ruse to get the girls naked. (Just kidding.) Tempest's size C breasts were surgically increased to size DD by "Dr. Eisenberg of Orlando, Florida." Howard has seen and felt the saline pleasures of Tempest's successful surgery.

Temple Ohabei Shalom   The Jewish synagogue in Brookline, Massachusetts, at which Howard Stern and Alison Berns were married on June 4, 1978.

Tension Myositis Syndrome   The ailment that Dr. John Sarno said caused Stern's back problems. Basically it is a psychosomatic problem—the mind represses emotional energy such as anger and anxiety and manifests it in some sort of physical ailment, especially back problems. This syndrome was a defense to divert his mind from his obsessive-compulsive behavior.

Tenuta, Judy   The comedienne who played Roseanne to Stern's Tom Arnold in a television skit. She once flashed one of her breasts at Stern, to his delight. When probed by Stern about possibly being a lesbian, she proclaimed, "I like men. I like penises."

Teresa and Rafael   A couple who met at Stern's *Miss America* book-signing event in San Francisco, and were married in March 1996. Teresa was a virgin, wears a padded brassiere, and they had sex one month after they met—and joined the "Mile High Club" for fornicating at over 5,280 feet. Teresa looks like "Linda Ronstadt when she was good-looking," and Rafael said that he was half-Jewish, half-Spanish.

Terio, Denny   Television's *Dance Fever* host who gave Stern insights on producer Merv Griffin's sexual proclivities.

Terrytoons Circus   A television kiddie show that Howard liked in his childhood. It was hosted by ringmaster Claude Kirchner and featured the puppet Clownie, noted for his wisecracks.

Tesh, John   The former *Entertainment Tonight* coanchor and keyboard player and composer who reminds Stern of a WASPy Frankenstein monster—"the blond Frankenstein." Tesh is an occasional phone-in guest who takes Stern's barbs well. When he introduced one of his New Wave CDs, Stern said, "John really tightened the bolts on his neck for this one."

Thicke, Alan   The Canadian-born actor-singer who Stern declared was "luckier than Pamela Anderson's toilet seat," based on Thicke's bachelor life.

The Thing With Two Heads   The 1972 movie, one of Howard's favorites, starring Roosevelt Grier and Ray Milland. It was about a white bigot whose head was transplanted onto a black man's body.

"Think Tank"   A group of men whom Howard assembled on Tuesday morning broadcasts in Washington, DC. The controversial, motley crew included lawyer Harry Kohl, salesman Steve Chaconas, and record store manager Steve Keiger. They "ranked out" mothers and other targets.

Thomas, Danny   *See Adams, Joey.*

Thomas, Jay   The deejay whom Stern replaced when he joined K-Rock radio in New York. Thomas was making $260,000 a year at the time. He appeared as Eddie Lebeck on *Cheers,* played Candice Bergen's ex-boyfriend on *Murphy Brown,* and has been on other television shows. He was also the morning man on KPWR-FM in Los Angeles.

Thomas, Marlo   When the television actress's father, Danny Thomas, died, Howard's first comment on air was, "Marlo's in for big bucks— for something big!" Thomas, a comedian, became a producer and did quite well financially in Hollywood.

Thongs   A Stern fetish—scanty women's underwear and bathing suit bottoms that feature almost no derriere coverage, maximizing exposure of the female posterior ("butt" in SternLanguage).

Tiffany's   The Fifth Avenue jeweler that owns office space below the old K-Rock studio at 600 Madison Avenue in New York City.

Time   The magazine that called Stern an "equal opportunity offender."

Timmy   "Head writer" Jackie Martling's cat, which was missing but soon found dead as "roadkill" in early January 1996. "Eff" Timmy!

Tinker, Grant   The Dartmouth-educated NBC executive (and former husband of actress of Mary Tyler Moore) who fired Howard from WNBC radio. When asked if he was responsible, Grant said, "Yes, I'm quite proud of that because he didn't represent what I thought NBC should being doing and the image that I thought NBC should have." He added, "Incidentally, I find him quite funny sometimes."

Tiny Tim   The famous ukulele player who was a regular guest on the Stern shows. Tiny gave Howard advice on hemorrhoids ("soap and water, Pazo cream, witch hazel, and Charmin") and admitted that he, like Howard, had a fear of germs. Tiny ate lots of beans, never slept on sheets, and always kept the lights on while sleeping. He rarely used towels but used Viva Job Squad. He used hemorrhoid cream as hand cream. He confessed that he had a "homosexual experience" at age twenty-three—he massaged a male friend's back—but no real sexual contact occurred. Tiny said he wore Depends diapers instead of underwear. Tiny mentioned that his father was Catholic and his mother was Jewish, and became noticeably upset when Howard routinely blurted out, "Jesus Christ!" His bride, "Miss Sue," had "environment illness"—she couldn't stand the smell of rugs, paint, furniture, etc. According to Tiny, she apparently serviced him once or twice a week and did not like him to perform cunnilingus. Tiny said he made more love in his last marriage than he had in the previous fifteen years. Politically, he supported the candidacy of Pat Buchanan and was against abortion. Tiny (a.k.a. Larry Love) loved his beer and was not averse to having a breakfast brew or two in the K-Rock studios. Tiny's real name was Herbert Khaury; he died in December 1996.

Tit   A word that Stern complains about because he can't use it, yet he says other stations use it.

"To Hell with Shell"   An on-air campaign Stern launched in Hartford during the 1979 gas shortages to boycott Shell, to protest high prices and long lines.

Tobiason, Arthur   The boy to whom Ray Stern gave Howard's valued collection of *Mad* magazines.

Tobin, Cathy   One of Howard's assistants, Cathy is fairly good-natured in what could be considered a chaotic environment, by most people's standards. Cathy said that she drank only three glasses of wine at Stern's *Private Parts* "wrap" party at Scores, but was remarkably incapacitated. She conjectured that she was "slipped a Mickey Finn," to use an old expression.

Tormé, Mel   The singer and songwriter whom Stern calls "The Velvet Frog," acknowledging the fact that Mel has gained "a few pounds" through the years, much of it in the neck.

Toupees   Howard bellyaches about actors and TV personalities wearing toupees, yet some of his biggest sponsors are hairpiece and hair-replacement companies, who cannot produce a better product than what most Hollywood leading men wear. Among the men whom Stern attacks for committing the sin (actual and perceived) have been Burt Reynolds, Andre Agassi, Chevy Chase, Cousin Brucie, Bob Grant, Charles Grodin, Burt Reynolds, David Lee Roth, and William Shatner.

Tracht, Doug   *See The Greaseman.*

Tracy   A stripper who looks somewhat like *Baywatch* actress Pam Anderson. She has 37-DD breasts (with implants), doesn't like hairy men, started having lesbian sex in 1995, and stripped down so Howard could take Polaroid photographs of her. Tracy has a tattoo of a black rose on her right shoulder.

Transcendental Meditation   Howard and his wife, Alison, regularly practice Transcendental Meditation (TM), as does his mother, Ray! TM, a technique used to find one's inner self, was founded by the Indian guru Maharishi Mahesh Yogi in 1957, ten years before the Beatles discovered him. (In college, Howard filmed a documentary on TM, and future wife Alison appeared in it.) According to Stern biographer Paul Colford, when living in Rockville Center, Stern had a framed photograph of the Maharishi hanging on his walls. About twenty minutes before each radio broadcast, Howard meditates. Other followers of TM have included the Beatles, actress Mia Farrow, and Mike Love of the Beach Boys. Sidekick Robin Quivers took TM courses at the Maharishi Vedic School in New York City.

Travolta, John   Although the popular movie actor has never been a guest on the Stern show, Howard periodically jokes about Travolta's "voodoo" religion, Scientology, and its founder, L. Ron Hubbard, yet never jokes about Transcendental Meditation, the Beatles' involvement with it, or their guru, Maharishi Mahesh Yogi.

Trellis, Bob   Stern's "phoney phone call" name when he called ex–church secretary Jessica Hahn posing as a book editor interested in her life story.

"Tribute to Breasts"   The theme of Stern's WWOR-TV show on April 25, 1992. The show achieved a respectable eleven rating and twenty-three share, beating out NBC's *Saturday Night Live*, setting the show record at the time.

Trotta, Kevin   An advertising salesman at WRNW, Briarcliff Manor, New York, where Howard held his first real professional deejay job. Trotta was one of the first off-air radio excess to be beckoned on the air by Stern, which usually resulted in embarrassing Trotta.

Trump, Blaine   Realtor Donald Trump's very attractive socialite sister-in-law, whom Stern and Quivers met at a party at Joan Rivers's apartment. Howard said that Blaine was "a hot little bitch" whom he wanted to "defile." Get in line, Howie!

Trump, Donald   An occasional phone-in guest, Realtor Donald Trump confessed to Stern that he lost his virginity at age fourteen and was also shocked to hear that Stern was still loyal to his wife when he asked him the question off-microphone. (Trump implied on Stern's subsequent radio show that he was loyal to Ivana at first. Trump also confessed that he initially liked Ivana's Czechoslovakian accent, but it later drove him crazy! Stern said that he originally liked wife Alison's "husky" voice but now dislikes it.) Stern loved it when Trump told talk-show host Larry King that he had bad breath!

Tula   The surprisingly attractive transsexual who acted in a James Bond movie and has appeared on Stern's show. He/she actually grabbed Stern's crotch in a way that Howard said excited him enough to get a "boner," and Howard admitted that he would let him perform oral sex on him.

Tur, Bob   The Los Angeles helicopter pilot who took the aerial videos of truck driver Reginald Denny being beaten up during the Rodney King riots in South Central L.A. Stern told Tur that "he should have machine-gunned" the rioters.

Turkowitz, Sandy   One of Stern's Rockville Centre, Long Island, high school classmates, who he thought was "beautiful." He said that she was "one hot mama" and often drove past her house to try to catch a glimpse of her. She now lives in Beverly Hills, California.

Turner, Paul   The voice-over announcer who does the intro and exit when the Stern show goes into and out of commercial breaks.

Turner, Ted   The cable television mogul whom Howard dismisses as "just another horny guy with money."

Tweed, Shannon   The *Playboy* "Playmate of the Year" who is rock singer Gene Simmons's common-law wife. When Stern probed her to find out if Simmons was a good lover, and mentioned his legendary long tongue, she smiled. "I never leave home without it." Tweed admitted to Howard that she once had a lesbian experience in a hot tub in a "party atmosphere." ***See Hefner, Hugh.***

2001: A Space Odyssey   The futuristic Stanley Kubrick movie that Howard saw while under the influence of LSD. Among his hallucinations, he thought the ceiling was melting. This occasion marked the last time Stern took drugs, but the beginning of his ritualistic behavior. ***See Obsessive-compulsive disorder.***

Tyson, Mike   The heavyweight boxing champion and ex-convict whom Stern makes fun of a lot. Howard launched into Tyson when he was interviewed by director Spike Lee and he suggested that he could have been a *brain surgeon* but the *white man* kept him back.

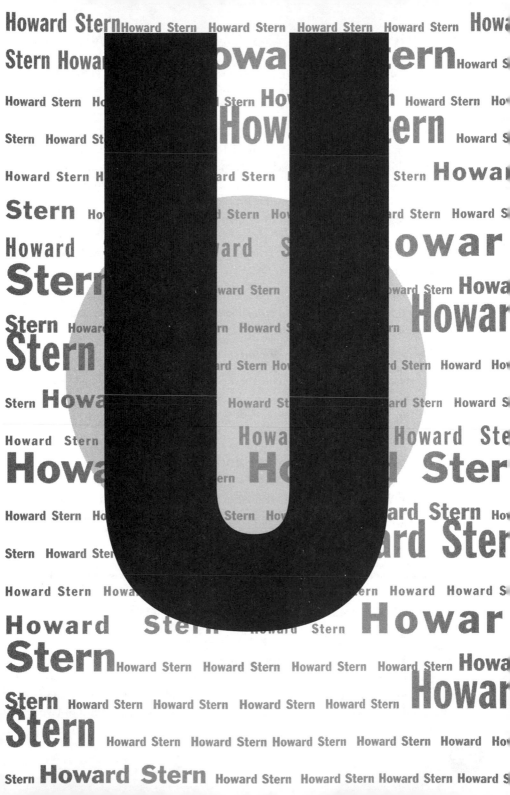

Udovitch, Mim   The *Village Voice* writer who described Howard as wearing "the best Joey-Ramone-Meets-Cher apparel that money can buy."

Uncle Ed   The pervert in Philadelphia who provided Howard with some material that wasn't fit for all listeners. Uncle Ed was one of these bachelors who had teenage boys coming and going to his apartment. He was into being peed on, defecated on, and collecting young boys' underwear and socks for olfactory purposes. Coprolagnia (sexual arousal at the thought or sight of excrement), coprophilia (love of excrement), and coprophagia (feeding off excrement, like a dung beetle!) are but a few of the psychological terms to describe some of friendly Uncle Ed's major problems.

Underdog Lady   Born Suzanne Muldowney, the occasional guest portrays the cartoon character Underdog in the form of dance. It is an understatement to note that she lacks a sense of humor.

"Uniballer"   *See Belzer, Richard.*

University of Maryland   The university where Robin Quivers earned her nursing degree in 1974.

U.S. Open Sores   Stern's second video release, shot at his Nassau Coliseum show.

Utz, Ted   A disc jockey at WRNW radio in Briarcliff Manor, New York, where Stern first worked professionally. He was later general manager of WNEW-FM when Stern became the highest-rated radio host in New York. About Howard, Utz remarked, "He really didn't show any of the characteristics that we now know. The devil was still hiding inside of him."

Uzo   The exotic Nigerian woman who occasionally visits Stern at the studio and is so in awe of him that she starts to cry when she looks him straight in the eye, and calls him God. She has her own cable TV show in New York (Channel 16 on Paragon Cable) during which she dances, mostly with other women (she's bisexual, if not mostly lesbian!). She complained that most black women have "fat asses" and most white women have "flat asses." She made the observation that "Jack Onassis was the biggest hooker alive." She also believes that any woman who has sex with a man for free should be jailed. In her bedroom Uzo has a sign on the wall: "Howard Stern rules." Her fan club address is:

Dance Ventures of Uzo, 1202 Lexington Avenue, Suite 280, New York, NY 10028. Phone: (212) 249-4226; fax: (212) 535-4055. She is known as "Uzo Candy Babe" on Prodigy. Not a big eater, she eats a lot of peanuts, rice, and pineapple juice. She thinks that Brad Pitt looks like "a fag" and she likes Irish guys. She also has a strong fondness for Carmen Electra.

Vacuum cleaners   A product that Robin Quivers (and singer Tom Jones, on a separate occasion) admitted selling door to door, and an item that Stern's father-in-law manufactured (Pullman Vacuum). Guest Willie Nelson also sold Kirby vacuum cleaners earlier in his life.

Vagina   Stern regards his use of the words *vagina* and *penis* as a major accomplishment in radio, words that Arthur Godfrey, Art Linkletter, Jack Benny, Edgar Bergen, and others seemed to have inadvertently overlooked in their long, distinguished careers in radio.

Valiant   The make of 1970 car that Stern owned at the time he deejayed in Washington, DC, before moving to WNBC in New York.

ValuJet   The airline whose flight 592 crashed in the Everglades, Florida, swamp, killing all passengers. Stern seemed genuinely sympathetic and was disturbed that even if anyone survived the crash, they would be killed by alligators, snakes, and mosquitoes.

Van Damme, Jean-Claude   The French action-movie actor *(Kickboxer)* whom Stern likes but called a "scumbag" because he flirted with Alexa, a nineteen-year-old stripper, in the station "green room." When Van Damme mentioned the word *temple* in a passing conversation about a movie, Stern jokingly asked if he was Jewish, to which he responded that he is one-fourth Jewish and volunteered that his fourth wife, Darcy La Pier, is Jewish.

Van Halen   One of Stern's all-time favorite rock groups. He does not like Sammy Hagar and likes David Lee Roth.

Vaughn, Robert   The television actor who played Napoleon Solo on the popular television spy spoof *The Man from U.N.C.L.E.* (1964–68), and an occasional Stern guest. About Vaughn, Howard said, "That guy was good."

Venus II   The masturbation machine given to Howard as a birthday present. After he tried out the gizmo, remarked, "The best sex I ever had . . . it was fantastic!" Jackie Martling was unable to be satisfied by Venus II.

Vetter, Eddie   The Pearl Jam rocker who is Jewish, according to Kurt Waldheim, Jr., during a "Guess Who's the Jew?" contest.

Vibrator   The battery-operated appliance "The Swedish Massager" that Stern says his wife has a regular need for. Cohost Robin Quivers admitted that Howard "used to buy me vibrators every year." Robin later referred to a "Magic Wand" as being a particularly good vibrator.

Victoria   The five-foot-nine-inch-tall Russian *Playboy* playmate and Stern guest who told Howard, "It's never too cold for sex" when he asked her, "Isn't it too cold to have sex in the Ukraine?" She lost her virginity at age fifteen to a man twenty-five, and was raped at age sixteen in the United States.

Videos   Stern's videos have included *Negligee and Underpants Party, U.S. Open Sores, Butt Bongo Fiesta,* and *Miss Howard Stern's New Year's Eve Party.*

Vidu   The four-foot-six-inch-tall part–Puerto Rican man who showed up at the studio to be considered as one of the three hundred men whom Jasmine Saint Clair would have sex with in her upcoming movie. Vidu seemed unimpressed by Jasmine's looks.

Viera, Meredith   The much-touted female broadcaster who joined CBS's *60 Minutes,* soon took a maternity leave, and soon was let go. Stern had no fond words for her.

Vietnam War   A war that Stern misleadingly tells his audience that he served in. His "comedic" riff, one of his worst, consists of bragging about how many "gooks" he killed and how many villages he helped destroy. He said, "My battalion was called 'The Jews.' " He has also said, "I had seventeen ears on my gook necklace." For listeners who do the math, the war in Vietnam ended while Stern was still trying to get "hand jobs" at Boston University.

Vile   Stern's favorite word, according to critic Marvin Kitman.

Villechaize, Herve   The diminutive television actor *(Fantasy Island)* was a guest on Stern's television show (8-3-91). Howard showed a clip of Herve as King Fausto in the 1980 cult film *Forbidden Zone,* making love to a woman. Herve mentioned that he was married to a full-size woman, but it lasted only a year and a half.

Vincent, Jan-Michael   One of Stern's favorite guests, the living-on-the-edge actor survived a broken neck from an auto accident in August 1996.

Vinton, Bobby   The singer known as "The Polish Prince," and a guest in early 1993. Stern subtly baited him about Poles and Jews. Vinton pointed out that Poland was a refuge for Jews for centuries when few other countries welcomed them. The singer also pointed out that he had many Jewish friends and business associates.

"Virgin Mary Kong"   A bit that Stern did in his first month at WNBC-AM radio in New York—for which he was suspended for a few days. It was a video game in which men chased the Virgin Mary around a singles bar.

Virginity   Howard says that he lost his virginity at age sixteen. The "lucky girl" was fifteen or sixteen. He used a condom and his father's apricot brandy to accomplish the historic deed. Robin Quivers said (3-4-91) that she had sex for the first time because she was the only one in her social circle who hadn't.

Vogel, Ludwig   The chairman of the Libertarian party when Howard decided to run for governor of New York. Vogel was "bronskied" by a large-breasted stripper named Colt 45 on the Stern campaign bus while parked next to Golofinger's, a Newburgh, New York club.

Von Beltz, Heidi   The call-in guest and stunt double who was critically injured in the Burt Reynolds movie *Cannonball Run* in an auto stunt (with the stunt double of actor Roger Moore) and lost the use of her legs. Through therapy and a $3 million award, she recovered. She admitted that the last time she had sex was with actor Ray Liotta.

"Wack Pack"   The entourage of Stern's wacky noncelebrity guests, which includes Vinnie D'Amico, Captain Janks, Fred the Elephant Boy, Kenneth Keith Kallenbach, King of All Messengers, Vinnie Mazzeo, Rachel the Spanker, Siobhan, and others.

Wagner, Dan   The man whom Stern called "a hero and Emmy winner" after Wagner appeared on the show. He told a long and tall story about saving the life of an Emmy Award executive, gave Howard a real Emmy, and then admitted it was a put-on. (He acquired the real Emmy five years before on a photography shoot.) Wagner admitted that he also sent Stern letters pretending to be a prison inmate, and a woman who could play a kazoo with her private parts. In any event, Stern finally received an Emmy. Wagner's nickname on Prodigy is "Bambi-cakes."

Wagner, Lori   The porn actress who told Stern, "You've made penis a household word!"

Wah, Ben   Stern's first movie role—as a nutty television anchorman for "Channel 14 News" in the 1986 movie *Ryder, P.I.* The name comes from Japanese *ben wah* balls used to enhance male pleasure during sexual intercourse. They are inserted in the male's anus and removed at the instant of orgasm, stimulating the prostate gland. A female version is inserted in the vagina to provide constant stimulation.

Wain, Norman   The owner of WNCX-EM in Cleveland, one of the Stern show affiliates.

Waiting to Exhale   According to Robin Quivers, the Whitney Houston film was "the stupidest movie I've ever seen!" When Howard probed her about the audience's reaction, she said that they (predominantly black women) talked to the screen: "Go girl," "Don't go there, girl!" and said it was like "a church service." (Robin saw Oliver Stone's *Nixon* during the same Christmas 1995 vacation and walked out of it because she thought it was so bad.)

Waldheim, Kurt, Jr.   The Nazi character in a favorite Stern bit, played by producer Fred "Eric" Norris. Waldheim makes comments like "I turn Jews into velvet" and admits, "I learned 'skull polo' in the German cavalry." He usually appears on the show for the "Who's the Jew?" contest. He addressed an Italian-American caller as "my shovel-wielding friend." When Howard asked Waldheim how he could tell who is a Jew, he answered, "It's a gift. I'm clairvoyant." **See "Guess Who's the Jew."**

Walker, Bree   The attractive female newscaster who once asked Stern for a job when he was program director of WRNW in Briarcliff Manor. (Her hands are deformed, which Stern has made fun of.)

Walker, Johnny   Not a Scotch whisky but the morning man at WFNR-AM in Baltimore with whom Robin Quivers worked.

Walker, Mike   *See "The Mike Walker Game."*

Wallace, Mike   The veteran *60 Minutes* reporter whose rough-looking skin fascinates Howard. Stern had Stuttering John ask him, "How could you be so old and still have pimples?" Stern called Wallace "the biggest phony on two feet. He's a game-show host, he's not a journalist." The former Myron Wallace, by the way, was known as "Chinky" in his youth because his eyes looked Oriental.

Walsh, Joe   A singer-guitar player, formerly with the Eagles, who became a frequent guest on the Stern show and later served a brief stint as a deejay at WXRK.

"The War Department"   A name that Howard sometimes uses for his wife because "we're always at war."

Warner, Ed   A director of one of Stern's E! shows.

Washington-Rose School   The name of the grammar school that Stern attended in Roosevelt, New York, through the sixth grade.

Washingtonian   The magazine that named Stern the year's best disc jockey in the early 1980s.

Watt, Danny   The oldest Stern show intern, who started in late August 1995. An ex-bartender and waiter, he "got tired of drunks" and enrolled at Nassau Community College to study theater and communications.

Wayne's World   Stern confidently predicts that his first movie easily will generate a greater gross than *Wayne's World.*

Waxman, Lawrence   The public-speaking teacher at South Side Senior High School in Rockville Centre, Long Island, who made Howard sing "Row, Row, Row Your Boat" in front of the class, humiliating Stern.

WBTU   The Boston University radio station that spawned the one and only Howard Stern.

WCBM-AM The Baltimore radio station that Robin Quivers worked at when Stern moved to New York from Washington, DC, until Howard helped negotiate her joining WNBC.

WCCC The AM/FM radio station that Stern worked for in Hartford in the late 1970s for $12,000 a year, while wife Alison worked as a social worker for more money. Here he met Fred Norris, who was a college student working at the station. Stern left in 1980 to go to Detroit.

WCMB-AM A Harrisburg, Pennsylvania, radio station that Robin Quivers worked at before returning to work at a Baltimore station.

Wedding ring Stern has been known to wear a lot of rings and a neck chain, but he, the loyal, faithful husband, does not wear a wedding ring.

Weinstein, Lew A childhood friend of Stern since the fifth grade, who became an ophthalmologist and occasional sponsor on Howard's radio show. "Dr. Lew" also went to Boston University with Stern—and was his only male friend at college. Stern said that he was fully mature at age twelve and had to shave "twice a day." His current practice is with Weinstein Receiving Center, (800-75-today). He operated on intern Steve Grillo's eyes.

Weinstein, Mrs. Howard's third grade teacher.

Weiss, Deborah Hayford A reporter at the Monmouth, Illinois, *Review Atlas* who called Stern "a grubby Lenny Bruce wanna-be who comes off like Peck's bad boy on methadrine." After seeing him on NBC's *The Tonight Show,* she wrote, "Stern's appearance was a slimy brew of racial and sexual vulgarisms, poo-poo humor and bargain-basement nihilism so far over the line even [Jay] Leno would later apologize."

Welch, Raquel The first woman to sock Stuttering John—after he asked, "Are they drooping yet?" To Raquel, the truth hurt. To John, the nose hurt.

Wells, Dawn The actress who played Mary Ann Summers on the television comedy series *Gilligan's Island.* When she appeared on Stern's WWOR-TV show, he told her that she was the first woman he masturbated to.

Wert, Lawrence J. The vice president and general manager of Chicago's WLUP, which carried the Stern show for ten months in the 1992–93 period, and then terminated it after Stern refused to accept a time slot when indecency issues would not be a concern. Hell has no fury like Stern being financially spurned and having his ego bruised. (His ratings in Chicago were low.) On-air he announced to Wert, "I wish AIDS on you, and I wish AIDS on your family." Stern crossed the line: He knows that you do not attack one's family. He would never accept any attack on his wife, children, and parents, yet on the air he broke a bigger rule than uttering any of the seven no-no words.

West, Adam   The TV actor who played Batman on the popular television series (1966–68), he was a guest on Howard's show the night he introduced Fartman to his television viewers. West made $4,500 a week during the last season of *Batman,* but received royalties only for the first two years of reruns. West once dated Lana Wood, sister of actress Natalie Wood, and admitted that he met a Doris Day look-alike in Madrid, while shooting a "spaghetti western," and in his hotel room he learned that "Doris" was a man! West's autobiography is entitled *Back to the Batcave.*

West, Billy   A Stern sidekick in the mid-1990s and great voice-over man (e.g., *Ren and Stimpy*). He does a good Judge Ito and an excellent "bad Jay Leno" (a Jay Leno who says things that Jay would never say in public). He also does the definitive imitations of Larry Fine of the Three Stooges, "Grandpa" Al Lewis, and Cincinnati Reds baseball club owner Marge Schott. West was the last person named in the acknowledgment section of *Private Parts.* West left the show in early November 1995 for reasons not fully explained. According to A. J. Benza of the *New York Daily News*, West's agency, William Morris, was negotiating (unbeknownst to Stern!) to get him on the show five days a week instead of three days a week, and for more money per day. Not only are his imitations very good—his ability to ad-lib with detail is excellent!) West will do fine (and Fine, as in Larry) on his own! Stern announced that he had no knowledge of West's negotiations with Infinity, nor did he influence the decision, although he obviously didn't go to bat for West. Stern said, "I love Billy and I love working with him . . . He's a great guy and a great talent," but added that his absence would not affect the show's ratings.

West, Leslie   Rock guitarist (Mountain) and friend of Stern who occasionally appears on the show. His big hit was "Mississippi Queen." He dropped out of school after nine and a half years. The bad news is that he takes injections to get erections. The good news is that they last a *long* time. (West's real last name, by the way, is Weinstein.)

Westcott, Al　The bearded, long-haired Las Vegas resident and studio musician who monitors Stern's radio show and reports all indecencies to the Federal Communications Commission. When Infinity Broadcasting agreed to pay $1.7 million in fines incurred by Stern, Westcott declared a victory.

Westheimer, Dr. Ruth　The heavily accented, tiny sex adviser who occasionally appears on Stern's shows. Stuttering John once sought her help when he told her, "I'm uncircumcised and have a smegma question." She quickly interjected, "Dat's a stupid qvestion!"

WFBR-AM　The radio station at which Robin Quivers worked as a newsreader when she was recruited to work with Howard in Washington.

What's Eating Gilbert Grape?　One of Stern's favorite movies, it starred Johnny Depp.

White, Vanna　See **You'll Never Make Love in This Town Again.**

Whitehead, Ann　A freshman at Boston University with whom Stern had a "passionate two weeks." She left B.U. and now works with elderly people in San Francisco. She said on the "Is This a Life?" show (2-9-91) that Howard was "sweet, shy, and sensitive."

Whitman, Christine Todd　The Republican governor of New Jersey whose candidacy Stern supported. She won and agreed to name a New Jersey rest stop after him. The plaque (at a rest stop on I 295 in Burlington County) was soon stolen and sent to Stern. Unlike President Bill Clinton, Whitman admitted that she smoked marijuana, actually inhaled, and then "upchucked."

Who Farted, I Smelt It　One of Jackie the Jokeman's many audiotapes that he sells and promotes daily on the Stern show and at his stand-up comedy appearances. A new title would easily double his sales!

WHOM-AM　The New York radio station where Howard's father, Ben, worked as an engineer. The station later became WKTU, then K-Rock, his current station.

Whore　The word for a prostitute or promiscuous woman, which Stern occasionally pronounces "hoo'er," a Brooklynism that Howard probably picked up from his father.

Who's the Poof?   A Stern show skit in which Howard, Robin, Jackie, Fred and Gary try to guess which of three men is a homosexual.

Whyte Lace   One of Stern's computer-sex girlfriends. She is thirty-four years old, weighs 135 pounds, is five-feet-five-inches tall, wears D-cup brassieres, and "looks like Ally Sheedy." She told Stern's audience that she once invited one of her computer-sex boyfriends to come to her house and "rape" her. As she lay in bed in panties and waist-high negligee, he entered her room, put a knife to her throat, and said, "Say one word and I'll slit your fuckin' throat." They had wild sex for three hours ("The best sex I ever had!"), which included oral sex, anal sex (her favorite act!), and S & M (he dripped hot candle wax on her chest and vaginal area). Some listeners called in and told Gary and Stuttering John that she had "a great ass" but was moody and temperamental. When prompted by Stern, she hinted that she once attempted suicide.

Wiggins, John   The man who receives the music credit for Stern's E! show.

WIIO-AM   A radio station in Carlisle, Pennsylvania, where Robin Quivers worked after attending a broadcasting school.

Wild, David   The *Rolling Stone* writer who wrote one of the few articles (6-14-90) about Stern that he actually liked. Fearing a negative article, Howard even went out to dinner with him and insisted on paying the bill. Wild, by the way, went to Cornell University with athlete-turned-actor Ed Marinaro.

Will   Howard had his last will and testament drafted on March 11, 1996. Although he publicly denounces people who have inherited wealth, it is assumed that his wife and three children will inherit at least an eight-figure amount (over $10 million and less than $100 million), enabling future shock jocks and commentators to take potshots at Alison, Emily, Debra, and Ashley in the same way he attacks the Kennedys, Fords, and Rockefellers. Howard's heirs will inherit the "mother lode" and live next door to Melissa Rivers, on Fifth Avenue.

Williams, Montel   The bald, light-skinned black talk-show host with "the big shiny cue-ball head," according to Stern. He is an ex-marine. When Howard found out that Montel bought Jackie Onassis's "bracelet of enameled tiger heads and black pearls" (Robin's description) for $17,500 at the Sotheby auction, Howard said, "I hate that guy having money. That show should have been off the air after a week."

235

Williams, Robin   The comedic actor *(Good Morning Vietnam)* and mime with whom Stern has had a long-standing feud. He said that it started when he criticized Williams for marrying his kids' baby-sitter. At Sting's "Rain Forest Concert" in April 1996, Williams walked down the aisle, ignored (or didn't see) Howard, but talked to Stern's daughter Debra.

Williams, Ted   The great Hall of Fame baseball player who was asked by Stuttering John, "Did you ever accidentally fart in the catcher's face?" Williams, accustomed to getting respect, responded, "Who the hell are you?" and cut the interview short, muttering, "That kind of shit . . . See ya later."

Wilson, Carnie   Beach Boy Brian Wilson's daughter and member of the Wilson Phillips singing group ("Hold On"). After she was a guest on Stern's show, her agent thought she held up well under pressure and managed to parlay the appearance into her own television talk show. During one visit to Stern's studio, she "mooned" Howard so he could feel her derriere, and he said, "It's tight as can be."

Winchell, Paul   The television ventriloquist whom Howard liked to watch in his youth. His dummy's name was Jerry Mahoney, and Howard owned one, along with marionettes. Winchell reportedly helped develop the artificial heart.

Windows 95   The software program that Microsoft introduced in late summer of 1995. Stern called it a "hunk of junk." By mid-1996, he mentioned that he was using the program!

Winfrey, Oprah   One of Stern's huge objects of hate. He's envious of the talk-show host's colossal income (over $90 million a year!) and complains that she can repeatedly use words like *vagina* with impunity. He calls her "a big dolt with an empty, oversized head and two hundred fifty million dollars." He has also said, "She's a pig. A big ugly beast . . . She is the biggest *schifosa* on the planet." He added, "I encourage all white people to boycott Oprah."

Winslow, Michael   See Hollywood Squares.

WJFK-FM   The call letters of Stern's Washington, DC, station when he reentered the market in late 1988, six years after the station fired him. Stern's kickoff line was: "Welcome to WJFK . . . Assassination

Radio," after which Fred Norris ran the sound effects of three bullet shots!

WLUP   The station in Chicago owned by Evergreen, which Stern is suing for $45 million for breach of contract. Stern began airing in 1992 and was taken off the air in August 1993.

WNBC-AM   The New York radio station that hired Ṣtern for about $200,000 a year in 1982. He was suspended briefly in 1984 for airing a bit about God playing the video game "Virgin Mary Kong." He was fired in September 1985, he thinks, for another oddball routine, "Bestiality Dial-a-Date." About WNBC Stern said, "We took an unhip radio station and completely changed it . . . For three years, we prevented the dinosaur from dying." He was making about $400,000 a year when he left. The station went off the air in October 1988, and its frequency 660 AM became WFAN. Bottom line: With or without Stern, WNBC radio was badly mismanaged and Infinity Broadcasting moved in swiftly!

WNRW   The radio station at which Stern worked as a deejay and program director in Briarcliff Manor, New York, before going to Hartford, Connecticut.

WNTN   A Newton, Massachusetts, radio station at which Stern worked for a few months after graduating from Boston University.

WNVE-FM   The Stern radio affiliate in Rochester, New York.

Wolcott, James   The *New Yorker* critic who wrote (11-15-93) that "Howard Stern is the flip side of Jerry Seinfeld, and the opposite of cute. Stern, his face curtained by his long heavy-metal-rocker hair, revels in the forbidden role of raw, subversive Jew . . ." He wrote further, "To enter Howard Stern's mind is to reenter the sticky mess of adolescence, a permanent stash of porn mags and airplane glue . . . He belches on the air, discusses his staff's bowel movements, tells his black female sidekick Robin Quivers he'd like to be her plantation massa."

Wolf, Peter   A member of the Giles Band who admitted to Stern that he had a fling with actress Faye Dunaway. (Trivia item: on location for the movie *Chinatown,* he saw director Roman Polanski pull a hair out of Dunaway's head, prompting her to storm off the set.)

"Wonder trash"   Another anagram of the name Howard Stern.

"Wood"   One of Stern's nicknames for an erection, as in "Did you start getting wood?"

Woodruff, Bob   The WWOR-TV vice president for program development who hired Stern in 1990 to do a weekly comedy show for about $10,000 a week.

Wood-Yi   The Stern show Woody Allen character who in mid-1996 began giving the weather reports.

"Woof down"   The term Howard uses when he means to say that he "wolfs down" his food, namely, devours his meals in a hurry (which is one of the reasons he always has a lot of gas!). The closer to 10:00 A.M., the more annoying his lip-smacking on mike gets. Even Robin and phone callers occasionally complain.

WRNW-FM   The radio station in Briarcliff Manor, New York, where Stern started his professional radio career as a ninety-six-dollar-a-week disk jockey.

WWDC-FM   The radio station (known as "DC-101") in Washington, DC, where Stern worked in the early 1980s at the starting salary of $40,000. He hired newsreader and former air force nurse Robin Quivers in 1981. When the show increased its ratings, Stern was allowed to hire Fred Norris from Hartford.

WWWW-FM   Also known as "W-4," the Detroit radio station that Stern joined in 1980 for a salary of $30,000. The October-November 1980 ratings book indicated that Stern had a 1.6 share, whereas his major competition, WRIF and WLLZ, received 4.7 and 4.6 respectively. He was fired, in effect, after nine months when, in his words, "I woke up and the station went country!" He was making $50,000 a year at the time.

WXRK-FM   Stern's flagship radio station, known as K-Rock, located at 600 Madison Avenue, New York, NY 10022. Stern biographer Paul Colford estimates in his book that Howard signed for $500,000 with annual escalations and incentives. Colford also writes that Robin Quivers started at $100,000, Fred Norris at $85,000, and Boy Gary Dell'Abate at $27,000. When Jackie Martling was hired in August 1986 he was paid about $1,500 a week. It was previously known as

WKTU ("Disco 92"). Their general switchboard phone number is (212) 750-0550, and the request/contest line is (212) 955-9292.

Wynn, Marla   A former Miss America and Miss Pennsylvania, she told Stern that Larry King said he wanted to make love to her.

Xchaotic, Johnny   A computer hacker who has jammed the E-mail of famous people whom he disliked, e.g., Howard Stern, Rush Limbaugh, and Bill Gates. He dismissed Stern as being "ignorant."

XTRA-FM   Stern's San Diego radio outlet (91.1 FM), whose general manager is Mike Glickenaus. The Stern show debuted on February 13, 1995, and more than tripled the station's previous audience. Glickenhaus said, "What Howard is, is a magnet, for business and for listeners."

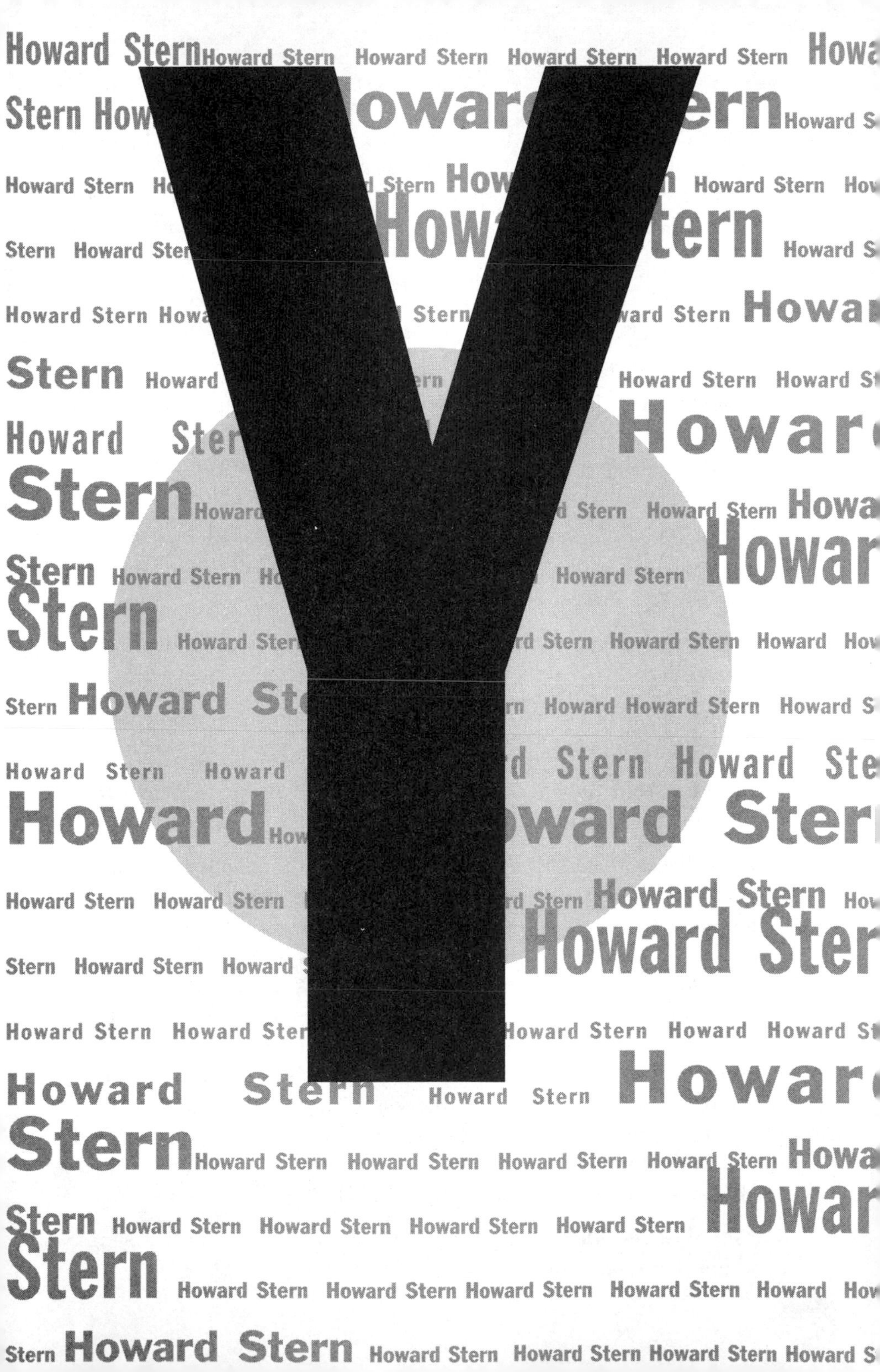
Y
Howard Stern

Yankoff, Major General A military character that Howard played on his television show (2-16-91). When asked by a bikini-clad woman, "How do you get on the Howard Stern show?" he flipped to a new chart showing a graphic of the producer of his show, Dan Forman, after which all the girls ran off in fright.

Yarmulke The skullcap that Stern wore at his Bar Mitzvah. Howard is one of few "half-Italians" who speaks Yiddish and has had a Bar Mitzvah.

Yiddishisms For a "half-Italian" guy from Long Island, Howard has an excellent knowledge of Yiddish and also tends to "Yiddify" certain English words such as "schnot" (for snot) and "schweenie" (for wee-nie.) He says that his wife, Alison, "schnores" in her sleep.

Yoga Attention, reporters! Stern practices Transcendental Medita-tion, not yoga (although his guru is named Yogi, as in the Maharishi Mahesh Yogi.) However, **see Carlisi, Anthony.**

Yogi Bear Howard's favorite television show as a child, but *not* his sister Ellen's favorite show. (They had to share a television set!)

Yogurt One of Fred's breakfast and snack staples, which he drinks rather than use a spoon.

"You Bet Your Ass" A spoof of the Grouch Marx show *You Bet Your Life* broadcast on Stern's January 4, 1992, television show.

You'll Never Make Love in This Town Again The Hollywood exposé written by women who have had firsthand (so to speak!) experience in the boudoirs of movie stars. After Stern interviewed Robin and Liza, two of the coauthors, a full-page ad for the book in *The New York Times Book Review* quoted Stern as saying, "This is an important book to read." Liza said that she met *Wheel of Fortune*'s Vanna White at Hugh Heffner's mansion, went back to Vanna's place, "did drugs," and en-gaged in lesbian frolic for thirty minutes. Liza also said that O. J. Simp-son pal Marcus Allen had "the biggest private parts you've ever seen on a man." She added, "I screamed when I saw it!" They also implied that rock singer Rod Stewart should be called, in Howard's words, "Rod-less Stewart," and that singer Don Henley likes sex toys.

"You'll Never Walk Alone" One of Howard's father's favorite songs, which Ben sings vigorously but slightly off key.

Young, Neil   The aging rock singer with big sideburns, about which Stern commented, "Those are real pork chops." Stern also said, "An old guy prancing around the stage isn't pretty."

Your Wedding Night   A "sex manual" that Howard found on his parents' bookshelf. He consulted the book to find out about "French kissing and petting."

"You've got some body!" "What do you do work out?" "Are you a C-cup?"   Stern's all-time most frequently asked questions of female guests. He thinks it flatters them, and it does if they've never heard Howard rattle off these all-too-familiar words every morning!

Z

Howard Stern Howard Stern Howard Stern Howard Stern Howard Stern Howar
Stern Howard Stern tern Howard St
oward Stern Howar rn Howard Stern How
tern Howard Stern Howard Stern tern Howard St
oward Stern Howard Stern Howar oward Stern Howar
Stern Howard Stern Howar n Howard Stern Howard Ste
oward Stern Ho Howar
Stern Howard Stern rd Stern Howard Stern Howar
Stern Howard Stern Howa n Howard Stern Howar
Stern Howard Ste ard Stern Howard Stern Howard Howa
tern Howard S tern Howard Howard Stern Howard Ste
oward Stern How ard Stern Howard Ster
Howard Howard Stern
oward Stern Howa n Howard Stern Howard Stern Howa
tern Howard Ste ard Stern
oward Stern H Howard Howard Ste
Howard Stern Howard Stern Howar
Stern Howard Stern Howard Stern Howard Stern Howard Stern Howar
tern Howard Stern Howard Stern Howard Stern Howard Stern Howar
Stern Howard Stern Howard Stern Howard Stern Howard Howa
tern Howard Stern Howard Stern Howard Stern Howard Stern Ste

Z-100   The New York rock station to which Stern's daughter Emily makes "phony phone calls." Jo Maeder, formerly the "Rock 'n' Roll Madam" at K-Rock, began working for Z-100 in early 1996. K-Rock's program director, Steve Kingston, previously worked at Z-100.

Zappa, Dweezil   The son of rock composer Frank Zappa, who drove Stern nuts because Dweezil dated (and had sex with) movie actress Sharon Stone—he was "bagging the cooch" (Dweezil's term!). When Stern asked if Stone was a *real* blonde (in other words, was her pubic hair blond?), Dweezil said, "Yeah!"

Zappa, Frank   The late rock composer whom Howard liked. Zappa was one of few celebrities to call him at home.

Zelda's   A Boston University hangout that Howard frequented to pick up girls.

Zeros   The rock group that wrote and recorded the song "H-O-W-A-R-D" back in his WNBC days.

Zimmerman, Ira   A representative of the National Stuttering Project who thought that Stern was exploiting Stuttering John. Stern rightfully pointed out that the show makes fun of Robin's breasts, Gary's teeth, and Jackie's belly—and he asked how many people would hire a stutterer in a high-profile job.

Zimmerman, Ron   A former stand-up comedian and writer who told Stern, "I always drank and did drugs to go onstage." He would drink four to five shots of Jack Daniel's whiskey and smoke a joint before his act. He dated actress Linda Doucette, formerly of the Gary Shandling show. Zimmerman was going to hang himself by jumping off his tub when Jay Leno called one Christmas Eve and invited Ron over to hang out. Zimmerman has twelve tattoos, many of which are on his arms.

Zombie, Rob   From the rock group White Zombie, one of Stern's favorite groups, Rob was termed "a musical genius" by Howard. He has many tattoos on his arms. His girlfriend Sheri got drunk at one of their concerts, punched a security guard, and had sex with Rob in the band bus.

Zucker, Danny A former Stern intern for the Fox TV pilot. He became a writer on television shows such as *Evening Shade, Roseanne,* and *Grace Under Fire.*

Zucker, Gail Alison Stern's friend, who has appeared on the Stern show. She currently has no husband, but Howard assured the audience that "Gail is a lot of fun."